Persistency, Consistency, and Polynomial Matrix Models in Least-Squares Identification

by

Matthew S. Holzel

A dissertation submitted in partial fulfillment
of the requirements for the degree of
Doctor of Philosophy
(Aerospace Engineering)
in The University of Michigan
2012

Doctoral Committee:

Professor Dennis S. Bernstein, Chair
Professor Pierre T. Kabamba
Professor Ilya V. Kolmanovsky
Professor Semyon M. Meerkov

With any luck, I will look back on everything I've done and realize how foolish I was.

-Matthew S. Holzel

I am deeply indebted to:

my wife - Bojana Drincic - for all of her love, and for putting up with me;

my parents - Frank and Jackie Holzel - for all of their love, for my wonderful childhood, and for all of the sacrifices they have made so that I can be the person I am today;

my brother - Greg Holzel - for always challenging (and usually beating) me in everything I do, even to this day;

my friends - Tony D'Amato, Marco Ceze, Tim Eymann, Matt Fledderjohn, Luke Hansen, Jesse Hoagg, Brandon Smith, Ashley Verhoff, and others - who have helped me maintain my sanity;

and my colleagues, who have helped me along this journey.

To all of the aforementioned, I would like to sincerely thank you; without you I could never have accomplished all that I have done. I am indebted to you just as much as the references in the bibliography. This work is not mine alone... it is ours.

TABLE OF CONTENTS

LIST OF FIGURES

ABSTRACT

Persistency, Consistency, and Polynomial Matrix Models in Least-Squares
Identification

by

Matthew S. Holzel

Chair: Dennis S. Bernstein

The ultimate goal of system identification is the identification of possibly nonlinear
systems in the presence of unknown deterministic and stochastic noise using robust,
efficient algorithms that are amenable to recursive implementation. Throughout the
dissertation, we will consider incrementally more difficult problems in system identification, with the aim of achieving this goal. Specifically, we begin by considering
the simplest case of identifying linear systems with no noise. Afterwards, we allow
for deterministic noise, followed by stochastic noise. Finally, we conclude by allowing
for an unknown Hammerstein nonlinearity, before attempting to solve the problem of
identifying a more general class of nonlinear systems.

Our motivation for considering these problems in system identification is control. Specifically, we are interested in implementing control algorithms which require
either a polynomial matrix model of the system or the Markov parameters of the
system, such as in retrospective cost adaptive control and model predictive control.
Furthermore, we seek to develop recursive algorithms for identification to allow for
online system identification, such as on aircraft in flight. Thus we focus exclusively on

least-squares-based estimation of Markov parameters and polynomial matrix models. The novel contributions of this work are: theory and algorithms for relating Markov parameters and polynomial matrix models, a finite-data analysis of persistency in time-domain identification, the zero buffering technique, an analysis of the consistency of μ-Markov-based least-squares estimates in errors-in-variables identification of linear and Hammerstein system identification, an algorithm for solving equality-constrained multivariate polynomial least-squares problems, an algorithm for computing the nullspace of large sparse matrices that retains sparsity, and an SVD-based algorithm for computing the zeros of polynomial matrices.

CHAPTER I

Introduction

The goal of system identification is to estimate a model of a system's dynamics based on a finite amount of input and output data sampled from the system. One of the simplest and oldest techniques for estimating a model is the method of least-squares, which despite being more than 200 years old, remains the backbone of the system identification literature for several reasons, most notably, the flexibility of its applicability, the simplicity and efficiency of computing its solution, and its amenability to recursive calculation. Furthermore, due to its longstanding use in the field, least-squares has been thoroughly investigated [1–8], usually as the amount of sampled data approaches infinity.

The case of infinite data is particularly interesting to researchers since, in the presence of random noise, the strong law of large numbers implies that the ensemble average of a sequence of independent and identically distributed random variables converges in the limit to its mean. Furthermore, the assumption that the random variables are independent and identically distributed is relaxed in several sources [5,6], allowing us to conclude, in a wide variety of cases, that the estimate of the system model converges with probability one to its true value, in which case we say that the estimate is *consistent*. However, one of the bedrock requirements in establishing such claims is *persistency*. Roughly speaking, if an input signal is persistent, then the

1

system is uniquely identifiable given the sampled data. In terms of the asymptotic nature of a signal, persistency has been studied in [9].

Circumstances in which the least-squares estimates are consistent are well-known, and limited mainly to the case where the system is of a special form such as the equation error model [6], or the noise autocorrelation function is known [10, 11]. In other cases, consistency can be established, although this usually requires solving a nonconvex form of the least-squares cost function, such as in prediction error methods [4].

However, despite its widespread use, there are still several unresolved questions in least-squares-based identification. For instance:

- How should persistency be defined in terms of finite data sets?

- How can we increase the persistency of a signal?

- Can deterministic noise processes be handled exactly when only finite data sets are available?

- Are there any invariant system parameters that can be estimated consistently, even when the system model cannot be consistently estimated?

- Can least squares be used for Hammerstein system identification even when a parametric form for the Hammerstein nonlinearity is unknown?

- Is it possible to solve more complex least-squares problems in semi-closed form, that is, guarantee that we can obtain the set of local and global minimizers?

Furthermore, although least-squares methods can be used to identify state-space and frequency domain models [2,12], presently we focus on the identification of polynomial matrices, which, despite also being extensively investigated several decades ago, still have some open problems [13–17], for example:

2

- What is the direct relationship between polynomial matrices and their Markov parameters?

- Are there reliable numerical methods for computing Markov parameters directly from polynomial matrices and vice versa?

1.1   T-2 Subscale Jet Transport Aircraft

In the remainder of this dissertation, we consider the identification of the T-2 subscale jet transport aircraft flying about a trim condition as an example of the type of system we can identify, where the T-2 subscale aircraft is a 5.5 percent, dynamically-scaled model of a generic commercial twin-engine jet transport aircraft [18–21]. The T-2 aircraft is shown in flight in Figure 1.1.

Figure 1.1: T-2 Subscale Jet Transport Aircraft. Credit: NASA Langley Research Center.

Specifically, we will attempt to identify the 50 Hz, zero-order-hold, linearized longitudinal model of the T-2 subscale aircraft from the elevator to the angle of attack given by

$$\left(1 - 1.862\mathbf{r} + 0.8798\mathbf{r}^2\right)\alpha(k) = \left(-0.009767\mathbf{r} - 0.006026\mathbf{r}^2\right)\delta_e(k), \qquad (1.1)$$

where $\delta_e \in \mathbb{R}$ denotes the elevator deflection in radians, $\alpha \in \mathbb{R}$ denotes the angle of attack in radians, and $\mathbf{r}$ denotes the backward shift operator, that is, for a general signal $y(k) \in \mathbb{R}^p$,

$$\mathbf{r}y(k) = y(k-1).$$

Our motivation for attempting to identify a discrete-time model of the T-2 aircraft is control. Specifically, we are interested in applying retrospective cost adaptive control [22] on the T-2 aircraft under various off-nominal flight conditions. However, to implement the retrospective cost algorithm, we require knowledge of either the polynomial matrix model (1.1) or its Markov parameters. Furthermore, we would like to develop robust recursive algorithms for identification in the case where the system model may change drastically in flight, for instance, when a control surface becomes stuck. Hence we focus exclusively on least-squares-based identification of the polynomial matrix model (1.1) and its Markov parameters.

1.2   Problem Statement

With the T-2 subscale aircraft model in mind, we will consider identification of the broader class of polynomial matrix systems of the form

$$A_0 y(k) + \cdots + A_n y(k-n) = B_0 u(k) + \cdots + B_n u(k-n), \tag{1.2}$$

where n is a nonnegative integer, $A_0, \ldots, A_n \in \mathbb{R}^{p \times p}$, $B_0, \ldots, B_n \in \mathbb{R}^{p \times m}$, $y(k) \in \mathbb{R}^p$ is the output, and $u(k) \in \mathbb{R}^m$ is the input. The T-2 aircraft model (1.1) can be seen as a special case of (2.3), where $n = 2$, $m = p = 1$, the elevator deflection δ_e is taken to be the input u, and the angle of attack α is taken to be the output y.

For identification, we assume that u and y are sampled for $k = 1, \ldots, N$. Also,

4

we let

$$\Theta \triangleq \left[\begin{array}{ccccccc} B_0, & \cdots, & B_n, & -A_1, & \cdots, & -A_n \end{array} \right],$$

$$\Phi_N \triangleq \left[\begin{array}{ccc} u(n+1) & \cdots & u(N) \\ \vdots & & \vdots \\ u(1) & \cdots & u(N-n) \\ y(n) & \cdots & y(N-1) \\ \vdots & & \vdots \\ y(1) & \cdots & y(N-n) \end{array} \right], \tag{1.3}$$

$$Y_N \triangleq \left[\begin{array}{ccc} y(n+1), & \cdots, & y(N) \end{array} \right],$$

where we consider the properties of the least-squares estimate $\hat{\Theta}_N$ of Θ given by

$$\hat{\Theta}_N = \arg\min_{\hat{\Theta}_N} \left\| Y_N - \hat{\Theta}_N \Phi_N \right\|_{\mathrm{F}},$$

where $\| \cdot \|_\mathrm{F}$ denotes the Frobenius norm of $(\cdot)$. Specifically, we consider the problem of determining in what sense $\hat{\Theta}_N$ is "close" to Θ, by addressing several variants of this problem:

i) Under what conditions does Φ_N have full rank? (Chapter III)

ii) How can we ensure that Φ_N has full rank? (Chapter IV)

iii) How does deterministic noise affect the least-squares estimate? (Chapter V)

iv) How does random noise affect the least-squares estimate? In what sense does $\hat{\Theta}_N$ approximate Θ? (Chapter VI)

v) In what sense does $\hat{\Theta}_N$ approximate Θ when nonlinearities are present? (Chapter VII)

5

vi) Can we solve more fundamentally nonlinear optimization problems in semi-closed form? (Chapter VIII)

1.3 Chapter Outlines

Since we focus on the identification of polynomial matrix systems, we begin with the necessary background concerning polynomial matrices and address several questions in realization theory, namely: How are polynomial matrices directly related to Markov parameters both theoretically and numerically? In later chapters, we use these interrelations to establish the μ-Markov model and to obtain semi-consistent polynomial matrix estimates from semi-consistent Markov parameter estimates.

Chapter II - Polynomial Matrices and Markov Parameters

Polynomial matrix and state-space models provide alternative and complementary parametric representations for multivariable linear systems, with transfer function models providing an easy-to-work-with link between the two [13–16]. Similarly, frequency response models and Markov parameter models provide additional, albeit nonparametric, representations for the same systems [2, 23].

The subject of realization theory then, is to transform one type of model into another [13,24,25]. For example, the transformation from a state-space model $(\tilde{A}, \tilde{B}, \tilde{C}, \tilde{D})$ to a polynomial matrix model (E, F) is given by $E(\mathbf{r}) = \det\left[\mathbf{r}I - \tilde{A}\right]I$ and $F(\mathbf{r}) = \tilde{C}\mathrm{adj}\left[\mathbf{r}I - \tilde{A}\right]\tilde{B} + \tilde{D}$, and the transformation from a Markov parameter model to a state-space model is established by the Ho-Kalman algorithm [1, 13, 26].

However, although many of these transformations are theoretically understood, some, such as transformation from a state-space model to a polynomial matrix model, may not be easy to compute, and numerical (rather than symbolic) algorithms are needed. To this end, [1] provides a robust numerical link between the Markov parameter and state-space models in the form of the eigensystem realization algorithm,

6

which utilizes the singular value decomposition and Ho-Kalman algorithm to construct a minimal state-space model from a sufficient number of Markov parameters. Similarly, other authors have developed numerical approaches to realization theory, such as [27], although most of the available literature tends to fall into the broad class of system identification, that is, numerical algorithms for transforming input/output data into a given model type [2–4, 6].

In this chapter, we develop the numerical and theoretical link between polynomial matrix and Markov parameter models, so as to provide a complete picture of the interrelationships between different linear system representations. Furthermore, this work is important in several modern control areas, such as adaptive control [28, 29] and model predictive control [30–32], where polynomial matrix models are still preferred over state-space models and where system identification may yield only Markov parameters of the system and not the polynomial matrix system directly [3, 33].

The development of numerical and theoretical links between polynomial matrix and Markov parameter models is carried out entirely within the context of polynomial matrices without the use of rational functions; consequently, rational transfer functions do not appear. This approach removes the need to explicitly discuss poles and zeros, singularities, and cancellations, thus allowing us to focus on the essential algebraic structure of the problem in terms of polynomial matrices. Furthermore, the algorithms that we develop do not depend on symbolic computation, but rather are entirely numerical. This approach circumvents possible ill-conditioning that can arise in symbolic computations that depend on exact cancellation of the coefficients of operator powers.

The contents of Chapter II are as follows. First, we present preliminaries concerning polynomial matrices. Next, after introducing the problem statement, we discuss the theoretical relationship between polynomial matrices and Markov parameters.

Finally, we present several numerical algorithms for transforming Markov parameter models into polynomial matrix models and vice versa, followed by numerical examples and conclusions.

Chapter III - Persistency

Persistency is a bedrock requirement of system identification. Roughly speaking, persistency guarantees that the inputs to the system and the resulting outputs have sufficient richness in spectral content to ensure that the system dynamics can be uniquely determined when no noise is present. These comments apply to both time-domain and frequency-domain identification objectives.

In the frequency-domain context, necessary and sufficient conditions are established in [9] for the degree of richness of the input to generate an informative experiment. One of these conditions is equivalent to the requirement that the spectral density of the input be nonzero at a specified number of frequencies. These conditions are also extended to closed-loop identification. In [34], signals that maximize persistency as defined by various cost criteria are examined, whereas in [35], persistency in the time-domain is based on the informative value of the state. Persistency within a behavioral context is developed in [36].

All of these persistency conditions are defined in terms of either the statistics of the input and output signals, or in terms of the asymptotic nature of these signals, see, for example, [9]. This approach is especially applicable to stochastic analysis in which unbiasedness (zero mean of the error probability distribution) and consistency (convergence with probability one to the true value in the limit of infinite data) are desired properties of the estimate.

In Chapter III we reconsider the notion of persistency within a deterministic, finite-data context. Instead of stochastic analysis, we approach persistency in terms of the condition number of the regressor matrix. Specifically, we consider autoregressive input models, and analyze the resulting rank and condition number of the regressor matrix. We make no assumption about the input or output of the system prior to the start of the data record, nor do we assume that the system begins at rest.

Chapter III also investigates the feasibility of estimating the degree of the system in terms of the rank of the regressor matrix. In particular, we show that the rank of the regressor matrix is related to the degree of persistency of the input, the degree of the model, and the degree of the true system, providing an easily implementable technique for estimating the degree of the true system. Although noise in the input and output signals corrupts this degree estimate, under moderate signal to noise ratios, the degree of the true system can be estimated with useful accuracy.

The contents of Chapter III are as follows. First, we provide a brief problem statement. Then we examine persistency from a regression point of view, analyzing the numerical persistency of several signals, defining the degree of persistency, and proving its relation to the rank of the regressor matrix. We also provide conditions on the degree of persistency of the input such that the regressor matrix has full rank, and introduce a degree-estimation technique along with two examples. Finally, we end with conclusions.

Chapter IV - Zero Buffering

While Chapter III addresses how to analyze previously collected data sets, Chapter IV examines a simple technique for choosing (or augmenting) the input before the data is collected so that the input is strongly persistent, and thus the data are more informative.

The novel contribution of Chapter IV is the technique of *zero buffering*, in which a signal is preceded by a sequence of zeros. Furthermore, we show that the degree of persistency of a signal is increased by zero buffering. In particular, we demonstrate the effectiveness of zero buffering in increasing the degree of persistency of a Schröder-phased signal [37], which, without zero buffering, yields a poorly conditioned regressor matrix. Thus, without zero buffering, the Schröder-phased signal has limited value in time-domain least-squares identification despite its ubiquity in the literature [37–40].

The contents of Chapter IV are as follows. First, we introduce zero buffering and show that it can increase the persistency of a signal. Then we give a numerical example in which a Schröder-phased signal is zero-buffered, show that zero buffering improves the conditioning of the regressor matrix, and show that the zero-buffered signal dramatically improves the quality of the estimation results in a numerical example. Finally we state some conclusions.

Chapter V - Deterministic Noise

In this chapter, we introduce a complementary definition to the degree of persistency called the *full degree of persistency*, and show that this notion is useful for understanding how deterministic signals propagate through polynomial matrix models. Furthermore, we show that both the system and deterministic noise can be identified exactly via overparameterization using ordinary least-squares. Specifically, by combining the noise and system model, we arrive at a single polynomial matrix model, which can be identified reliably using computationally efficient techniques. Furthermore, the system and noise process can be decoupled using one of the many matrix fraction decomposition techniques available in the literature [41–43].

The contents of this chapter are as follows. First, we define the *full degree of persistency*, and show how this concept is related to how signals propagate through polynomial matrix models. Then we show that, by combining the system and noise model, we can identify the coupled model reliably using ordinary least-squares, followed by conclusions.

10

Chapter VI - Consistency and Semi-Consistency

In the previous chapters, we developed a framework for handling deterministic processes in identification. In this chapter, we allow for random noise processes. Specifically, we consider the identification of polynomial matrix models in the presence of input and output measurement noise, a longstanding problem in system identification known as errors-in-variables identification [2, 44, 45]. A challenging aspect of this problem is to obtain consistent parameter estimates, that is, parameter estimates that converge to the true values with probability 1 as the amount of data increases without bound. When the autocorrelation function of the noise on the input and output is known to within a scaling, consistent parameter estimation is possible by using the Koopman-Levins algorithm [11]. This approach has been revisited and refined over the years; numerous references are given in [10].

When the noise properties are unknown, instrumental variables techniques can be applied, and consistency is achievable under specific assumptions [46, 47]. Another approach is to use prediction error methods, which depend on the ability to compute the global minimizer of a nonconvex function [6]. The frequency domain approach given in [48] also yields consistency, although the model order is required to increase rapidly as the amount of data increases.

The approach that we consider in this chapter is based on the μ-Markov model, which is a μ-step prediction model that has the property that μ coefficients of the numerator polynomial are Markov parameters of the system [49]. The usefulness of this model structure is the fact that, under arbitrary output noise and with an input signal that is a realization of a white stochastic process, least-squares estimates of the Markov parameters are consistent. This result is noted without proof in [50], and a related result is given in [51], although the proof given in [51] is incomplete.

Interest in consistent estimates of the Markov parameters stems from the fact that the Markov parameters can be used to construct a consistent state-space model by

11

using the Ho-Kalman algorithm [1], or to construct a consistent polynomial matrix model using the algorithms developed in Chapter II. In this chapter we consider a least-squares technique for extracting polynomial matrices from Markov parameters, which is based on the results of Chapter II. Furthermore, we show that, given consistent Markov parameter estimates, the polynomial matrix estimates are also consistent. Several methods for estimating Markov parameters are compared in [52].

The first goal of this chapter is to provide an extension and complete proof of the result mentioned above, namely, that the μ Markov parameters of a μ-Markov model can be estimated consistently when the input is a realization of a white noise process and the outputs are corrupted by noise with arbitrary unknown statistics and spectrum. Since the proof is formulated in a MIMO setting using polynomial matrices, this result extends the results of [50, 51]. The second goal of this chapter is to prove that the Markov parameters can be estimated consistently to within an unknown scale factor when the input is a realization of a white noise process and the inputs are corrupted by a white noise process independent of the input, in which case we say that the Markov parameters estimates are *semi-consistent*. Furthermore, we show that *semi-consistent* polynomial matrix estimates are obtainable from *semi-consistent* Markov parameter estimates.

The contents of the chapter are as follows. First, we present preliminaries concerning the μ-Markov model and convergence with probability one. Then we present the problem statement, and show two circumstances in which either the system coefficients or Markov parameters can be identified consistently. Finally, we show how to obtain semi-consistent linear system estimates from semi-consistent Markov parameter estimates, followed by conclusions.

12

Chapter VII - Parametric and Nonparametric Hammerstein System Identification

Hammerstein system identification is a block-structured method of nonlinear system identification, which parameterizes the system as a static nonlinearity, followed by a linear dynamic system. Hammerstein models are widely used in the literature because of their ability to capture a wider variety of phenomenon than linear dynamic systems alone, and the relative ease with which they can be identified. Indeed, several prominent methods are available for Hammerstein system identification such as [53–65]. However, at their core, there are essentially two main competing methods:

1. Methods that parameterize the Hammerstein nonlinearity, then solve a least-squares-type optimization problem using zig-zag optimization.

2. Methods that employ separable inputs such that identification of the linear system and Hammerstein nonlinearity become decoupled.

The primary purpose of the chapter is to demonstrate that ersatz nonlinearities are ubiquitous in Hammerstein system identification. Furthermore, we present a method for identifying the linear system with no knowledge of the Hammerstein nonlinearity. This method is based on identifying the Markov parameters in the μ-Markov model. We then show numerically that for finite data, this method yields Markov parameter estimates with a lower variance than correlation-based methods. We also show that this method is capable of producing accurate estimates for unstable systems, while the correlation-based method yields estimates with an unacceptably large variance.

The contents of the chapter are as follows. First, we present the problem statement, and show that when a parametric form for the Hammerstein is known, identification of the Hammerstein nonlinearity and linear system can be formed as a linear optimization problem via overparameterization. Then we show how to decouple the Hammerstein nonlinearity and linear system. Finally, we establish conditions under which the Markov parameters of the linear system can be identified with no knowledge of the Hammerstein nonlinearity using correlation-type methods.

Chapter VIII - Nonlinear Least-Squares

As system identification stretches the boundaries of optimal estimation toward ever more complicated scenarios, that is, with nonlinearities present and under more difficult noise assumptions, the optimization problems that need be solved also begin to push the boundaries of what is possible. Specifically, system identification is typically concerned with posing an optimization problem and attributing properties such as unbiasedness or consistency to its global minimizer [2, 3, 6]. However, as the identification problems become more difficult, the applicability of advanced system identification theory becomes harder to justify when the global minimizer also becomes increasingly difficult to ascertain. Indeed, many minimization methods guarantee that we find only a local minimizer, while also exhibiting a sometimes severe dependence on the initial guess.

Here we present a method for solving equality-constrained multivariate polynomial least-squares problems in a general manner. Specifically, although this problem has been addressed in algebraic geometry, all of the available literature appears to revolve around Gröbner bases and symbolic multivariate polynomial division algorithms [66, 67]. Here we show how to solve the same problem using linear algebra techniques. Specifically, we show that this problem amounts to nothing more than the computation of the nullspace of a large sparse matrix, and then computing the zeros of a scalar, univariate polynomial. Furthermore, the method we present does not rely on an initial guess, and yields the set of local and global minimizers to equality-constrained multivariate polynomial optimization problems when there exist a finite number of local and global minimizers.

14

CHAPTER II

Polynomial Matrices and Markov Parameters

We consider polynomial matrix representations of MIMO linear systems and their connection to Markov parameters. Specifically, we develop theory and numerical algorithms for transforming polynomial matrix models into Markov parameter models, and vice versa. We also provide numerical examples to illustrate the proposed algorithms.

2.1 Introduction

Polynomial matrix and state-space models provide alternative and complementary parametric representations for multivariable linear systems, with transfer function models providing an easy-to-work-with link between the two [13–16]. Similarly, frequency response models and Markov parameter models provide additional, albeit nonparametric, representations for the same systems [2,23].

The subject of realization theory then, is to transform one type of model into another [13,24,25]. For example, the transformation from a state-space model $(\tilde{A}, \tilde{B}, \tilde{C}, \tilde{D})$ to a polynomial matrix model (E, F) is given by $E(\mathbf{r}) = \det[\mathbf{r}I - \tilde{A}]I$ and $F(\mathbf{r}) = \tilde{C}\text{adj}[\mathbf{r}I - \tilde{A}]\tilde{B} + \tilde{D}$, and the transformation from a Markov parameter model to a state-space model is established by the Ho-Kalman algorithm [1,13,26].

However, although many of these transformations are theoretically understood,

15

some, such as transformation from a state-space model to a polynomial matrix model, may not be easy to compute, and numerical (rather than symbolic) algorithms are needed. To this end, [1] provides a robust numerical link between the Markov parameter and state-space models in the form of the eigensystem realization algorithm, which utilizes the singular value decomposition and Ho-Kalman algorithm to construct a minimal state-space model from a sufficient number of Markov parameters. Similarly, other authors have developed numerical approaches to realization theory, such as [27], although most of the available literature tends to fall into the broad class of system identification, that is, numerical algorithms for transforming input/output data into a given model type [2–4, 6].

The goal of the present chapter is to develop the numerical and theoretical link between polynomial matrix and Markov parameter models, so as to provide a complete picture of the interrelationships between different linear system representations. Furthermore, this work is important in several modern control areas, such as adaptive control [28, 29] and model predictive control [30–32], where polynomial matrix models are still preferred over state-space models and where system identification may yield only Markov parameters of the system and not the polynomial matrix system directly [3, 33].

The development of numerical and theoretical links between polynomial matrix and Markov parameter models is carried out entirely within the context of polynomial matrices without the use of rational functions; consequently, rational transfer functions do not appear. This approach removes the need to explicitly discuss poles and zeros, singularities, and cancellations, thus allowing us to focus on the essential algebraic structure of the problem in terms of polynomial matrices. Furthermore, the algorithms that we develop do not depend on symbolic computation, but rather are entirely numerical. This approach circumvents possible ill-conditioning that can arise in symbolic computations that depend on exact cancellation of the coefficients of operator powers.

The contents of this chapter are as follows. First, we present preliminaries concerning polynomial matrices. Next, after introducing the problem statement, we discuss the theoretical relationship between polynomial matrices and Markov parameters. Finally, we present several numerical algorithms for transforming Markov parameter models into polynomial matrix models and vice versa, followed by numerical examples and conclusions.

2.2 Polynomial Matrices

In this section, we introduce polynomial matrices in the backward shift operator $\mathbf{r}$, employing the standard notation

$$\mathbf{r}^n y(k) = y(k - n),$$

where $\mathbf{r}\,[y(k)]$ represents the signal that results from $\mathbf{r}$ operating on the signal y. For a complete treatment of matrices, polynomial matrices, and realization theory, refer to any of the excellent books [16, 17, 68, 69].

Remark 2.2.1. Alternatively, throughout the chapter, one could view $\mathbf{r}$ as an indeterminate. However, in this case, definitions such as that of a causal system (Definition 2.2.10) have no physical meaning. □

We begin by introducing infinite polynomial matrices, or polynomial matrix expansions, since polynomial matrices can be viewed as a special case of infinite polynomial matrices.

Definition 2.2.1. Let $G_0, G_1, G_2, \ldots \in \mathbb{R}^{p \times m}$ and

$$G(\mathbf{r}) \triangleq \sum_{i=0}^{\infty} G_i \mathbf{r}^i. \tag{2.1}$$

17

Then we denote $G \in \mathbb{R}_{\infty}^{p \times m}[\mathbf{r}]$. Furthermore, by convention, $G(\mathbf{r}) = 0_{p \times m}$ if and only if $G_i = 0_{p \times m}$ for all $i \geq 0$.

Definition 2.2.2. Let $C_0, C_1, \ldots, C_s \in \mathbb{R}^{p \times m}$ and

$$C(\mathbf{r}) \triangleq C_0 + C_1 \mathbf{r} + \cdots + C_s \mathbf{r}^s. \tag{2.2}$$

Then we denote $C \in \mathbb{R}^{p \times m}[\mathbf{r}]$. Furthermore,

i) We say that $C(\mathbf{r})$ is *diagonal* if $m = p$ and $C_0, \ldots, C_s$ are diagonal. If, in addition, there exists $\eta \in \mathbb{R}[\mathbf{r}]$ such that $C(\mathbf{r}) = \eta(\mathbf{r}) I_p$, then $C(\mathbf{r})$ is *quasi-scalar*.

ii) We say that C_j is the *trailing coefficient of* $C(\mathbf{r})$ if C_j is nonzero and $C_0 = \cdots = C_{j-1} = 0_{p \times m}$. If, in addition, $m = p$ and C_j is nonsingular, then we say that $C(\mathbf{r})$ is *regular*. If, in addition, $C_j = I_p$, then we say that $C(\mathbf{r})$ is *comonic*.

Remark 2.2.2. Given $F \in \mathbb{R}^{p \times m}[\mathbf{r}]$ or $F \in \mathbb{R}_{\infty}^{p \times m}[\mathbf{r}]$, we sometimes refer to F_i without explicitly defining a form for $F(\mathbf{r})$ such as (2.1) or (2.2). It should be clear that F_i refers to the ith coefficient matrix of $F(\mathbf{r})$, that is, the coefficient matrix which multiplies $\mathbf{r}^i$. □

Next, note that for all $C \in \mathbb{R}^{p \times p}[\mathbf{r}]$, the determinant and adjugate of $C(\mathbf{r})$ can be computed with addition, subtraction, and multiplication operations. Hence $\det [C(\mathbf{r})] \in \mathbb{R}[\mathbf{r}]$ and $\mathrm{adj}\,[C(\mathbf{r})] \in \mathbb{R}^{p \times p}[\mathbf{r}]$.

Definition 2.2.3. Let $C \in \mathbb{R}^{p \times p}[\mathbf{r}]$. Then $C(\mathbf{r})$ has *full normal rank* if

$$\det [C(\mathbf{r})] \neq 0.$$

Fact 2.2.1. Let $C, E \in \mathbb{R}^{p \times p}[\mathbf{r}]$ and $F(\mathbf{r}) \triangleq C(\mathbf{r})E(\mathbf{r})$. Then $F(\mathbf{r})$ has full normal rank if and only if $C(\mathbf{r})$ and $E(\mathbf{r})$ have full normal rank.

Proof. $\det [F(\mathbf{r})] = \det [C(\mathbf{r})] \det [E(\mathbf{r})]$. □

Fact 2.2.2. Let $C \in \mathbb{R}^{p \times p}[\mathbf{r}]$ have full normal rank and let $G, H \in \mathbb{R}_{\infty}^{p \times m}[\mathbf{r}]$. Then $C(\mathbf{r})G(\mathbf{r}) = 0_{p \times m}$ if and only if $G(\mathbf{r}) = 0_{p \times m}$. Furthermore, $C(\mathbf{r})G(\mathbf{r}) = C(\mathbf{r})H(\mathbf{r})$ if and only if $G(\mathbf{r}) = H(\mathbf{r})$.

Proof. First, note that $\det[C(\mathbf{r})]$ is nonzero since $C(\mathbf{r})$ has full normal rank. Also, let α_i be the trailing coefficient of $\det[C(\mathbf{r})]$.

Next, let $C(\mathbf{r})G(\mathbf{r}) = 0_{p \times m}$. Then

$$F(\mathbf{r}) \triangleq \mathrm{adj}[C(\mathbf{r})]C(\mathbf{r})G(\mathbf{r}) = \det[C(\mathbf{r})]G(\mathbf{r}) = 0_{p \times m},$$

and hence $F_i = \alpha_i G_0 = 0_{p \times m}$. However, since α_i is nonzero, $G_0 = 0_{p \times m}$. Furthermore, since $G_0 = 0_{p \times m}$, it follows that $F_{i+1} = \alpha_i G_1 = 0_{p \times m}$, and therefore $G_1 = 0_{p \times m}$. Hence, by induction we have that $G_i = 0_{p \times m}$ for all $i \geq 0$, that is, $G(\mathbf{r}) = 0_{p \times m}$.

Third, let $G(\mathbf{r}) = 0_{p \times m}$. Then $C(\mathbf{r})G(\mathbf{r}) = 0_{p \times m}$ follows immediately. Similarly, if $G(\mathbf{r}) = H(\mathbf{r})$, then $C(\mathbf{r})G(\mathbf{r}) = C(\mathbf{r})H(\mathbf{r})$.

Finally, let $C(\mathbf{r})G(\mathbf{r}) = C(\mathbf{r})H(\mathbf{r})$. Then

$$C(\mathbf{r})[G(\mathbf{r}) - H(\mathbf{r})] = 0_{p \times m},$$

and hence, as we already showed, $G(\mathbf{r}) - H(\mathbf{r}) = 0_{p \times m}$, that is, $G(\mathbf{r}) = H(\mathbf{r})$. $\quad\square$

Fact 2.2.3. If $C \in \mathbb{R}^{p \times p}[\mathbf{r}]$ is regular, then $C(\mathbf{r})$ has full normal rank.

Proof. Let C_j be the trailing coefficient of $C(\mathbf{r})$ and let $C(\mathbf{r}) \triangleq \mathbf{r}^j C'(\mathbf{r})$ where

$$C'(\mathbf{r}) \triangleq C_j + C_{j+1}\mathbf{r} + \cdots + C_{j+k}\mathbf{r}^k.$$

Next, since $C(\mathbf{r})$ is regular, C_j is nonsingular. Hence

$$\det[C'(0)] = \det[C_j] \neq 0,$$

19

and thus $C'(\mathbf{r})$ has full normal rank.

Finally, since $\mathbf{r}^j$ has full normal rank, from Fact 2.2.1, we have that $C(\mathbf{r})$ has full normal rank. $\qquad \square$

Fact 2.2.4. If $C \in \mathbb{R}^{p \times p}[\mathbf{r}]$ is nonzero and quasi-scalar, then $C(\mathbf{r})$ has full normal rank.

Proof. Since $C(\mathbf{r})$ is nonzero and quasi-scalar, $C(\mathbf{r})$ is regular. Hence, from Fact 2.2.3, $C(\mathbf{r})$ has full normal rank. $\qquad \square$

Definition 2.2.4. Let $C \in \mathbb{R}^{p \times p}[\mathbf{r}]$. Then $C(\mathbf{r})$ is *unimodular* if there exists $E \in \mathbb{R}^{p \times p}[\mathbf{r}]$ such that $E(\mathbf{r})C(\mathbf{r}) = I_p$.

Remark 2.2.3. Equivalently, from Definition 2.2.4, we have that $C(\mathbf{r})$ is unimodular if and only if $\det[C(\mathbf{r})]$ is a nonzero constant. $\qquad \square$

Definition 2.2.5. Let $C, L \in \mathbb{R}^{p \times p}[\mathbf{r}]$ and $D \in \mathbb{R}^{p \times m}[\mathbf{r}]$. Then

i) $L(\mathbf{r})$ is a *left factor of* (C, D) if there exist $E \in \mathbb{R}^{p \times p}[\mathbf{r}]$ and $F \in \mathbb{R}^{p \times m}[\mathbf{r}]$ such that $C(\mathbf{r}) = L(\mathbf{r})E(\mathbf{r})$ and $D(\mathbf{r}) = L(\mathbf{r})F(\mathbf{r})$.

ii) $L(\mathbf{r})$ is a *greatest left factor of* (C, D) if $L(\mathbf{r})$ is a left factor of (C, D) and, for every left factor $L'(\mathbf{r})$ of (C, D), there exists $U \in \mathbb{R}^{p \times p}[\mathbf{r}]$ such that $L(\mathbf{r}) = L'(\mathbf{r})U(\mathbf{r})$.

iii) $L(\mathbf{r})$ is a *greatest quasi-scalar factor of* (C, D) if $L(\mathbf{r})$ is a quasi-scalar left factor of (C, D) and, for every quasi-scalar left factor $L'(\mathbf{r})$ of (C, D), there exists $\eta \in \mathbb{R}[\mathbf{r}]$ such that $L(\mathbf{r}) = L'(\mathbf{r})\eta(\mathbf{r})$.

iv) (C, D) is *left coprime* if every left factor of (C, D) is unimodular.

Analogous definitions apply for right factors, greatest right factors, and right coprime.

Note that, when referring to a pair (C, D), we drop the argument $\mathbf{r}$, for conciseness. Also, note that for every (C, D), there exist greatest left and right factors of (C, D) [15].

20

Fact 2.2.5. Let $C \in \mathbb{R}^{p \times p}[\mathbf{r}]$ and $D \in \mathbb{R}^{p \times p}[\mathbf{r}]$. The zero polynomial is a left factor of (C, D) if and only if $C(\mathbf{r})$ and $D(\mathbf{r})$ are both zero.

Proof. First, let $L(\mathbf{r}) = 0_{p \times p}$ be a left factor of (C, D). Then there exist $C' \in \mathbb{R}^{p \times p}[\mathbf{r}]$ and $D' \in \mathbb{R}^{p \times m}[\mathbf{r}]$ such that $C(\mathbf{r}) = L(\mathbf{r})C'(\mathbf{r})$ and $D(\mathbf{r}) = L(\mathbf{r})D'(\mathbf{r})$. However, since $L(\mathbf{r})C'(\mathbf{r}) = 0_{p \times p}$ and $L(\mathbf{r})D'(\mathbf{r}) = 0_{p \times m}$ for every $C' \in \mathbb{R}^{p \times p}[\mathbf{r}]$ and $D' \in \mathbb{R}^{p \times m}[\mathbf{r}]$, it follows that $C(\mathbf{r})$ and $D(\mathbf{r})$ are both zero.

Second, let $C(\mathbf{r})$ and $D(\mathbf{r})$ both be zero. Then for every $C' \in \mathbb{R}^{p \times p}[\mathbf{r}]$ and $D' \in \mathbb{R}^{p \times m}[\mathbf{r}]$, $C(\mathbf{r}) = [0_{p \times p}] C'(\mathbf{r})$ and $D(\mathbf{r}) = [0_{p \times p}] D'(\mathbf{r})$. Hence $L(\mathbf{r}) = 0_{p \times p}$ is a left factor of (C, D). $\square$

Fact 2.2.6. Let $C \in \mathbb{R}^{p \times p}[\mathbf{r}]$ and $D \in \mathbb{R}^{p \times p}[\mathbf{r}]$, where $C(\mathbf{r})$ and $D(\mathbf{r})$ are not both zero. Then the greatest comonic quasi-scalar factor of (C, D) is unique.

Proof. First, since $C(\mathbf{r})$ and $D(\mathbf{r})$ are not both zero, then from Fact 2.2.5, the zero polynomial is not a left factor of (C, D). Hence greatest quasi-scalar factors of (C, D) are nonzero.

Next, let $L, L' \in \mathbb{R}^{p \times p}[\mathbf{r}]$ be greatest comonic quasi-scalar factors of (C, D). Then $L(\mathbf{r})$ and $L'(\mathbf{r})$ are nonzero, and from Definition 2.2.5, there exist $\eta, \mu \in \mathbb{R}[\mathbf{r}]$ such that $L(\mathbf{r}) = L'(\mathbf{r})\eta(\mathbf{r})$ and $L'(\mathbf{r}) = L(\mathbf{r})\mu(\mathbf{r})$. Furthermore, $\eta(\mathbf{r})$ and $\mu(\mathbf{r})$ are nonzero since $L(\mathbf{r})$ and $L'(\mathbf{r})$ are nonzero.

Third, note that $L(\mathbf{r}) = \eta(\mathbf{r})\mu(\mathbf{r})L(\mathbf{r})$. Furthermore, since $L(\mathbf{r})$ is nonzero and quasi-scalar, then from Fact 2.2.4, $L(\mathbf{r})$ has full normal rank, and from Fact 2.2.2, it follows that $\eta(\mathbf{r})\mu(\mathbf{r}) = 1$. Hence $\eta, \mu \in \mathbb{R}$.

Finally, since $L(\mathbf{r})$ and $L'(\mathbf{r})$ are both comonic, it follows that $\eta(\mathbf{r}) = \mu(\mathbf{r}) = 1$, that is, $L(\mathbf{r}) = L'(\mathbf{r})$. Thus the greatest comonic quasi-scalar factor of (C, D) is unique. $\square$

Definition 2.2.6. Let $C \in \mathbb{R}^{p \times p}[\mathbf{r}]$ and $D \in \mathbb{R}^{p \times m}[\mathbf{r}]$. Then the *principal factor* of (C, D) is I_p if $C(\mathbf{r}) = 0_{p \times p}$ and $D(\mathbf{r}) = 0_{p \times m}$. Otherwise, the *principal factor* of

21

(C, D) is the greatest comonic quasi-scalar factor of (C, D).

Definition 2.2.7. Let $C \in \mathbb{R}^{p \times p}[\mathbf{r}]$ and let $D(\mathbf{r}) \in \mathbb{R}^{p \times p}[\mathbf{r}]$ be the principal factor of

$(\text{adj}[C], \det[C]I_p)$. Then $E(\mathbf{r})$ is the *minimal adjugate of* $C(\boldsymbol{r})$ if $\text{adj}[C(\mathbf{r})] = D(\mathbf{r})E(\mathbf{r})$, and $\beta(\mathbf{r})$ is the *minimal determinant of* $C(\boldsymbol{r})$ if $\det[C(\mathbf{r})]I_p = D(\mathbf{r})\beta(\mathbf{r})$. Specifically, we write

$$\text{adj}[C(\mathbf{r})] = D(\mathbf{r})\text{madj}[C(\mathbf{r})],$$
$$\det[C(\mathbf{r})]I_p = D(\mathbf{r})\text{mdet}[C(\mathbf{r})].$$

Fact 2.2.7. Let $C \in \mathbb{R}^{p \times p}[\mathbf{r}]$. Then the minimal adjugate and minimal determinant of $C(\mathbf{r})$ are unique.

Proof. Let $D(\mathbf{r})$ be the principal factor of $(\text{adj}[C], \det[C]I_p)$ and suppose that $E, F \in \mathbb{R}^{p \times p}[\mathbf{r}]$ are both minimal adjugates of $C(\mathbf{r})$. Then $\text{adj}[C(\mathbf{r})] = D(\mathbf{r})E(\mathbf{r}) = D(\mathbf{r})F(\mathbf{r})$. Furthermore, since the principal factor $D(\mathbf{r})$ is defined to be comonic, it is nonzero. Therefore, from Fact 2.2.4, $D(\mathbf{r})$ has full normal rank, and it follows from Fact 2.2.2 that $E(\mathbf{r}) = F(\mathbf{r})$, that is, the minimal adjugate is unique.

Similarly, if $\beta, \gamma \in \mathbb{R}[\mathbf{r}]$ are both minimal determinants of $C(\mathbf{r})$, then $\det[C(\mathbf{r})]I_p = D(\mathbf{r})\beta(\mathbf{r}) = D(\mathbf{r})\gamma(\mathbf{r})$, and from Fact 2.2.2, $\beta(\mathbf{r}) = \gamma(\mathbf{r})$, that is, the minimal determinant is unique. $\square$

Remark 2.2.4. $\det[C(\mathbf{r})] = \text{mdet}[C(\mathbf{r})] = 0$ if and only if $C \in \mathbb{R}^{p \times p}[\mathbf{r}]$ does not have full normal rank. $\square$

Example 2.2.1. Let $\alpha, \beta, \gamma \in \mathbb{R}[\mathbf{r}]$ be nonzero, let α_i be the trailing coefficient of $\alpha(\mathbf{r})$, and let (β, γ) be left coprime, that is, $\beta(\mathbf{r})$ and $\gamma(\mathbf{r})$ have no common zeros.

Finally, let

$$E(\mathbf{r}) \triangleq \alpha(\mathbf{r}) \begin{bmatrix} \beta(\mathbf{r}) & 0 \\ 0 & \gamma(\mathbf{r}) \end{bmatrix}.$$

Then

1) The determinant of $E(\mathbf{r})$ is given by

$$\det[E(\mathbf{r})] = \alpha^2(\mathbf{r})\beta(\mathbf{r})\gamma(\mathbf{r}).$$

2) The adjugate of $E(\mathbf{r})$ is given by

$$\text{adj}[E(\mathbf{r})] = \alpha(\mathbf{r}) \begin{bmatrix} \gamma(\mathbf{r}) & 0 \\ 0 & \beta(\mathbf{r}) \end{bmatrix}.$$

3) The principal factor of $(\text{adj}[E], \det[E]I_p)$ is given by

$$\left[\frac{1}{\alpha_i}\right]\alpha(\mathbf{r})I_p.$$

4) The minimal determinant of $E(\mathbf{r})$ is given by

$$\text{mdet}[E(\mathbf{r})] = \alpha_i\alpha(\mathbf{r})\beta(\mathbf{r})\gamma(\mathbf{r}).$$

5) The minimal adjugate of $E(\mathbf{r})$ is given by

$$\text{madj}[E(\mathbf{r})] = \alpha_i \begin{bmatrix} \gamma(\mathbf{r}) & 0 \\ 0 & \beta(\mathbf{r}) \end{bmatrix}.$$

□

23

Definition 2.2.8. Let $C, E \in \mathbb{R}^{p \times p}[\mathbf{r}]$ and $D, F \in \mathbb{R}^{p \times m}[\mathbf{r}]$. Then (E, F) is a *multiple of* (C, D) if there exists $L \in \mathbb{R}^{p \times p}[\mathbf{r}]$ with full normal rank such that $E(\mathbf{r}) = L(\mathbf{r})C(\mathbf{r})$ and $F(\mathbf{r}) = L(\mathbf{r})D(\mathbf{r})$. Furthermore,

i) (E, F) is a *comonic multiple of* (C, D) if $E(\mathbf{r})$ is comonic.

ii) (E, F) is a *quasi-scalar multiple of* (C, D) if $E(\mathbf{r})$ is quasi-scalar.

Remark 2.2.5. A quasi-scalar multiple is analogous to a transfer function representation of a MIMO system since the system can be written as a rational polynomial matrix. For instance, if $(\alpha I_p, F)$ is a quasi-scalar multiple of (C, D), where $\alpha \in \mathbb{R}[\mathbf{r}]$ and

$$
F(\mathbf{r}) \triangleq \begin{bmatrix} f_{1,1}(\mathbf{r}) & \cdots & f_{1,m}(\mathbf{r}) \\ \vdots & & \vdots \\ f_{p,1}(\mathbf{r}) & \cdots & f_{p,m}(\mathbf{r}) \end{bmatrix} \in \mathbb{R}^{p \times m}[\mathbf{r}],
$$

then a transfer function representation of the system (C, D) would be

$$
\begin{bmatrix} \dfrac{f_{1,1}(\mathbf{r})}{\alpha(\mathbf{r})} & \cdots & \dfrac{f_{1,m}(\mathbf{r})}{\alpha(\mathbf{r})} \\ \vdots & & \vdots \\ \dfrac{f_{p,1}(\mathbf{r})}{\alpha(\mathbf{r})} & \cdots & \dfrac{f_{p,m}(\mathbf{r})}{\alpha(\mathbf{r})} \end{bmatrix}.
$$

Note however, that we have made no definition of the meaning $1/\mathbf{r}$, and one must be particularly careful in defining rational functions of operators since in general, an operator is not a one-to-one mapping. $\qquad\square$

Definition 2.2.9. Let $C \in \mathbb{R}^{p \times p}[\mathbf{r}]$ and $D \in \mathbb{R}^{p \times m}[\mathbf{r}]$. Also, let s be the smallest nonnegative integer such that $C(\mathbf{r})$ is of the form (2.2). Then the *degree of* $C(\boldsymbol{r})$ is s if $C(\mathbf{r})$ is nonzero, and $-\infty$ if $C(\mathbf{r})$ is zero. Finally, let s be the degree of $C(\mathbf{r})$ and let t be the degree of $D(\mathbf{r})$. Then the *degree of* (C, D) is $\max(s, t)$.

Next we show that the minimal adjugate provides us with a quasi-scalar multiple $(C^\star, D^\star)$ of (C, D) with the lowest possible degree, where $C^\star(\mathbf{r})$ is the minimal determinant of $C(\mathbf{r})$.

Proposition 2.2.1. Let $C \in \mathbb{R}^{p \times p}[\mathbf{r}]$ have full normal rank, $D \in \mathbb{R}^{p \times m}[\mathbf{r}]$, $E(\mathbf{r}) \triangleq$ madj$\big[C(\mathbf{r})\big]$, $\beta(\mathbf{r}) \triangleq$ mdet$\big[C(\mathbf{r})\big]$, and β_i be the trailing coefficient of $\beta(\mathbf{r})$. Then

$$(C^\star, D^\star) \triangleq (EC/\beta_i, ED/\beta_i) = (\beta/\beta_i I_p, ED/\beta_i),$$

is the unique comonic quasi-scalar multiple of (C, D) of the lowest degree.

Proof. First, since $C(\mathbf{r})$ has full normal rank, $\beta(\mathbf{r}) \neq 0$. Hence, from Fact 2.2.4, $\beta(\mathbf{r})I_p$ has full normal rank. Furthermore, since $\beta(\mathbf{r})I_p$ has full normal rank and $E(\mathbf{r})C(\mathbf{r}) = \beta(\mathbf{r})I_p$, then from Fact 2.2.1, $E(\mathbf{r})$ also has full normal rank. Hence $(EC, ED) = (\beta I_p, ED)$ is a quasi-scalar multiple of (C, D).

Next, from Fact 2.2.7, the minimal adjugate is unique. Hence (FC, FD) is a quasi-scalar multiple of (C, D) if and only if there exists a nonzero $\mu \in \mathbb{R}[\mathbf{r}]$ such that $F(\mathbf{r}) = \mu(\mathbf{r})E(\mathbf{r})$. Furthermore, if the degree of $\mu(\mathbf{r})$ is greater than zero, the degree of (FC, FD) is greater than the degree of $(C^\star, D^\star)$. Hence $(C^\star, D^\star)$ is the unique comonic quasi-scalar multiple of (C, D) of the lowest degree. $\square$

Definition 2.2.10. Let $C \in \mathbb{R}^{p \times p}[\mathbf{r}]$ and $D \in \mathbb{R}^{p \times m}[\mathbf{r}]$. Also, assume there exists $G \in \mathbb{R}_\infty^{p \times m}[\mathbf{r}]$ such that

$$C(\mathbf{r})G(\mathbf{r}) = D(\mathbf{r}).$$

Then (C, D) is *causal*, $G(\mathbf{r})$ is a *Markov parameter polynomial of* (C, D), and G_i is an ith *Markov parameter of* (C, D).

Remark 2.2.6. In section 2.8, we show that this definition of Markov parameters is consistent with the usual state-space definition of Markov parameters. $\square$

Fact 2.2.8. Let $C, E \in \mathbb{R}^{p \times p}[\mathbf{r}]$ and $D, F \in \mathbb{R}^{p \times m}[\mathbf{r}]$. Also, let (E, F) be a multiple of (C, D). Then (E, F) is causal if and only if (C, D) is causal.

Proof. First, since (E, F) is a multiple of (C, D), there exists $L \in \mathbb{R}^{p \times p}[\mathbf{r}]$ with full normal rank such that $(E, F) = (LC, LD)$.

Next, let (E, F) be causal. Then there exists $G \in \mathbb{R}_\infty^{p \times m}[\mathbf{r}]$ such that

$$E(\mathbf{r})G(\mathbf{r}) = L(\mathbf{r})C(\mathbf{r})G(\mathbf{r}) = L(\mathbf{r})D(\mathbf{r}) = F(\mathbf{r}).$$

Hence from Fact 2.2.2, $C(\mathbf{r})G(\mathbf{r}) = D(\mathbf{r})$, that is, (C, D) is causal.

Finally, let (C, D) be causal. Then there exists $G' \in \mathbb{R}_\infty^{p \times m}[\mathbf{r}]$ such that $C(\mathbf{r})G'(\mathbf{r}) = D(\mathbf{r})$. Hence

$$L(\mathbf{r})C(\mathbf{r})G'(\mathbf{r}) = E(\mathbf{r})G'(\mathbf{r}) = F(\mathbf{r}) = L(\mathbf{r})D(\mathbf{r}),$$

and therefore, (E, F) is causal. $\qquad\square$

Fact 2.2.9. Let $E \in \mathbb{R}^{p \times p}[\mathbf{r}]$ be comonic, let $F \in \mathbb{R}^{p \times m}[\mathbf{r}]$, and let

$$E(\mathbf{r}) = I_p \mathbf{r}^\ell + E_{\ell+1} \mathbf{r}^{\ell+1} + \cdots + E_s \mathbf{r}^s,$$
$$F(\mathbf{r}) = F_0 + F_1 \mathbf{r} + \cdots + F_s \mathbf{r}^s,$$

where $0 \le \ell \le s$. If (E, F) is causal, then $F_0 = \cdots = F_{\ell-1} = 0_{p \times m}$ and the Markov parameter polynomial of (E, F) is given later in Theorem 2.4.1.

Proof. Since (E, F) is causal, there exists $G \in \mathbb{R}_\infty^{p \times m}[\mathbf{r}]$ such that $E(\mathbf{r})G(\mathbf{r}) = F(\mathbf{r})$. Hence, computing the product $E(\mathbf{r})G(\mathbf{r})$, it follows that $F_0 = \cdots = F_{\ell-1} = 0_{p \times m}$. $\qquad\square$

Fact 2.2.10. Let $C \in \mathbb{R}^{p \times p}[\mathbf{r}]$ have full normal rank, let $D \in \mathbb{R}^{p \times m}[\mathbf{r}]$, and let (C, D) be left coprime and causal. Then C_0 is nonsingular.

26

Proof. First, from Proposition 2.2.1, there exists a comonic multiple $(E, F) = (LC, LD)$ of (C, D). Furthermore, from Fact 2.2.8, since (C, D) is causal, (E, F) is causal. Hence, letting E_ℓ denote the trailing coefficient of $E(\mathbf{r})$, from Fact 2.2.9 we have that $F_0 = \cdots = F_{\ell-1} = 0_{p \times m}$. Therefore $\mathbf{r}^\ell I_p$ is a left factor of (E, F).

Next, since (C, D) is left coprime, $L(\mathbf{r})$ is a greatest left factor of (E, F). Hence there exists $L' \in \mathbb{R}^{p \times p}[\mathbf{r}]$ such that $L(\mathbf{r}) = \mathbf{r}^\ell L'(\mathbf{r})$.

Finally, letting $(E', F') \triangleq (L'C, L'D)$, we have that $E'_0 = I_p$. Furthermore, since $E'_0 = L'_0 C_0 = I_p$, it follows that C_0 is nonsingular. $\qquad\square$

Fact 2.2.11. Let $C \in \mathbb{R}^{p \times p}[\mathbf{r}]$ have full normal rank and let $C_0 \in \mathbb{R}^{p \times p}$ be nonsingular. Also, let

$$\beta(\mathbf{r}) \triangleq \mathrm{mdet}\,[C(\mathbf{r})] = \beta_0 + \beta_1 \mathbf{r} + \cdots + \beta_s \mathbf{r}^s.$$

Then β_0 is nonzero.

Proof. Let $D(\mathbf{r}) = \mu(\mathbf{r}) I_p$ denote the principal factor of $(\mathrm{adj}[C], \det[C]I_p)$, where $\mu \in \mathbb{R}[\mathbf{r}]$. Then $\det[C(\mathbf{r})] = \mu(\mathbf{r})\beta(\mathbf{r})$. Furthermore, since C_0 is nonsingular, we have that

$$0 \neq \det[C_0] = \det[C(0)] = \mu(0)\beta(0).$$

Hence $\beta_0 = \beta(0)$ is nonzero. $\qquad\square$

2.3 Problem Formulation

Consider the linear time-invariant system

$$A(\mathbf{r})y(k) = B(\mathbf{r})u(k), \tag{2.3}$$

where **r** is the backward shift operator, $A \in \mathbb{R}^{p \times p}[\mathbf{r}]$ has full normal rank, $B \in \mathbb{R}^{p \times m}[\mathbf{r}]$, $y \in \mathbb{R}^p$ is the output, $u \in \mathbb{R}^m$ is the input, (A, B) is left coprime and causal, and (2.3) holds for all $k \in \mathbb{K}$. Also, let $(A^\star, B^\star)$ be the unique comonic quasi-scalar multiple of (A, B) given by Proposition 2.2.1, and let

$$A(\mathbf{r}) \triangleq A_0 + A_1\mathbf{r} + \cdots + A_n\mathbf{r}^n,$$

$$B(\mathbf{r}) \triangleq B_0 + B_1\mathbf{r} + \cdots + B_n\mathbf{r}^n,$$

$$A^\star(\mathbf{r}) \triangleq I_p + a_1^\star I_p\mathbf{r} + \cdots + a_{n^\star}^\star I_p\mathbf{r}^{n^\star},$$

$$B^\star(\mathbf{r}) \triangleq B_0^\star + B_1^\star\mathbf{r} + \cdots + B_{n^\star}^\star\mathbf{r}^{n^\star},$$

where $a_1^\star, \ldots, a_{n^\star}^\star \in \mathbb{R}$. This notation is assumed for the rest of the chapter.

Throughout the chapter, we have two objectives in mind, namely

1) Given a not necessarily left coprime multiple of (A, B), compute the Markov parameters of (A, B).

2) Given a sufficient number of the Markov parameters of (A, B), compute a multiple of (A, B).

We show how to obtain both of these objectives numerically.

Remark 2.3.1. The trailing coefficient of $A^\star(\mathbf{r})$ is the identity as a result of Proposition 2.2.1, Fact 2.2.10, and Fact 2.2.11. □

Remark 2.3.2. Let (C, D) be a multiple of (A, B). Since $A(\mathbf{r})$ has full normal rank, then from Fact 2.2.1, $C(\mathbf{r})$ also has full normal rank. □

2.4 Markov Parameters

In this section, we develop Markov parameters algebraically from polynomial matrices. Furthermore, we show that the Markov parameters of (A, B) and the Markov parameters of every multiple of (A, B) are equal and unique.

28

Theorem 2.4.1. Let (E, F) be a comonic multiple of (A, B) given by

$$E(\mathbf{r}) \triangleq I_p \mathbf{r}^\ell + E_{\ell+1} \mathbf{r}^{\ell+1} + \cdots + E_s \mathbf{r}^s,$$

$$F(\mathbf{r}) \triangleq F_0 + F_1 \mathbf{r} + \cdots + F_s \mathbf{r}^s,$$

where $0 \leq \ell \leq s$. Also, let $H(\mathbf{r}) \triangleq \sum_{i=0}^\infty H_i \mathbf{r}^i$, where, for all $i \geq 0$,

$$H_i \triangleq F_{\ell+i} - \sum_{j=1}^{\min(s-\ell,i)} E_{\ell+j} H_{i-j}, \tag{2.4}$$

and $F_j \triangleq 0_{p \times m}$ for $j > s$. Then $H(\mathbf{r})$ is the Markov parameter polynomial of (A, B) and every multiple of (A, B).

Proof. First, from Proposition 2.2.1, there exists a comonic multiple of (A, B). Furthermore, recalling that (A, B) is causal, Fact 2.2.8 implies that (E, F) is also causal. Hence, from Fact 2.2.9, $F_0 = \cdots = F_{\ell-1} = 0_{p \times m}$.

Next, let $G(\mathbf{r}) \triangleq E(\mathbf{r})H(\mathbf{r})$. Then for $i \geq 0$, we have that

$$G_{\ell+i} = H_i + \sum_{j=1}^{\min(s-\ell,i)} E_{\ell+j} H_{i-j}. \tag{2.5}$$

Hence from (2.4) and (2.5), it follows that

$$G_i = \begin{cases} F_i, & \ell \leq i \leq s, \\ 0_{p \times m}, & \text{otherwise,} \end{cases}$$

that is, $G(\mathbf{r}) = F(\mathbf{r})$. Therefore $E(\mathbf{r})H(\mathbf{r}) = F(\mathbf{r})$, and thus $H(\mathbf{r})$ is a Markov parameter polynomial of (E, F).

Next, since (E, F) is a multiple of (A, B), there exists $L \in \mathbb{R}^{p \times p}[\mathbf{r}]$ with full normal

29

rank such that $E(\mathbf{r}) = L(\mathbf{r})A(\mathbf{r})$ and $F(\mathbf{r}) = L(\mathbf{r})B(\mathbf{r})$. Hence

$$E(\mathbf{r})H(\mathbf{r}) = L(\mathbf{r})A(\mathbf{r})H(\mathbf{r}) = L(\mathbf{r})B(\mathbf{r}) = F(\mathbf{r}),$$

and from Fact 2.2.2, $A(\mathbf{r})H(\mathbf{r}) = B(\mathbf{r})$. Thus $H(\mathbf{r})$ is a Markov parameter polynomial of (A, B). Furthermore, if $H'' \in \mathbb{R}^{p \times m}[\mathbf{r}]$ is also a Markov parameter polynomial of (A, B), then $A(\mathbf{r})H''(\mathbf{r}) = B(\mathbf{r})$, and hence $A(\mathbf{r})H(\mathbf{r}) = A(\mathbf{r})H''(\mathbf{r})$. Thus from Fact 2.2.2, $H''(\mathbf{r}) = H(\mathbf{r})$, and it follows that $H(\mathbf{r})$ is the unique Markov parameter polynomial of (A, B).

Finally, for every multiple (A', B') of (A, B), there exists $M \in \mathbb{R}^{p \times p}[\mathbf{r}]$ with full normal rank such that $A'(\mathbf{r}) = M(\mathbf{r})A(\mathbf{r})$ and $B'(\mathbf{r}) = M(\mathbf{r})B(\mathbf{r})$. Hence $A(\mathbf{r})H(\mathbf{r}) = B(\mathbf{r})$ implies $M(\mathbf{r})A(\mathbf{r}) = A'(\mathbf{r})H(\mathbf{r}) = B'(\mathbf{r}) = M(\mathbf{r})B(\mathbf{r})$, and it follows that $H(\mathbf{r})$ is a Markov parameter polynomial of (A', B'). Furthermore, if $H''' \in \mathbb{R}^{p \times m}[\mathbf{r}]$ is also a Markov parameter polynomial of (A', B'), then $A'(\mathbf{r})H'''(\mathbf{r}) = B'(\mathbf{r})$, and hence $A'(\mathbf{r})H(\mathbf{r}) = A'(\mathbf{r})H'''(\mathbf{r})$. Thus from Fact 2.2.2, $H'''(\mathbf{r}) = H(\mathbf{r})$, and it follows that $H(\mathbf{r})$ is the unique Markov parameter polynomial of (A', B'). $\qquad\square$

Theorem 2.4.2. Let $C \in \mathbb{R}^{p \times p}[\mathbf{r}]$ have full normal rank, let $D \in \mathbb{R}^{p \times m}[\mathbf{r}]$, and let $H \in \mathbb{R}^{p \times m}_{\infty}[\mathbf{r}]$ be the Markov parameter polynomial of (A, B) and (C, D), that is,

$$A(\mathbf{r})H(\mathbf{r}) = B(\mathbf{r}),$$
$$C(\mathbf{r})H(\mathbf{r}) = D(\mathbf{r}).$$

Then (C, D) is a multiple of (A, B).

Proof. Let $C_R \in \mathbb{R}^{p \times p}[\mathbf{r}]$ be a greatest right factor of (A, C). Then there exist

$A_L \in \mathbb{R}^{p \times p}[\mathbf{r}]$ and $C_L \in \mathbb{R}^{p \times p}[\mathbf{r}]$, such that

$$A(\mathbf{r}) = A_L(\mathbf{r})C_R(\mathbf{r}),$$
$$C(\mathbf{r}) = C_L(\mathbf{r})C_R(\mathbf{r}).$$

Furthermore, since $A(\mathbf{r})$ and $C(\mathbf{r})$ have full normal rank, from Fact 2.2.1, we have that $A_L(\mathbf{r})$, $C_L(\mathbf{r})$, and $C_R(\mathbf{r})$ have full normal rank.

Next, let $E(\mathbf{r}) \triangleq \mathrm{madj}\big[A_L(\mathbf{r})\big]$ and $\beta(\mathbf{r}) \triangleq \mathrm{mdet}\big[A_L(\mathbf{r})\big]$. Since $A(\mathbf{r}) = A_L(\mathbf{r})C_R(\mathbf{r})$, then $E(\mathbf{r})A(\mathbf{r}) = \beta(\mathbf{r})C_R(\mathbf{r})$, and hence

$$C_L(\mathbf{r})E(\mathbf{r})A(\mathbf{r}) = C_L(\mathbf{r})\beta(\mathbf{r})C_R(\mathbf{r}) = \beta(\mathbf{r})C(\mathbf{r}).$$

Third, since $C(\mathbf{r})H(\mathbf{r}) = D(\mathbf{r})$, then

$$\beta(\mathbf{r})C(\mathbf{r})H(\mathbf{r}) = \beta(\mathbf{r})D(\mathbf{r}) = C_L(\mathbf{r})E(\mathbf{r})A(\mathbf{r})H(\mathbf{r}) = C_L(\mathbf{r})E(\mathbf{r})B(\mathbf{r}),$$

and hence $(C_L E A, C_L E B) = (\beta C, \beta D)$.

Next, since (A, B) is left coprime and $C_L(\mathbf{r})E(\mathbf{r})$ has full normal rank, $C_L(\mathbf{r})E(\mathbf{r})$ is a greatest left factor of $(C_L E A, C_L E B)$. Furthermore, since $\beta(\mathbf{r})I_p$ is also a left factor of $(C_L E A, C_L E B)$, it follows that there exists $F \in \mathbb{R}^{p \times p}[\mathbf{r}]$ such that $C_L(\mathbf{r})E(\mathbf{r}) = \beta(\mathbf{r})F(\mathbf{r})$ and hence $(\beta F A, \beta F B) = (\beta C, \beta D)$.

Finally, since $A_L(\mathbf{r})$ has full normal rank, βI_p has full normal rank. Thus from Fact 2.2.2, $F(\mathbf{r})A(\mathbf{r}) = C(\mathbf{r})$ and $F(\mathbf{r})B(\mathbf{r}) = D(\mathbf{r})$. Furthermore, since $C_L(\mathbf{r})E(\mathbf{r})$ has full normal rank and $C_L(\mathbf{r})E(\mathbf{r}) = \beta(\mathbf{r})F(\mathbf{r})$, from Fact 2.2.1 it follows that $F(\mathbf{r})$ has full normal rank. □

2.5 Numerical Manipulation of Polynomial Matrices

In this section, we introduce notation and definitions that we use to numerically manipulate polynomial matrices.

Definition 2.5.1. Let $F \in \mathbb{R}^{p \times m}[\mathbf{r}]$ have degree n and be given by

$$F(\mathbf{r}) \triangleq F_0 + F_1 \mathbf{r} + \cdots + F_n \mathbf{r}^n.$$

Then for $s \geq 0$ and $t \geq 0$,

$$\theta(F) \triangleq \begin{bmatrix} F_0 & \cdots & F_n \end{bmatrix} \in \mathbb{R}^{p \times m(n+1)},$$

$$\theta_s(F) \triangleq \begin{bmatrix} F_0 & \cdots & F_s \end{bmatrix} \in \mathbb{R}^{p \times m(s+1)},$$

$$\mathcal{T}_s(F) \triangleq \begin{bmatrix} F_0 & F_1 & \cdots & F_s \\ 0_{p \times m} & \ddots & \ddots & \vdots \\ \vdots & \ddots & \ddots & F_1 \\ 0_{p \times m} & \cdots & 0_{p \times m} & F_0 \end{bmatrix} \in \mathbb{R}^{p(s+1) \times m(s+1)},$$

$$\mathcal{T}_{s,t}(F) \triangleq \begin{bmatrix} F_0 & F_1 & \cdots & F_s & F_{s+1} & \cdots & F_{s+t} \\ 0_{p \times m} & \ddots & \ddots & \vdots & \vdots & & \vdots \\ \vdots & \ddots & \ddots & F_1 & F_2 & & \vdots \\ 0_{p \times m} & \cdots & 0_{p \times m} & F_0 & F_1 & \cdots & F_t \end{bmatrix} \in \mathbb{R}^{p(s+1) \times m(s+t+1)},$$

$$\mathcal{K}_{s,t}(F) \triangleq \begin{bmatrix} \mathcal{T}_{s,t}(F) \\ \begin{bmatrix} I_{m(s+1)} & 0_{m(s+1) \times mt} \end{bmatrix} \end{bmatrix} \in \mathbb{R}^{(p+m)(s+1) \times m(s+t+1)},$$

$$\overline{\mathcal{K}}_{s,t}(F) \triangleq \begin{bmatrix} 0_{(m[s+1]+ps) \times p} & I_{(m[s+1]+ps)} \end{bmatrix} \mathcal{K}_{s,t}(F) \in \mathbb{R}^{(m[s+1]+ps) \times m(s+t+1)},$$

where $F_i = 0_{p \times m}$ for all $i > n$, and we drop the argument $\mathbf{r}$ for conciseness.

Remark 2.5.1. Note that $\theta(F) = \theta_n(F)$ and $\overline{\mathcal{K}}_{s,t}(F)$ is obtained by removing the first p rows of $\mathcal{K}_{s,t}(F)$. $\qquad\qquad\qquad\qquad\qquad\qquad\qquad$ $\square$

Fact 2.5.1. Let $E \in \mathbb{R}^{p \times m}[\mathbf{r}]$ be of degree n and let $C \in \mathbb{R}^{m \times l}[\mathbf{r}]$ be of degree s. Then the first $n + 1$ matrix coefficients of the product $D(\mathbf{r}) \triangleq E(\mathbf{r})C(\mathbf{r})$ are given by

$$\theta_n\left(D\right) = \theta\left(E\right)\mathcal{T}_n\left(C\right),$$

and all of the $n + s + 1$ matrix coefficients of $D(\mathbf{r})$ are given by

$$\theta\left(D\right) = \theta\left(E\right)\mathcal{T}_{n,s}\left(C\right).$$

Proof. For all $i = 0, \ldots, n + s$, we have that

$$D_i = \sum_{j=\max(0,i-s)}^{\min(n,i)} E_j C_{i-j},$$

from which Fact 2.5.1 follows. $\qquad\qquad\qquad\qquad\qquad\qquad\qquad\qquad\qquad$ $\square$

Fact 2.5.2. Let $E \in \mathbb{R}^{p \times m}[\mathbf{r}]$ be of degree n, $F \in \mathbb{R}^{m \times l}_{\infty}[\mathbf{r}]$, and $t \geq 0$. Then the first $n + t + 1$ matrix coefficients of the product $G(\mathbf{r}) \triangleq E(\mathbf{r})F(\mathbf{r})$ are given by

$$\theta_{n+t}\left(G\right) = \theta\left(E\right)\mathcal{T}_{n,t}\left(F\right),$$

Proof. For all $i = 0, \ldots, n + t$, we have that

$$G_i = \sum_{j=0}^{\min(n,i)} E_j F_{i-j},$$

from which Fact 2.5.2 follows. $\qquad\qquad\qquad\qquad\qquad\qquad\qquad\qquad\qquad$ $\square$

Remark 2.5.2. Let $D \in \mathbb{R}^{p \times m}[\mathbf{r}]$ be given by

$$D(\mathbf{r}) \triangleq \left[\begin{array}{ccc} d_1(\mathbf{r}) & \cdots & d_m(\mathbf{r}) \end{array}\right],$$

33

where $d_1, \ldots, d_m \in \mathbb{R}^{p \times 1}[\mathbf{r}]$. Then

$$\text{vec}\big[D(\mathbf{r})\big] \triangleq \begin{bmatrix} d_1(\mathbf{r}) \\ \vdots \\ d_m(\mathbf{r}) \end{bmatrix} \in \mathbb{R}^{pm \times 1}[\mathbf{r}],$$

$$I_s \otimes D(\mathbf{r}) \triangleq \begin{bmatrix} D(\mathbf{r}) & & \\ & \ddots & \\ & & D(\mathbf{r}) \end{bmatrix} \in \mathbb{R}^{ps \times ms}[\mathbf{r}].$$

$\square$

Fact 2.5.3. Let $C \in \mathbb{R}^{p \times m}[\mathbf{r}]$ and $D \in \mathbb{R}^{m \times \ell}[\mathbf{r}]$. Then

$$\text{vec}\big[C(\mathbf{r})D(\mathbf{r})\big] = \big[I_\ell \otimes C(\mathbf{r})\big]\text{vec}\big[D(\mathbf{r})\big].$$

Proof. See [68]. $\square$

2.6 Numerical Algorithms for Computing the Markov Parameters

Here we demonstrate how to compute the Markov parameters of (A, B) from a multiple of (A, B) numerically. Since Theorem 2.4.1 is constructive given a comonic multiple of (A, B), first we present two methods of computing a comonic multiple of (A, B) numerically.

Proposition 2.6.1. Let (C, D) be a multiple of (A, B). Then there exists a nonnegative t such that

$$\text{rank}\begin{bmatrix} \begin{bmatrix} 0_{p \times pt} & I_p \end{bmatrix} \\ \mathcal{T}_t(C) \end{bmatrix} = \text{rank}\big[\mathcal{T}_t(C)\big]. \tag{2.6}$$

34

Furthermore, let $U \in \mathbb{R}^{p \times p(t+1)}$ be a solution of

$$\begin{bmatrix} 0_{p \times pt} & I_p \end{bmatrix} = U \mathcal{T}_t (C),\tag{2.7}$$

and let $L \in \mathbb{R}^{p \times p}[\mathbf{r}]$ be the polynomial matrix of degree t such that

$$\theta (L) \triangleq U.$$

Then $(E, F) = (LC, LD)$ is a comonic multiple of (A, B) and (C, D).

Proof. From Proposition 2.2.1, there exists a comonic multiple $(E', F') = (L'C, L'D)$ of (A, B) and (C, D). Hence, letting E_γ be the trailing coefficient of $E'(\mathbf{r})$, we have that

$$\theta_\gamma (E') = \begin{bmatrix} 0_{p \times p\gamma} & I_p \end{bmatrix},$$

where, from Fact 2.5.1, it follows that

$$\theta_\gamma (E') = \begin{bmatrix} 0_{p \times p\gamma} & I_p \end{bmatrix} = \theta_\gamma (L') \mathcal{T}_\gamma (C).$$

Thus there exists a nonnegative t such that (2.6) holds.

Finally, since there exists a nonnegative t such that (2.6) holds, there exists a $U \in \mathbb{R}^{p \times p(t+1)}$ such that (2.7) holds ($\theta_t(L')$ being one such U). Hence,

$$\theta (L) \mathcal{T}_t (C) = \theta_t(E) = \begin{bmatrix} 0_{p \times pt} & I_p \end{bmatrix},$$

that is, $E(\mathbf{r})$ is comonic. Therefore (E, F) is a comonic multiple of (A, B) and (C, D). $\square$

Algorithm 2.6.1. Let (C, D) be a given multiple of (A, B) of degree s. The fol-

35

lowing algorithm yields a comonic multiple $(E, F) = (LC, LD)$ of (A, B), as described in Proposition 2.6.1.

1) $t = -1$.

2) $t = t + 1$.

3) $u = \text{rank}\left[\mathcal{T}_t(C)\right]$.

4) $v = \text{rank}\left[\begin{array}{c} \left[\begin{array}{cc} 0_{p \times pt} & I_p \end{array}\right] \\ \mathcal{T}_t(C) \end{array}\right]$.

5) If $u < v$, go to step 2. Otherwise, continue.

6) $\theta(L) = \left[\begin{array}{cc} 0_{p \times pt} & I_p \end{array}\right] \mathcal{T}_t^+(C)$, where $(\cdot)^+$ denotes the Moore-Penrose generalized inverse.

7) $\theta(E) = \theta(L)\mathcal{T}_{t,s}(C)$.

8) $\theta(F) = \theta(L)\mathcal{T}_{t,s}(D)$.

Next, we present an alternative method for computing a comonic multiple of (A, B). Specifically, we show how to compute a comonic quasi-scalar multiple of (A, B) from an arbitrary multiple (C, D) of (A, B).

Proposition 2.6.2. Let (C, D) be a multiple of (A, B) of degree s and let

$$L(\mathbf{r}) \triangleq I_m \otimes C^T(\mathbf{r}),$$
$$M(\mathbf{r}) \triangleq \text{vec}\left[D(\mathbf{r})\right]^T.$$

Then there exists a nonnegative t such that

$$\text{nullity}\left(W_t^T\right) \geq 1. \tag{2.8}$$

where

$$W_t \triangleq \begin{bmatrix} \mathcal{T}_{t,s}\left(M\right) \\ \mathcal{T}_{t,s}\left(L\right) \end{bmatrix}.$$

Furthermore, let $U \in \mathbb{R}^{(pm+1)(t+1)}$ be a nonzero vector in the nullspace of W_t^T, and let $\gamma' \in \mathbb{R}[\mathbf{r}]$ and $F' \in \mathbb{R}^{p \times m}[\mathbf{r}]$ be the polynomial matrices of degree t such that

$$\theta\left(\gamma'\right) \triangleq U^T \begin{bmatrix} I_{t+1} \\ 0_{pm(t+1) \times t+1} \end{bmatrix},$$

$$\theta\left(\text{vec}\left[F'\right]^T\right) \triangleq -U^T \begin{bmatrix} 0_{t+1 \times pm(t+1)} \\ I_{pm(t+1)} \end{bmatrix}.$$

Then $\gamma'(\mathbf{r})$ is nonzero. Finally, let γ_i be the trailing coefficient of $\gamma'(\mathbf{r})$, and let $\gamma(\mathbf{r}) \triangleq \gamma'(\mathbf{r})/\gamma_i$ and $F(\mathbf{r}) \triangleq F'(\mathbf{r})/\gamma_i$. Then $(\gamma I_p, F)$ is a comonic quasi-scalar multiple of (A, B).

Proof. First, letting $E(\mathbf{r}) \triangleq \text{madj}\left[C(\mathbf{r})\right]$ and $\beta(\mathbf{r}) \triangleq \text{mdet}\left[C(\mathbf{r})\right]$, it follows that

$$C(\mathbf{r})E(\mathbf{r})D(\mathbf{r}) = \beta(\mathbf{r})D(\mathbf{r}).$$

Hence, from Fact 2.5.3, we have that

$$\left[I_m \otimes C(\mathbf{r})\right]\text{vec}\left[E(\mathbf{r})D(\mathbf{r})\right] = \beta(\mathbf{r})\text{vec}\left[D(\mathbf{r})\right],$$

where $\beta(\mathbf{r})$ is nonzero since $C(\mathbf{r})$ has full normal rank. Thus, letting η denote the degree of $(\beta I_p, ED)$, from Fact 2.5.1 we have that

$$\theta\left(\text{vec}\left[ED\right]^T\right)\mathcal{T}_{\eta,s}\left(L\right) = \theta(\beta)\mathcal{T}_{\eta,s}\left(M\right).$$

37

Thus there exists a nonnegative t such that (2.8) holds.

Next, since there exists a nonnegative t such that (2.8) holds, there exists a nonzero $U \in \mathbb{R}^{(pm+1)(t+1)}$ in the nullspace of W_t^T. Furthermore, from the definition of $\gamma'(\mathbf{r})$ and $F'(\mathbf{r})$, it follows that

$$\theta\left(\mathrm{vec}\left[F'\right]^T\right)\mathcal{T}_{t,s}(L) = \theta\left(\gamma'\right)\mathcal{T}_{t,s}(M),$$

and hence from Fact 2.5.1, we have that $C(\mathbf{r})F'(\mathbf{r}) = \gamma'(\mathbf{r})D(\mathbf{r})$.

Next, suppose that $\gamma'(\mathbf{r})$ is zero. Then $C(\mathbf{r})F'(\mathbf{r}) = 0_{p \times m}$ and therefore, since $C(\mathbf{r})$ has full normal rank, from Fact 2.2.2, $F'(\mathbf{r}) = 0_{p \times m}$. However this contradicts the fact that U is nonzero. Hence $\gamma'(\mathbf{r})$ is nonzero.

Finally, letting $H \in \mathbb{R}^{p \times m}[\mathbf{r}]$ denote the Markov parameter polynomial of (A, B) and (C, D), it follows that

$$C(\mathbf{r})H(\mathbf{r}) = D(\mathbf{r}),$$
$$C(\mathbf{r})\gamma(\mathbf{r})H(\mathbf{r}) = \gamma(\mathbf{r})D(\mathbf{r}) = C(\mathbf{r})F(\mathbf{r}).$$

Therefore from Fact 2.2.2, $\gamma(\mathbf{r})H(\mathbf{r}) = F(\mathbf{r})$. Furthermore, since $\gamma(\mathbf{r})I_p$ is comonic and quasi-scalar, from Fact 2.2.4, $\gamma(\mathbf{r})$ has full normal rank. Therefore, from Theorem 2.4.2, $(\gamma I_p, F)$ is a comonic quasi-scalar multiple of (A, B). $\qquad\square$

Algorithm 2.6.2. Let (C, D) be a given multiple of (A, B) of degree s. The following algorithm yields a comonic quasi-scalar multiple $(\gamma I_p, F)$ of (A, B), as described in Proposition 2.6.2.

1) $t = -1$.

2) $L(\mathbf{r}) = I_m \otimes C^T(\mathbf{r})$.

3) $M(\mathbf{r}) = \mathrm{vec}\left[D(\mathbf{r})\right]^T$.

38

4) $t = t + 1$.

5) Compute the singular value decomposition of

$$
W_t = \begin{bmatrix} \mathcal{T}_{t,s}(M) \\ \mathcal{T}_{t,s}(L) \end{bmatrix}.
$$

6) If nullity $\left(W_t^T\right) = 0$, go to step 4. Otherwise, continue.

7) Choose a nonzero vector $U \in \mathbb{R}^{(pm+1)(t+1)}$ in the nullspace of W_t^T, and scale U such that the first nonzero component is 1.

8) $\theta(\gamma) = U^T \begin{bmatrix} I_{t+1} \\ 0_{pm(t+1) \times t+1} \end{bmatrix}$.

9) $\theta\left(\text{vec}\,[F]^T\right) = -U^T \begin{bmatrix} 0_{t+1 \times pm(t+1)} \\ I_{pm(t+1)} \end{bmatrix}$.

Remark 2.6.1. Proposition 2.6.1 and 2.6.2 provide two alternative ways of obtaining a comonic multiple of (A, B) numerically, with the main difference being that Proposition 2.6.1 provides a comonic multiple of both (A, B) and (C, D), while Proposition 2.6.2 provides a quasi-scalar comonic multiple that is only guaranteed to be a multiple of (A, B). Typically, Proposition 2.6.1 will provide a comonic multiple of lower degree than Proposition 2.6.2, due to the quasi-scalar requirement in Proposition 2.6.2, however this is not always the case. One of the benefits of Proposition 2.6.2 is that quasi-scalar multiples exhibit a direct link to transfer function, and thus state-space, models, as shown in Section 2.8, albeit at the expense of increased computational complexity. $\qquad \square$

Now that we have shown how to compute a comonic multiple of (A, B) numerically, Theorem 2.4.1 can be used to compute the Markov parameters of (A, B) algebraically. Specifically, we have the following proposition:

39

Proposition 2.6.3. Let (C, D) be a multiple of (A, B) and let (E, F) be a comonic multiple of (A, B) computed using either Proposition 2.6.1 (Algorithm 2.6.1) or Proposition 2.6.2 (Algorithm 2.6.2). Then the Markov parameters of (A, B) are given by (2.4).

2.7 Numerical Algorithms for Computing a Multiple of (A, B)

Here we present two methods of computing a multiple of (A, B) numerically from the Markov parameters of (A, B).

Proposition 2.7.1. Let $H \in \mathbb{R}_\infty^{p \times m}[\mathbf{r}]$ be the Markov parameter polynomial of (A, B) and let $\bar{n} \geq n^*$. Then for all nonnegative t,

$$\operatorname{rank}\left[\mathcal{K}_{t,n^*}(H)\right] = \operatorname{rank}\left[\mathcal{K}_{t,\bar{n}}(H)\right], \tag{2.9}$$

$$\operatorname{rank}\left[\overline{\mathcal{K}}_{t,n^*}(H)\right] = \operatorname{rank}\left[\overline{\mathcal{K}}_{t,\bar{n}}(H)\right]. \tag{2.10}$$

Furthermore, there exists a nonnegative $s \leq n^*$ such that

$$\operatorname{rank}\left[\overline{\mathcal{K}}_{s,n^*}(H)\right] = \operatorname{rank}\left[\mathcal{K}_{s,n^*}(H)\right]. \tag{2.11}$$

Finally, letting (2.11) hold, letting $E \in \mathbb{R}^{p \times p}[\mathbf{r}]$ have full normal rank, letting $F \in \mathbb{R}^{p \times m}[\mathbf{r}]$, and

$$\begin{bmatrix} \theta\,(E) & -\theta\,(F) \end{bmatrix} \mathcal{K}_{s,\bar{n}}(H) = 0_{p \times m(s + \bar{n} + 1)}, \tag{2.12}$$

then (E, F) is a multiple of (A, B).

Proof. First, since (A^*, B^*) is a quasi-scalar multiple of (A, B), then

$$A^*(\mathbf{r})H(\mathbf{r}) = B^*(\mathbf{r}).$$

40

Furthermore, from (2.4), for all $j \geq 1$ we have that

$$a_{n^*}^* H_j + \cdots + a_1^* H_{n^*+j-1} + H_{n^*+j} = 0_{p \times m},$$

where, since $a_1^*, \ldots, a_{n^*}^* \in \mathbb{R}$,

$$H_j a_{n^*}^* + \cdots + H_{n^*+j-1} a_1^* + H_{n^*+j} = 0_{p \times m}. \tag{2.13}$$

Next, suppose that $\bar{n} = n^* + 1$. Then from (2.13), the columns of $\mathcal{K}_{t,\bar{n}}(H)$ beginning with H_{t+n^*+1} are in the column space of the previous mn^* columns, specifically,

$$\begin{bmatrix} H_{t+1} \\ \vdots \\ H_1 \\ 0_{m(t+1) \times m} \end{bmatrix} a_n^* + \cdots + \begin{bmatrix} H_{t+n^*} \\ \vdots \\ H_{n^*} \\ 0_{m(t+1) \times m} \end{bmatrix} a_1^* + \begin{bmatrix} H_{t+n^*+1} \\ \vdots \\ H_{n^*+1} \\ 0_{m(t+1) \times m} \end{bmatrix} = 0_{(p+m)(t+1) \times m}.$$

Similarly, for all $j \geq 1$, the columns of $\mathcal{K}_{t,n^*+j}(H)$ beginning with H_{t+n^*+j} are in the column space of the previous mn^* columns. Hence, by induction, we have (2.9). Furthermore, (2.10) follows directly from (2.9) since $\overline{\mathcal{K}}_{t,\bar{n}}(H)$ is obtained by removing the first p rows of $\mathcal{K}_{t,\bar{n}}(H)$.

Next, since (A^*, B^*) is a comonic quasi-scalar multiple of (A, B), from Fact 2.5.2, we have that

$$\theta(A^*) \mathcal{T}_{n^*,n^*}(H) = \theta_{2n^*}(B^*) = \begin{bmatrix} \theta(B^*) & 0_{p \times mn^*} \end{bmatrix},$$

and hence

$$\begin{bmatrix} \theta(A^*) & -\theta(B^*) \end{bmatrix} \mathcal{K}_{n^*,n^*}(H) = 0_{p \times m(2n^*+1)},$$

41

where, since $A^*(\mathbf{r})$ is comonic with $A_0^* = I_p$, we have (2.11).

Finally, let $E(\mathbf{r})$ have full normal rank and let (2.12) hold. Then from (2.9), for all $j \geq 1$, we have that

$$\left[\begin{array}{cc} \theta\,(E) & -\theta\,(F) \end{array}\right] \mathcal{K}_{s,\bar{n}+j}(H) = 0_{p \times m(s+\bar{n}+j+1)},$$

and hence

$$\theta\big(E\big)\mathcal{T}_{s,\bar{n}+j}\big(H\big) = \left[\begin{array}{cc} \theta\big(F\big) & 0_{p \times m(\bar{n}+j)} \end{array}\right].$$

Therefore, from Fact 2.5.2, $E(\mathbf{r})H(\mathbf{r}) = F(\mathbf{r})$, and from Theorem 2.4.2, (E, F) is a multiple of (A, B). $\qquad\square$

Algorithm 2.7.1. Let $\bar{n}$ be a known upper bound for n^*, that is, $\bar{n} \geq n^*$. Also, let $H(\mathbf{r})$ be the Markov parameter polynomial of (A, B), and let $H_0, \ldots, H_{2\bar{n}+1}$ be given. Then following algorithm yields a comonic multiple (E, F) of (A, B), as described in Proposition 2.7.1.

1) $s = 0$.

2) $s = s + 1$.

3) $u = \operatorname{rank}\left[\overline{\mathcal{K}}_{s,\bar{n}}(H)\right]$.

4) $v = \operatorname{rank}\left[\mathcal{K}_{s,\bar{n}}(H)\right]$.

5) If $u < v$, go to step 2. Otherwise, continue.

6) $W = \theta_{s+\bar{n}}(H)\overline{\mathcal{K}}_{s,\bar{n}}^{+}(H)$, where $(\cdot)^+$ denotes the Moore-Penrose generalized inverse.

7) $\theta\,(E) = \left[\begin{array}{cc} I_p & -W \left[\begin{array}{c} I_{ps} \\ 0_{m(s+1) \times ps} \end{array}\right] \end{array}\right].$

8) $\theta(F) = W \begin{bmatrix} 0_{ps \times m(s+1)} \\ I_{m(s+1)} \end{bmatrix}$.

Next, we present an alternative method for computing a comonic multiple of (A, B). Specifically, we show how to compute a comonic quasi-scalar multiple of (A, B) from the Markov parameters of (A, B).

Proposition 2.7.2. Let $H \in \mathbb{R}^{p \times m}_\infty[\mathbf{r}]$ be the Markov parameter polynomial of (A, B), $\bar{n} \geq n^\star$, and $H^\star(\mathbf{r}) \triangleq \mathrm{vec}[H(\mathbf{r})]^T$. Then for all nonnegative t,

$$\mathrm{rank}[\mathcal{K}_{t,n^\star}(H^\star)] = \mathrm{rank}[\mathcal{K}_{t,\bar{n}}(H^\star)]. \tag{2.14}$$

Furthermore, there exists a nonnegative $s \leq n^\star$ such that

$$\mathrm{nullity}[\mathcal{K}^T_{s,n^\star}(H^\star)] \geq 1. \tag{2.15}$$

Finally, letting $\gamma \in \mathbb{R}[\mathbf{r}]$ be nonzero, $D \in \mathbb{R}^{1 \times pm}[\mathbf{r}]$, and

$$\begin{bmatrix} \theta(\gamma) & -\theta(D) \end{bmatrix} \mathcal{K}_{s,\bar{n}}(H^\star) = 0_{1 \times pm(s+\bar{n}+1)}, \tag{2.16}$$
$$F(\mathbf{r}) \triangleq \mathrm{unvec}[D^T(\mathbf{r})],$$

then $(\gamma I_p, F)$ is a quasi-scalar multiple of (A, B).

Proof. First, since $(A^\star, B^\star)$ is a quasi-scalar multiple of (A, B), then

$$A^\star(\mathbf{r})H(\mathbf{r}) = B^\star(\mathbf{r}).$$

Hence letting $\overline{B}^\star(\mathbf{r}) \triangleq \mathrm{vec}[B(\mathbf{r})]^T$, from Fact 2.5.3, we have that

$$a^\star(\mathbf{r})H^\star(\mathbf{r}) = \overline{B}^\star(\mathbf{r}).$$

43

Therefore, from (2.4), for all $j \geq 1$ we have that

$$a_{n^*}^* H_j^* + \cdots + a_1^* H_{n^*+j-1}^* + H_{n^*+j}^* = 0_{1 \times pm},$$

where, since $a_1^*, \ldots, a_{n^*}^* \in \mathbb{R}$,

$$H_j^* a_{n^*}^* + \cdots + H_{n^*+j-1}^* a_1^* + H_{n^*+j}^* = 0_{1 \times pm}.$$

Thus (2.14) follows directly from the proof of Proposition 2.7.1.

Next, since (A^*, B^*) is a comonic quasi-scalar multiple of (A, B), from Fact 2.5.2, we have that

$$\theta(a^*) \mathcal{T}_{n^*, n^*}(H^*) = \theta_{2n^*}\left(\overline{B}^*\right) = \left[\begin{array}{cc} \theta\left(\overline{B}^*\right) & 0_{1 \times pmn^*} \end{array}\right],$$

and hence

$$\left[\begin{array}{cc} \theta(a^*) & -\theta\left(\overline{B}^*\right) \end{array}\right] \mathcal{K}_{n^*, n^*}(H^*) = 0_{1 \times pm(2n^*+1)},$$

where, since $a^*(\mathbf{r})$ is comonic with $a_0^* = 1$, we have (2.15).

Finally, let $\gamma(\mathbf{r})$ be nonzero and let (2.16) hold. Then from (2.14), for all $j \geq 1$, we have that

$$\left[\begin{array}{cc} \theta(\gamma) & -\theta(D) \end{array}\right] \mathcal{K}_{s, \bar{n}+j}(H^*) = 0_{1 \times pm(s+\bar{n}+j+1)},$$

and hence

$$\theta(\gamma) \mathcal{T}_{s, \bar{n}+j}(H^*) = \left[\begin{array}{cc} \theta(D) & 0_{1 \times pm(\bar{n}+j)} \end{array}\right].$$

44

Therefore, from Fact 2.5.2, $\gamma(\mathbf{r})H^*(\mathbf{r}) = D(\mathbf{r})$, and from Fact 2.5.3,

$$\gamma(\mathbf{r})H(\mathbf{r}) = F(\mathbf{r}).$$

Furthermore, since $\gamma(\mathbf{r})$ is nonzero and quasi-scalar, from Fact 2.2.4, $\gamma(\mathbf{r})I_p$ has full normal rank. Hence, from Theorem 2.4.2, $(\gamma I_p, F)$ is a multiple of (A, B). $\square$

Algorithm 2.7.2. Let $\bar{n}$ be a known upper bound for n^*, that is, $\bar{n} \geq n^*$. Also, let $H(\mathbf{r})$ be the Markov parameter polynomial of (A, B), and let $H_0, \ldots, H_{2\bar{n}+1}$ be given. Finally, for all $i = 0, \ldots, 2\bar{n} + 1$, let $H_i^* \triangleq \text{vec}\left[H_i\right]^T$. Then the following algorithm yields a quasi-scalar comonic multiple $(\gamma I_p, F)$ of (A, B), as described in Proposition 2.7.2.

1) $s = 0$.

2) $s = s + 1$.

3) Compute the singular value decomposition of $\mathcal{K}_{s,\bar{n}}(H^*)$.

4) If nullity $\left(\mathcal{K}_{s,\bar{n}}^T(H^*)\right) = 0$, go to step 2. Otherwise, continue.

5) Choose a nonzero vector $U \in \mathbb{R}^{1 \times (pm+1)(s+1)}$ in the left nullspace of $\mathcal{K}_{s,\bar{n}}(H^*)$.

6) $\theta(\gamma) = U \begin{bmatrix} I_{s+1} \\ 0_{pm(s+1) \times (s+1)} \end{bmatrix}$.

7) $\theta(D) = -U \begin{bmatrix} 0_{(s+1) \times pm(s+1)} \\ I_{pm(s+1)} \end{bmatrix}$.

8) $F(\mathbf{r}) = \text{unvec}\left[D^T(\mathbf{r})\right]$.

Remark 2.7.1. As in the previous section, Proposition 2.7.1 and 2.7.2 provide two alternative ways of obtaining a comonic multiple of (A, B) numerically from the Markov parameters, with the main difference being that Proposition 2.7.1 provides a

45

comonic multiple, while Proposition 2.7.2 provides a quasi-scalar comonic multiple. Proposition 2.7.1 will always provide a comonic multiple of degree less than or equal to Proposition 2.7.2, due to the quasi-scalar requirement in Proposition 2.7.2. However, one of the benefits of Proposition 2.7.2 is that quasi-scalar multiples exhibit a direct link to transfer function, and thus state-space, models, as we demonstrate in the following section, albeit at the expense of increased computational complexity. □

Remark 2.7.2. In both Algorithm 2.7.1 and Algorithm 2.7.2, it is required that an upper bound $\bar{n}$ for $n^\star$ is known. However, in practice, this may be difficult or impossible to ascertain. In this case, we would advise the reader to take an initial guess of for the upper bound, say n_1, and run the algorithms as proposed. If in Algorithms 2.7.1 and 2.7.2, the rank conditions are not satisfied for $s \leq n_1$, then increase n_1, provide more Markov parameters, and run the algorithms again. □

2.8 Connection with State-Space Models

Here we consider the connection between polynomial matrix models, state-space models, and Markov parameters. Specifically, we review the well-known method of obtaining a polynomial matrix model from a state-space model, and then show that, using the Markov parameters of the state-space model, we can obtain the same polynomial matrix model using the algorithms in the present chapter, particularly Proposition 2.7.1. Furthermore, we show that all of the same rank properties presented in Proposition 2.7.1 still hold when the Markov parameters are generated from a state-space model, where $n^\star$ is replaced by the degree of the state-space model which generates the Markov parameters.

46

Proposition 2.8.1. Consider the state-space system

$$x(t) = \mathbf{r}\tilde{A}x(t) + \mathbf{r}\tilde{B}u(t),$$

$$y(t) = \tilde{C}x(t) + \tilde{D}u(t),$$

where $\tilde{A} \in \mathbb{R}^{n\times n}$, $\tilde{B} \in \mathbb{R}^{n\times m}$, $\tilde{C} \in \mathbb{R}^{p\times n}$, and $\tilde{D} \in \mathbb{R}^{p\times m}$, $x \in \mathbb{R}^n$ is the state, $u \in \mathbb{R}^m$ is the input, and $y \in \mathbb{R}^p$ is the output. Also, let

$$A(\mathbf{r}) \triangleq \det\left[I_n - \mathbf{r}\tilde{A}\right],$$

$$E(\mathbf{r}) \triangleq \mathrm{adj}\left[I_n - \mathbf{r}\tilde{A}\right],$$

$$B(\mathbf{r}) \triangleq \mathbf{r}\tilde{C}E(\mathbf{r})\tilde{B} + A(\mathbf{r})\tilde{D}.$$

Then $A(\mathbf{r})y(t) = B(\mathbf{r})u(t)$.

Proof.

$$A(\mathbf{r})y(t) = \tilde{C}A(\mathbf{r})x(t) + A(\mathbf{r})\tilde{D}u(t) = \tilde{C}\left[E(\mathbf{r})\mathbf{r}\tilde{B}u(t)\right] + A(\mathbf{r})\tilde{D}u(t) = B(\mathbf{r})u(t).$$

$\square$

Definition 2.8.1. Let $\tilde{A} \in \mathbb{R}^{n\times n}$, $\tilde{B} \in \mathbb{R}^{n\times m}$, $\tilde{C} \in \mathbb{R}^{p\times n}$, and $\tilde{D} \in \mathbb{R}^{p\times m}$. Also, for $i \geq 1$, let

$$H_0 \triangleq \tilde{D}, \quad H_1 \triangleq \tilde{C}\tilde{B}, \quad H_2 = \tilde{C}\tilde{A}\tilde{B}, \quad \cdots, \quad H_i \triangleq \tilde{C}\tilde{A}^{i-1}\tilde{B}.$$

Then H_j is the jth *Markov parameter* of $(\tilde{A}, \tilde{B}, \tilde{C}, \tilde{D})$, and

$$H(\mathbf{r}) \triangleq \sum_{j=0}^{\infty} H_j\mathbf{r}^j,$$

is the *Markov parameter polynomial* of $(\tilde{A}, \tilde{B}, \tilde{C}, \tilde{D})$.

Proposition 2.8.2. Consider the controllable state-space model

$$x(t) = \mathbf{r}\tilde{A}x(t) + \mathbf{r}\tilde{B}u(t),$$

$$y(t) = \tilde{C}x(t) + \tilde{D}u(t),$$

where $\tilde{A} \in \mathbb{R}^{n \times n}$, $\tilde{B} \in \mathbb{R}^{n \times m}$, $\tilde{C} \in \mathbb{R}^{p \times n}$, and $\tilde{D} \in \mathbb{R}^{p \times m}$, $x \in \mathbb{R}^n$ is the state, $u \in \mathbb{R}^m$ is the input, and $y \in \mathbb{R}^p$ is the output. Furthermore, let $\bar{n} \geq n$ and let $H \in \mathbb{R}_\infty^{p \times m}[\mathbf{r}]$ be the Markov parameter polynomial of $(\tilde{A}, \tilde{B}, \tilde{C}, \tilde{D})$. Then for all nonnegative t,

$$\text{rank}\Big[\mathcal{K}_{t,n}(H)\Big] = \text{rank}\Big[\mathcal{K}_{t,\bar{n}}(H)\Big], \tag{2.17}$$

$$\text{rank}\Big[\overline{\mathcal{K}}_{t,n}(H)\Big] = \text{rank}\Big[\overline{\mathcal{K}}_{t,\bar{n}}(H)\Big]. \tag{2.18}$$

Furthermore, letting

$$A(\mathbf{r}) \triangleq \det\Big[I_n - \mathbf{r}\tilde{A}\Big],$$

$$E(\mathbf{r}) \triangleq \text{adj}\Big[I_n - \mathbf{r}\tilde{A}\Big],$$

$$B(\mathbf{r}) \triangleq \mathbf{r}\tilde{C}E(\mathbf{r})\tilde{B} + A(\mathbf{r})\tilde{D},$$

then

$$\Big[\ \theta_n\,(AI_p)\ \ -\theta_n\,(B)\ \Big]\mathcal{K}_{n,\bar{n}}\,(H) = 0_{p \times m(n+\bar{n}+1)}, \tag{2.19}$$

and there exists a nonnegative $s \leq n$ such that

$$\text{rank}\Big[\overline{\mathcal{K}}_{s,n}(H)\Big] = \text{rank}\Big[\mathcal{K}_{s,n}(H)\Big]. \tag{2.20}$$

Proof. First, note that from Definition 2.5.1 and Definition 2.8.1, for all $\bar{n} \geq n$

48

and $t \geq 0$, we have that

$$\mathcal{K}_{t,\bar{n}}(H) = \left[\begin{array}{cc} \mathcal{T}_t(H) & \mathcal{O}_t\left(\tilde{A}, \tilde{C}\right)\mathcal{C}_{\bar{n}}\left(\tilde{A}, \tilde{B}\right) \\ I_{m(t+1)} & 0_{m(t+1)\times m\bar{n}} \end{array} \right],$$

$$\mathcal{O}_t\left(\tilde{A}, \tilde{C}\right) \triangleq \left[\begin{array}{cccc} \left(\tilde{C}\tilde{A}^t\right)^T & \cdots & \left(\tilde{C}\tilde{A}\right)^T & \tilde{C}^T \end{array} \right]^T,$$

$$\mathcal{C}_{\bar{n}}\left(\tilde{A}, \tilde{B}\right) \triangleq \left[\begin{array}{cccc} \tilde{B} & \tilde{A}\tilde{B} & \cdots & \tilde{A}^{\bar{n}-1}\tilde{B} \end{array} \right],$$

where $\mathcal{O}_n\left(\tilde{A}, \tilde{C}\right)$ is the reordered observability matrix of $(\tilde{A}, \tilde{C})$, and $\mathcal{C}_n\left(\tilde{A}, \tilde{B}\right)$ is the controllability matrix of $(\tilde{A}, \tilde{B})$. Furthermore, since $(\tilde{A}, \tilde{B}, \tilde{C}, \tilde{D})$ is controllable, then for all $\bar{n} \geq n$, $\mathcal{C}_{\bar{n}}\left(\tilde{A}, \tilde{B}\right)$ has full row rank. Hence for all $\bar{n} \geq n$, it follows that

$$\mathrm{rank}\left[\mathcal{O}_t\left(\tilde{A}, \tilde{C}\right)\mathcal{C}_n\left(\tilde{A}, \tilde{B}\right)\right] = \mathrm{rank}\left[\mathcal{O}_t\left(\tilde{A}, \tilde{C}\right)\mathcal{C}_{\bar{n}}\left(\tilde{A}, \tilde{B}\right)\right] = \mathrm{rank}\left[\mathcal{O}_t\left(\tilde{A}, \tilde{C}\right)\right] \leq n,$$

that is, the final $m(\bar{n}-n)$ columns of $\mathcal{K}_{t,\bar{n}}(H)$ are in the column space of the previous mn columns and therefore (2.17). Similarly, we have (2.18).

Next, note that

$$B(\mathbf{r}) - A(\mathbf{r})H(\mathbf{r}) = \mathbf{r}\tilde{C}E(\mathbf{r})\tilde{B} + A(\mathbf{r})\tilde{D} - A(\mathbf{r})\left(\tilde{D} + \sum_{i=1}^{\infty}\tilde{C}\tilde{A}^{i-1}\tilde{B}\mathbf{r}^i\right),$$

$$= \mathbf{r}\tilde{C}\left(E(\mathbf{r}) - A(\mathbf{r})\sum_{i=0}^{\infty}\tilde{A}^i\mathbf{r}^i\right)\tilde{B}.$$

Furthermore, since

$$\left[I_n - \mathbf{r}\tilde{A}\right]\sum_{i=0}^{\infty}\tilde{A}^i\mathbf{r}^i = I_n,$$

it follows that

$$\left[I_n - \mathbf{r}\tilde{A}\right]\left(E(\mathbf{r}) - A(\mathbf{r})\sum_{i=0}^{\infty}\tilde{A}^i\mathbf{r}^i\right) = \det\left[I_n - \mathbf{r}\tilde{A}\right] - A(\mathbf{r}) = 0_{n\times n},$$

49

where, since $\left[I_n - \mathbf{r}\tilde{A}\right]$ is regular, from Fact 2.2.3, $\left[I_n - \mathbf{r}\tilde{A}\right]$ has full row rank. Hence, from Fact 2.2.2,

$$E(\mathbf{r}) - A(\mathbf{r}) \sum_{i=0}^{\infty} \tilde{A}^i \mathbf{r}^i = 0_{n \times n},$$

and therefore

$$B(\mathbf{r}) - A(\mathbf{r})H(\mathbf{r}) = \mathbf{r}\tilde{C}\left(0_{n \times n}\right)\tilde{B} = 0_{p \times m},$$

that is, $A(\mathbf{r})H(\mathbf{r}) = B(\mathbf{r})$.

Finally, note that $A(\mathbf{r})$ has degree less than or equal n from the definition of the determinant, and from the definition of the adjugate in terms of the cofactor matrix, it follows that $E(\mathbf{r})$ has degree less than or equal $n - 1$. Hence $B(\mathbf{r})$ has degree less than or equal to n. Therefore, since (A, B) has degree less than or equal n, and $A(\mathbf{r})H(\mathbf{r}) = B(\mathbf{r})$, we have (2.19). Furthermore, since

$$A(0) = \det\left[I_n - 0 \times \tilde{A}\right] = 1 = A_0,$$

we have (2.20). □

2.9 Numerical Examples

In the following, we illustrate Algorithm 2.6.1, Algorithm 2.6.2, Proposition 2.6.3, Algorithm 2.7.1, and Algorithm 2.7.2 with a low-degree example for conciseness. Let

$$A(\mathbf{r}) \triangleq \begin{bmatrix} (2+\mathbf{r}) & (3+\mathbf{r}) \\ (5+\mathbf{r}) & (7+\mathbf{r}) \end{bmatrix}, \tag{2.21}$$

$$B(\mathbf{r}) \triangleq \begin{bmatrix} (1+\mathbf{r}) & (2+\mathbf{r}) & (3+\mathbf{r}) \\ (4+\mathbf{r}) & (5+\mathbf{r}) & (6+\mathbf{r}) \end{bmatrix}, \tag{2.22}$$

$$N(\mathbf{r}) \triangleq \begin{bmatrix} (1+\mathbf{r}) & (2+\mathbf{r}) \\ (3+\mathbf{r}) & (6+\mathbf{r}) \end{bmatrix}, \tag{2.23}$$

and $(C, D) \triangleq (NA, NB)$. Then (C, D) is a multiple of (A, B), and

$$C(\mathbf{r}) = \begin{bmatrix} 12 + 10\mathbf{r} + 2\mathbf{r}^2 & 17 + 13\mathbf{r} + 2\mathbf{r}^2 \\ 36 + 16\mathbf{r} + 2\mathbf{r}^2 & 51 + 19\mathbf{r} + 2\mathbf{r}^2 \end{bmatrix}, \tag{2.24}$$

$$D(\mathbf{r}) = \begin{bmatrix} 9 + 8\mathbf{r} + 2\mathbf{r}^2 & 12 + 10\mathbf{r} + 2\mathbf{r}^2 & 15 + 12\mathbf{r} + 2\mathbf{r}^2 \\ 27 + 14\mathbf{r} + 2\mathbf{r}^2 & 36 + 16\mathbf{r} + 2\mathbf{r}^2 & 45 + 18\mathbf{r} + 2\mathbf{r}^2 \end{bmatrix}. \tag{2.25}$$

Furthermore,

$$\theta(C) = \begin{bmatrix} 12 & 17 & 10 & 13 & 2 & 2 \\ 36 & 51 & 16 & 19 & 2 & 2 \end{bmatrix},$$

$$\theta(D) = \begin{bmatrix} 9 & 12 & 15 & 8 & 10 & 12 & 2 & 2 & 2 \\ 27 & 36 & 45 & 14 & 16 & 18 & 2 & 2 & 2 \end{bmatrix},$$

where we insert vertical lines in $\theta(\cdot)$ to separate coefficients.

Example 2.9.1. Let $C(\mathbf{r})$ and $D(\mathbf{r})$ be given by (2.24) and (2.25), respectively.

The following example illustrates Algorithm 2.6.1.

First, the following table displays the normalized singular values ($\bar{\sigma}_i \triangleq \sigma_i/\sigma_{\max}$) of $T_t(C)$ and

$$\mathcal{I}_t(C) \triangleq \left[\begin{array}{c} \left[\begin{array}{cc} 0_{p \times pt} & I_p \end{array} \right] \\ T_t(C) \end{array} \right],$$

for $t = 0$ and $t = 1$. Since the ranks both equal 3 for $t = 1$, we move to step 6.

	$\bar{\sigma}[T_t(C)]$			$\bar{\sigma}[\mathcal{I}_t(C)]$		
t	$\bar{\sigma}_2$	$\bar{\sigma}_3$	$\bar{\sigma}_4$	$\bar{\sigma}_2$	$\bar{\sigma}_3$	$\bar{\sigma}_4$
0	6.2×10^{-17}			0.015		
1	0.65	3.7×10^{-4}	2.0×10^{-21}	0.65	1.2×10^{-2}	1.6×10^{-17}

Next, from Step 6, we have that

$$\theta(L) = \left[\begin{array}{cc|cc} -25.5 & 8.5 & 1 & 3 \\ 18 & -6 & -0.7 & -2.1 \end{array} \right],$$

and from Step 7 and 8, we have that

$$\theta(E) = \left[\begin{array}{cc|cc|cc|cc} \epsilon_1 & \epsilon_1 & 1 & \epsilon_1 & 24 & 36 & 8 & 8 \\ \epsilon_2 & \epsilon_2 & \epsilon_3 & 1 & -16.6 & -25 & -5.6 & -5.6 \end{array} \right],$$

$$\theta(F) = \left[\begin{array}{ccc|ccc|ccc|ccc} \epsilon_2 & \epsilon_1 & \epsilon_1 & 5 & 1 & -3 & 16 & 24 & 32 & 8 & 8 & 8 \\ \epsilon_4 & \epsilon_2 & \epsilon_2 & -3 & \epsilon_3 & 3 & -11 & -16.6 & -22.2 & -5.6 & -5.6 & -5.6 \end{array} \right],$$

52

where

$$\epsilon_1 \triangleq 1.1369 \times 10^{-13},$$

$$\epsilon_2 \triangleq -5.6843 \times 10^{-14},$$

$$\epsilon_3 \triangleq 9.9476 \times 10^{-14},$$

$$\epsilon_4 \triangleq -2.8422 \times 10^{-14}.$$

Therefore, we can see that the multiple $(E, F) = (LC, LD) = (LNA, LNB)$ is comonic. $\quad\square$

Example 2.9.2. Let $C(\mathbf{r})$ and $D(\mathbf{r})$ be given by (2.24) and (2.25), respectively. The following example illustrates Algorithm 2.6.2.

First, we begin by constructing $L(\mathbf{r}) = I_3 \otimes C^T(\mathbf{r})$ and $M(\mathbf{r}) = \text{vec}\,[D(\mathbf{r})]^T$. Then, examining the following table, which displays the inverse condition number of W_t for $t = 0$ and $t = 1$, we see that nullity $\left(W_t^T\right) > 0$ for $t = 1$.

t	$\sigma_{\min}\left[W_t^T\right]/\sigma_{\max}\left[W_t^T\right]$
0	8.8×10^{-4}
1	8.9×10^{-17}

Hence, proceeding to Steps 7-10 with $t = 1$, we find that

$$\theta(\gamma) = \left[\begin{array}{c|c} 1 & -1 \end{array}\right],$$

$$\theta(F) = \left[\begin{array}{ccc|ccc} 5 & 1 & -3 & -1 & -1 & -1 \\ -3 & 5 \times 10^{-14} & 3 & -9 \times 10^{-14} & -5 \times 10^{-15} & -4 \times 10^{-14} \end{array}\right].$$

Next, we would like to verify that $(\gamma I_2, F)$ is indeed a multiple of (A, B). To accomplish this, note that if $H \in \mathbb{R}_\infty^{2 \times 3}[\mathbf{r}]$ is the Markov parameter polynomial of

(A, B), we should have that

$$A(\mathbf{r})H(\mathbf{r}) = B(\mathbf{r}),$$

$$\gamma(\mathbf{r})H(\mathbf{r}) = F(\mathbf{r}),$$

and therefore

$$\gamma(\mathbf{r})A(\mathbf{r})H(\mathbf{r}) = A(\mathbf{r})\gamma(\mathbf{r})H(\mathbf{r}) = A(\mathbf{r})F(\mathbf{r}) = \gamma(\mathbf{r})B(\mathbf{r}).$$

Thus, to compare the accuracy of our computed quasi-scalar comonic multiple, let $\varepsilon_1(\mathbf{r}) \triangleq A(\mathbf{r})F(\mathbf{r}) - \gamma(\mathbf{r})B(\mathbf{r})$ and $\varepsilon_2(\mathbf{r}) \triangleq A(\mathbf{r})F(\mathbf{r})$. Then one type of percent error metric is

$$\frac{\left\|\theta(\varepsilon_1)\right\|_{\mathrm{F}}}{\left\|\theta(\varepsilon_2)\right\|_{\mathrm{F}}} = 1.018 \times 10^{-14},$$

where $\|\cdot\|_{\mathrm{F}}$ denotes the Frobenius norm of $(\cdot)$, and this type of percent error is meant to give us some indication of how far the product $\gamma(\mathbf{r})B(\mathbf{r})$ is from $A(\mathbf{r})F(\mathbf{r})$. Since this number is small, numerically we have that $A(\mathbf{r})F(\mathbf{r}) = \gamma(\mathbf{r})B(\mathbf{r})$.

Finally, since $A(\mathbf{r})F(\mathbf{r}) = \gamma(\mathbf{r})B(\mathbf{r})$, we have that

$$\gamma(\mathbf{r})B(\mathbf{r}) = A(\mathbf{r})F(\mathbf{r}) = A(\mathbf{r})\gamma(\mathbf{r})H(\mathbf{r}),$$

and hence from Fact 2.2.2, it follows that $\gamma(\mathbf{r})H(\mathbf{r}) = F(\mathbf{r})$. Furthermore, since $\gamma(\mathbf{r})$ is nonzero and quasi-scalar, from Fact 2.2.4, $\gamma(\mathbf{r})I_2$ has full normal rank. Hence from Theorem 2.4.2, $(\gamma I_2, F)$ is a comonic quasi-scalar multiple of (A, B). $\qquad\square$

Remark 2.9.1. The comonic multiple of (A, B) generated in Example A.2.1 has a higher degree, 3, than the quasi-scalar comonic multiple of (A, B) generated in Example 2.9.2, which has a degree of 1. While this may seem counterintuitive since the

54

constraint of generating a quasi-scalar comonic multiple appears to be more restrictive, the reason lies in how the multiple is generated. Specifically, in Algorithm 2.6.1 (Proposition 2.6.1 and Example A.2.1), we search for a comonic multiple of (C, D). Hence the degree of the multiple generated by Algorithm 2.6.1 will always be greater than or equal to the degree of (C, D). However, in Algorithm 2.6.2 (Proposition 2.6.2 and Example 2.9.2), we search for a quasi-scalar multiple of (A, B) directly, that is, the quasi-scalar comonic multiple (γ, F) of (A, B) is in general not a multiple of (C, D). $\square$

Example 2.9.3. Let $C(\mathbf{r})$ and $D(\mathbf{r})$ be given by (2.24) and (2.25), respectively. The following example illustrates Proposition 2.6.3.

First, we compute the Markov parameters of (A, B) using the multiples of (A, B) generated in Examples A.2.1 and 2.9.2. For both multiples we find that

$$
H_0 = \begin{bmatrix} 5 & 1 & -3 \\ -3 & 0 & 3 \end{bmatrix},
$$

$$
H_1 = \begin{bmatrix} 4 & 0 & -4 \\ -3 & 0 & 3 \end{bmatrix},
$$

and $H_i = H_1$ for every $i \geq 1$.

Next, computing the error $\varepsilon(\mathbf{r}) \triangleq A(\mathbf{r})H(\mathbf{r}) - B(\mathbf{r})$, we find that

$$
\frac{\|\theta_9(\varepsilon)\|_{\mathrm{F}}}{\|\theta(B)\|_{\mathrm{F}}} = 1.191 \times 10^{-13}.
$$

Hence numerically, we find that $A(\mathbf{r})H(\mathbf{r}) = B(\mathbf{r})$, that is, the Markov parameters are indeed the Markov parameters of (A, B). $\square$

Example 2.9.4. Let $C(\mathbf{r})$ and $D(\mathbf{r})$ be given by (2.24) and (2.25), respectively. The following example illustrates Algorithm 2.7.1.

First, assume that $\bar{n} = 4$ is an upper bound for n^*. Then, since $\bar{n} = 4$, we use the first 9 Markov parameters from Example 2.9.3.

Next, the following table displays the third through eighth normalized singular values ($\bar{\sigma}_i \triangleq \sigma_i/\sigma_{\max}$) of $\overline{\mathcal{K}}_{s,\bar{n}}(H)$ and $\mathcal{K}_{s,\bar{n}}(H)$ for $s = 0$ and $s = 1$. Since the ranks are equal for $s = 1$, we proceed to Step 6.

s	$\bar{\sigma}[\overline{\mathcal{K}}_{s+\bar{n}}(H)]$					$\bar{\sigma}[\mathcal{K}_{s+\bar{n}}(H)]$					
	$\bar{\sigma}_3$	$\bar{\sigma}_4$	$\cdots$	$\bar{\sigma}_7$	$\bar{\sigma}_8$	$\bar{\sigma}_3$	$\bar{\sigma}_4$	$\bar{\sigma}_5$	$\bar{\sigma}_6$	$\bar{\sigma}_7$	$\bar{\sigma}_8$
0	1					0.04	0.04	8×10^{-16}			
1	0.05	0.05	$\cdots$	0.04	8×10^{-16}	0.05	0.05	0.03	0.03	0.03	3×10^{-15}

Next, from Steps 6-8, we have that

$$\theta(E) = \left[\begin{array}{cc|cc} 1 & 0 & -4/13 & 12/13 \\ 0 & 1 & +3/13 & -9/13 \end{array}\right],$$

$$\theta(F) = \left[\begin{array}{ccc|ccc} +5 & +1 & -3 & -4/13 & -4/13 & -4/13 \\ -3 & -5\times10^{-16} & +3 & +3/13 & +3/13 & +3/13 \end{array}\right].$$

Furthermore, letting

$$L(\mathbf{r}) \triangleq I_2 + \left[\begin{array}{cc} 12/13 & 16/13 \\ 12/13 & 16/13 \end{array}\right]\mathbf{r},$$

it follows that $(E, F) = (LA, LB)$. Hence (E, F) is a comonic multiple of (A, B). $\square$

Example 2.9.5. Let $C(\mathbf{r})$ and $D(\mathbf{r})$ be given by (2.24) and (2.25), respectively. The following example illustrates Algorithm 2.7.2.

First, assume that $\bar{n} = 4$ is an upper bound for n^*. Then, since $\bar{n} = 4$, we use the first 9 Markov parameters from Example 2.9.3. Furthermore, for every $i \in [0, 8]$, we construct $H_i^\star = \text{vec}\,[H_i]^T$, that is,

$$H_0^\star = \begin{bmatrix} 5 & -3 & 1 & 0 & -3 & 3 \end{bmatrix},$$

$$H_1^\star = \begin{bmatrix} 4 & -3 & 0 & 0 & -4 & 3 \end{bmatrix},$$

and so on.

Next, examining the following table, which displays the inverse condition number of $\mathcal{K}_{s,\bar{n}}(H^\star)$ for $s = 0$ and $s = 1$, we see that nullity $\left[\mathcal{K}_{s,\bar{n}}^T(H^\star)\right] > 0$ for $s = 1$.

s	$\sigma_{\min}\left[\mathcal{K}_{s,\bar{n}}(H^\star)\right]/\sigma_{\max}\left[\mathcal{K}_{s,\bar{n}}(H^\star)\right]$
0	0.042
1	2.9×10^{-15}

Hence, proceeding to Steps 5-8 with $s = 1$, we find that

$$\theta(\gamma) = \begin{bmatrix} 1 & \bigg| & -1 \end{bmatrix},$$

$$\theta(F) = \begin{bmatrix} 5 & 1 & -3 & -1 & -1 & -1 \\ -3 & 5 \times 10^{-16} & 3 & 3 \times 10^{-13} & 8 \times 10^{-17} & -3 \times 10^{-13} \end{bmatrix},$$

which is similar to the quasi-scalar comonic multiple $(\gamma I_2, F)$ generated in Example 2.9.2 up to rounding errors.

Finally, as in Example 2.9.2, we should find that $A(\mathbf{r})F(\mathbf{r}) = \gamma(\mathbf{r})B(\mathbf{r})$. Thus, letting $\varepsilon_1(\mathbf{r}) \triangleq A(\mathbf{r})F(\mathbf{r}) - \gamma(\mathbf{r})B(\mathbf{r})$ and $\varepsilon_2(\mathbf{r}) \triangleq A(\mathbf{r})F(\mathbf{r})$, we find that

$$\frac{\|\theta\,(\varepsilon_1)\|_{\mathrm{F}}}{\|\theta\,(\varepsilon_2)\|_{\mathrm{F}}} = 2.041 \times 10^{-14},$$

and hence, numerically we have that $A(\mathbf{r})F(\mathbf{r}) = \gamma(\mathbf{r})B(\mathbf{r})$. Furthermore, as in Example 2.9.2, we find that this implies that $(\gamma I_2, F)$ is a comonic quasi-scalar multiple of (A, B). □

Remark 2.9.2. As evidenced by the previous examples, all of the proposed algorithms require, at some point, one to determine the rank of a matrix, which is always a very delicate task, even for these small examples. Furthermore, we do not suggest rigid guidelines for choosing tolerances for rank conditions, since presumably these choices would be motivated by the problem at hand, specifically the conditioning of the problem. For instance, suppose that a row or column of the Markov parameter polynomial was significantly smaller than the others. Then the results would be influenced by the practioner's determination whether the row or column in question is due to round-off errors or not. □

Remark 2.9.3. In the examples presented here, access to the original system allows us to ascertain the accuracy of the computed object. However, this is not possible for the practitioner, who may need to develop reliability tests. These should be motivated by how the end object is to be used. For instance, if the practitioner has access to the Markov parameters of a system, and computes a multiple of (A, B) from the Markov parameters, one could save the final x Markov parameters, that is, not include them in the algorithms, then check how small $A(\mathbf{r})H(\mathbf{r}) - B(\mathbf{r})$ is using the saved Markov parameters. However, if one is interested in the accuracy of the spectral content of the system (A, B), then some other test may be required. □

2.10 Conclusions

We have considered polynomial matrix representations of MIMO linear systems and their connection to Markov parameters. Specifically, we have developed theory and numerical algorithms for transforming polynomial matrix models into Markov parameter models, and vice verse. We have also provided numerical examples to illustrate the given algorithms.

CHAPTER III

Persistency

In this chapter, we consider the notion of persistency within a deterministic, finite-data context, namely, in terms of the rank and condition number of the regressor matrix Φ_N, which contains input and output data. We also investigate the feasibility of estimating the degree of a system in terms of the singular values of the regressor matrix by showing that the rank of the regressor matrix Φ_N is related to the degree of persistency of the input, the degree of the model, and the degree of the true system.

3.1 Introduction

Persistency is a bedrock requirement of system identification. Roughly speaking, persistency guarantees that the inputs to the system and the resulting outputs have sufficient richness in spectral content to ensure that the system dynamics can be uniquely determined when no noise is present. These comments apply to both time-domain and frequency-domain identification objectives.

In the frequency-domain context, necessary and sufficient conditions are established in [9] for the degree of richness of the input to generate an informative experiment. One of these conditions is equivalent to the requirement that the spectral density of the input be nonzero at a specified number of frequencies. These conditions are also extended to closed-loop identification. In [34], signals that maximize persis-

59

tency as defined by various cost criteria are examined, whereas in [35], persistency in the time-domain is based on the informative value of the state. Persistency within a behavioral context is developed in [36].

All of these persistency conditions are defined in terms of either the statistics of the input and output signals, or in terms of the asymptotic nature of these signals, see, for example, [9]. This approach is especially applicable to stochastic analysis in which unbiasedness (zero mean of the error probability distribution) and consistency (convergence with probability one to the true value in the limit of infinite data) are desired properties of the estimate.

In the present chapter we reconsider the notion of persistency within a deterministic, finite-data context. Instead of stochastic analysis, we approach persistency in terms of the condition number of the regressor matrix. Specifically, we consider autoregressive input models, and analyze the resulting rank and condition number of the regressor matrix. We make no assumption about the input or output of the system prior to the start of the data record, nor do we assume that the system begins at rest.

This chapter also investigates the feasibility of estimating the degree of the system in terms of the rank of the regressor matrix. In particular, we show that the rank of the regressor matrix is related to the degree of persistency of the input, the degree of the model, and the degree of the true system, providing an easily implementable technique for estimating the degree of the true system. Although noise in the input and output signals corrupts this degree estimate, under moderate signal to noise ratios, the degree of the true system can be estimated with useful accuracy.

The contents of this chapter are as follows. In Section 3.2, we provide a brief problem statement. Then in Section 3.3, we examine persistency from a regression point of view, analyzing the numerical persistency of several signals, defining the degree of persistency, and proving its relation to the rank of the regressor matrix. In

60

Section 3.4, we provide conditions on the degree of persistency of the input such that the regressor matrix has full rank, and introduce a degree-estimation technique along with two examples. Finally, we end with conclusions in Section 3.5.

3.2 Problem Statement

Consider the system

$$A(\mathbf{r})y(k) = B(\mathbf{r})u(k), \tag{3.1}$$

where $A \in \mathbb{R}^{p \times p}[\mathbf{r}]$, $B \in \mathbb{R}^{p \times m}[\mathbf{r}]$, (A, B) is of degree n, $y \in \mathbb{R}^p$, $u \in \mathbb{R}^m$, and u and y are sampled for $k = 1, \ldots, N$. Then the problem is to determine conditions on the signal u such that the system (3.1) is uniquely identifiable from the samples of the signals u and y.

3.3 Persistency in Regression

We begin by considering the *finite impulse response model*, and show how to construct the regression equations. Specifically, consider the system

$$y(k) = B(\mathbf{r})u(k), \tag{3.2}$$

where $B \in \mathbb{R}^{p \times m}[\mathbf{r}]$, $y \in \mathbb{R}^p$, $u \in \mathbb{R}^m$, and

$$B(\mathbf{r}) \triangleq B_0 + B_1\mathbf{r} + \cdots + B_n\mathbf{r}^n.$$

Then from (3.2), we have that

$$\Theta \Phi_N = Y_N, \tag{3.3}$$

61

where

$$\Theta \triangleq \left[\begin{array}{ccc} B_0, & \cdots, & B_n \end{array} \right] \in \mathbb{R}^{p \times m(n+1)}, \tag{3.4}$$

$$\Phi_N \triangleq \left[\begin{array}{ccc} u(n+1) & \cdots & u(N) \\ \vdots & & \vdots \\ u(1) & \cdots & u(N-n) \end{array} \right] \in \mathbb{R}^{m(n+1) \times (N-n)}, \tag{3.5}$$

$$Y_N \triangleq \left[\begin{array}{ccc} y(n+1), & \cdots, & y(N) \end{array} \right] \in \mathbb{R}^{p \times (N-n)}. \tag{3.6}$$

Furthermore, the matrix Φ_N in (3.3) is typically called the *regressor (or regression) matrix*, and (3.3) is called the *regression equation*.

Remark 3.3.1. We use the terms *regressor matrix* and *regression equation* loosely since *regression* simply refers to the process of sampling signals, and stacking up data in matrices. For instance if we consider a system of the form (3.1) instead of (3.2), then the regression equations are still given by (3.3), only with the regressor matrix Φ_N given by (1.3) as opposed to (3.5). □

3.3.1 Numerical Persistency

When $B(\mathbf{r})$ is unknown, $B(\mathbf{r})$ can be found simply be solving the linear system of equations given by (3.3) for Θ, which contains the coefficients of $B(\mathbf{r})$. However, when Φ_N does not have full row rank, Θ can not be uniquely determined. Thus our notion of persistency is related to the rank of the regressor matrix (3.5). Roughly speaking, if the regressor matrix (3.5) has a moderate condition number for large n, then u is highly persistent, since systems of high degree can be identified using the same input signal u. On the other hand, if the regressor matrix (3.5) has a large condition number or does not have full row rank for moderate values of n, then u is weakly persistent, and very few systems can be identified using that signal. Next, we examine the singular values of the regressor matrix for several signals.

Example 3.3.1. Consider the multi-sine signals

$$u(k) = \sum_{i=1}^{n_s} \cos\left(0.5\left[\frac{2\pi i}{T}\right]k\right), \tag{3.7}$$

$$v(k) = \sum_{i=1}^{n_s} \cos\left(1.0\left[\frac{2\pi i}{T}\right]k\right), \tag{3.8}$$

$$w(k) = \sum_{i=1}^{n_s} \cos\left(2.0\left[\frac{2\pi i}{T}\right]k\right), \tag{3.9}$$

where $n_s = 20$, $T = 200$, and $k = 1, \ldots, 2T$. Then Figures 3.1-3.3 display signals (3.7)-(3.9) along with their power spectral densities. Note that all of the signals have 20 sinusoidal components, although their frequency content is spread out differently.

Finally, letting $n = 40$ in the regressor matrix (3.5), Figure 3.4 displays the normalized singular values ($\bar{\sigma}_i \triangleq \sigma_i/\sigma_{\max}$) of the regressor matrix (3.5) for all of the signals (3.7)-(3.9). From Figure 3.4, we can see that the regressor matrix (3.5) is poorly conditioned for all of the signals (3.7)-(3.9). However, note that, in Figure 3.4, the signal $w(k)$, which has the largest bandwidth of (3.7)-(3.9), is also the most persistent, that is, the regressor matrix is better conditioned. Therefore, Figure 3.4 and additional examples suggest that multi-sine signals with larger bandwidths are more persistent than those with dense frequency spectra.

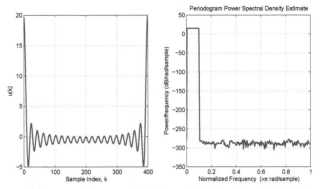

Figure 3.1: The signal $u(k)$ (left) and its power spectral density (right).

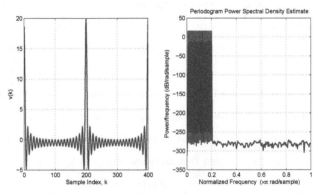

Figure 3.2: The signal $v(k)$ (left) and its power spectral density (right).

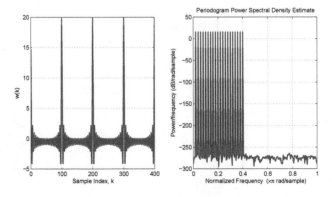

Figure 3.3: The signal $w(k)$ (left) and its power spectral density (right).

64

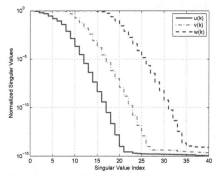

Figure 3.4: Normalized singular values of the regressor matrix (3.5) with $n = 40$ and the signals (3.7)-(3.9).

□

Example 3.3.2. Consider the unit impulse

$$u(k) = \begin{cases} 1, & k = 1, \\ 0, & k > 1, \end{cases} \tag{3.10}$$

which yields the regressor matrix

$$\Phi_N = \begin{bmatrix} 0 & 0 & \cdots & 0 \\ \vdots & \vdots & & \vdots \\ 0 & \vdots & & \vdots \\ 1 & 0 & \cdots & 0 \end{bmatrix}. \tag{3.11}$$

Then since $\operatorname{rank}\big[\Phi_N\big] = 1$, the solution Θ of (3.3) is unique if and only if $n = 0$. Hence the unit impulse (3.10) is weakly persistent.

65

Next, consider the shifted impulse

$$u_s(k) = \begin{cases} 0, & 1 \le k \le n, \\ 1, & k = n+1, \\ 0, & k > n+1, \end{cases} \tag{3.12}$$

which yields the regressor matrix

$$\Phi_N = \begin{bmatrix} I_{n+1} & 0_{(n+1) \times N} \end{bmatrix}. \tag{3.13}$$

Then since $\mathrm{rank}\begin{bmatrix} \Phi_N \end{bmatrix} = n + 1$, Φ_N has full row rank. Hence shifting the impulse n time steps yields a unique solution Θ of (3.3). Thus the shifted impulse (3.12) is highly persistent. $\qquad\square$

3.3.2 Degree of Persistency

In the previous section, we examined persistency from a numerical point of view by examining the singular values of the regression matrix. Here we formalize a theoretical notion of the degree of persistency. Furthermore, we show that numerical persistency and the theoretical notion of the degree of persistency are related in Theorem 3.3.1. We begin by defining the degree of persistency:

Definition 3.3.1. Let $u \in \mathbb{R}^m$, where u is sampled for $k = 1, \ldots, N$. Then the *degree of persistency of* u is the smallest nonnegative integer ℓ such that there exist $C_0, \ldots, C_\ell \in \mathbb{R}^{m \times m}$ which are not all zero and satisfy

$$C_0 u(k + \ell) + \cdots + C_\ell u(k) = 0_{m \times 1}, \tag{3.14}$$

for all $k = 1, \ldots, N - \ell$.

Fact 3.3.1. Let $u \in \mathbb{R}^m$ have a degree of persistency of ℓ, where $C_0, \ldots, C_\ell \in \mathbb{R}^{m \times m}$

66

are not all zero and

$$C_0 u(k + \ell) + \cdots + C_\ell u(k) = 0_{m \times 1},$$

for all $k = 1, \ldots, N - \ell$. Then C_0 is nonzero.

Proof. Suppose $C_0 = 0_{m \times m}$. Then

$$C_1 u(k + \ell - 1) + \cdots + C_\ell u(k) = 0_{m \times 1},$$

and hence u has a degree of persistency of $\ell - 1$, which is a contradiction. □

Theorem 3.3.1. Let $u \in \mathbb{R}^m$ have a degree of persistency of ℓ, where $C_0, \ldots, C_\ell \in \mathbb{R}^{m \times m}$ are not all zero and

$$C_0 u(k + \ell) + \cdots + C_\ell u(k) = 0_{m \times 1},$$

for all $k = 1, \ldots, N - \ell$. Then Φ_N has full row rank if and only if $\ell > n$. Specifically,

$$\text{rank}[\Phi_N] \geq m \cdot \min(\ell, n + 1).$$

Furthermore, if C_0 is nonsingular, then

$$\text{rank}[\Phi_N] = m \cdot \min(\ell, n + 1).$$

Proof. First, let $\ell > n$. From Definition 3.3.1, if there exist $D_0, \ldots, D_n \in \mathbb{R}^{m \times m}$, such that

$$\begin{bmatrix} D_0, & \cdots, & D_n \end{bmatrix} \Phi_N = 0_{m \times 1},$$

then $D_0 = \cdots = D_n = 0_{m \times m}$. Hence Φ_N has full row rank.

Next, let $\ell \leq n$ and

$$\phi_N \triangleq \begin{bmatrix} u(\ell) & \cdots & u(N-n+\ell-1) \\ \vdots & & \vdots \\ u(1) & \cdots & u(N-n) \end{bmatrix},$$

where ϕ_N is a submatrix of Φ_N. Furthermore, note that from the first part of this proof, we have that ϕ_N has full row rank. Hence

$$\mathrm{rank}\big[\Phi_N\big] \geq \mathrm{rank}\big[\phi_N\big] = m\ell.$$

Finally, let $\ell \leq n$ and let C_0 be nonsingular. Also, let

$$\vec{\phi}_N \triangleq \begin{bmatrix} u(n+1), & \cdots, & u(N) \end{bmatrix},$$

where $\mathbf{r}^i \vec{\phi}_N$ is the ith block-row of Φ_N. Then for every $i \in [0, n-\ell]$, we have that

$$\mathbf{r}^i \vec{\phi}_N = -C_0^{-1} \sum_{j=1}^{\ell} C_j \big[\mathbf{r}^{i+j} \vec{\phi}_N \big],$$

that is, $\mathbf{r}^i \vec{\phi}_N$ is linearly dependent on the following ℓ block-rows. Hence

$$\mathrm{rank}\big[\Phi_N\big] = \mathrm{rank}\big[\phi_N\big] = m\ell.$$

$\square$

Remark 3.3.2. When considering SISO systems ($m = 1$), we can drop the requirement that C_0 is nonsingular in the latter half of Theorem 3.3.1, since the trailing coefficient of a scalar nonzero polynomial is always nonsingular. $\square$

Fact 3.3.2. Let $u, v \in \mathbb{R}^m$ have a degree of persistency of ℓ_1 and ℓ_2, respectively,

68

where $C_0, \ldots, C_{\ell_1} \in \mathbb{R}^{m \times m}$ are not all zero, $D_0, \ldots, D_{\ell_2} \in \mathbb{R}^{m \times m}$ are not all zero, and

$$C_0 u(k_1 + \ell_1) + \cdots + C_{\ell_1} u(k_1) = 0_{m \times 1}, \tag{3.15}$$

$$D_0 u(k_2 + \ell_2) + \cdots + D_{\ell_2} u(k_2) = 0_{m \times 1}, \tag{3.16}$$

for all $k_1 = 1, \ldots, N - \ell_1$ and $k_2 = 1, \ldots, N - \ell_2$. Also, let

$$C(\mathbf{r}) \triangleq C_0 + C_1 \mathbf{r} + \cdots + C_{\ell_1} \mathbf{r}^{\ell_1},$$

$$D(\mathbf{r}) \triangleq D_0 + D_1 \mathbf{r} + \cdots + D_{\ell_2} \mathbf{r}^{\ell_2},$$

where $C(\mathbf{r})$ and $D(\mathbf{r})$ commute. Then the degree of persistency of $u + v$ is less than or equal to $\ell_1 + \ell_2$.

Proof. From (3.15)-(3.16), and the fact that $C(\mathbf{r})$ and $D(\mathbf{r})$ commute, we have that

$$C(\mathbf{r})D(\mathbf{r}) \left[u(k) + v(k) \right] = D(\mathbf{r}) \left[C(\mathbf{r})u(k) \right] + C(\mathbf{r}) \left[D(\mathbf{r})v(\mathbf{r}) \right] = 0_{m \times 1},$$

for all $k = 1, \ldots, N - \ell_1 - \ell_2$. Hence the degree of persistency of $u + v$ must be less than or equal to $\ell_1 + \ell_2$. $\qquad \square$

Remark 3.3.3. In the SISO case, we can obtain an even tighter bound on the degree of persistency $u + v$. Specifically, let $E(\mathbf{r})$ be the comonic polynomial which contains the common roots of $C(\mathbf{r})$ and $D(\mathbf{r})$, and let $C'(\mathbf{r})$ and $D'(\mathbf{r})$ contain the unique parts of $C(\mathbf{r})$ and $D(\mathbf{r})$, respectively, that is,

$$C(\mathbf{r}) \triangleq C'(\mathbf{r})E(\mathbf{r}), \quad D(\mathbf{r}) \triangleq D'(\mathbf{r})E(\mathbf{r}).$$

Finally, let n_c', n_d', and n_e denote the degree of $C'(\mathbf{r})$, $D'(\mathbf{r})$, and $E(\mathbf{r})$, respectively. Then the degree of persistency of $u + v$ is less than or equal $n_c' + n_d' + n_e$. $\qquad \square$

Remark 3.3.4. Scalar sinusoids have a degree of persistency of 2. Hence from Fact 3.3.2, the degree of persistency of each of the signals (3.7)-(3.9) in Example 3.3.1 is 40.

Unfortunately, while Theorem 3.3.1 guarantees that the regressor matrix (3.5) has full row rank in Example 3.3.1, numerically the regressor matrix is poorly conditioned. Thus one must be careful about choosing input signals in practice, since the numerical and theoretical rank of the regressor matrix (3.5) may be vastly different. In the next chapter, we present a method which reliably increases the degree of persistency of an arbitrary signal. □

3.4 Degree Estimation

Degree estimation is often performed by using the eigensystem realization algorithm, where the degree estimate is taken to be the rank of the Markov block Hankel matrix [1,70]. However, this approach pre-supposes knowledge of the system's Markov parameters. Here we show that a degree estimate can be obtained directly from the regressor matrix (3.18). We begin by considering persistency in the context of the more general system (3.1). Specifically, consider the comonic system

$$A(\mathbf{r})y(k) = B(\mathbf{r})u(k), \tag{3.17}$$

where $A(\mathbf{r})$ and $B(\mathbf{r})$ are given by

$$A(\mathbf{r}) \triangleq I_p + A_1\mathbf{r} + \cdots + A_{n-1}\mathbf{r}^{n-1} + A_n\mathbf{r}^n,$$
$$B(\mathbf{r}) \triangleq B_0 + B_1\mathbf{r} + \cdots + B_{n-1}\mathbf{r}^{n-1} + B_n\mathbf{r}^n,$$

and the regressor matrix Φ_N is now given by

$$\Phi_N \triangleq \begin{bmatrix} \Phi_{u,N} \\ \Phi_{y,N} \end{bmatrix}, \tag{3.18}$$

$$\Phi_{u,N} \triangleq \begin{bmatrix} u(n+1) & \cdots & u(N) \\ \vdots & & \vdots \\ u(1) & \cdots & u(N-n) \end{bmatrix} \in \mathbb{R}^{m(n+1)\times(N-n)}, \tag{3.19}$$

$$\Phi_{y,N} \triangleq \begin{bmatrix} y(n) & \cdots & y(N) \\ \vdots & & \vdots \\ y(1) & \cdots & y(N-n) \end{bmatrix} \in \mathbb{R}^{np\times(N-n)}. \tag{3.20}$$

Furthermore, the regression equation is still given by (3.3), although Θ is now given by

$$\Theta \triangleq \begin{bmatrix} B_0, & \cdots, & B_n, & -A_1, & \cdots, & -A_n \end{bmatrix}.$$

Also, note that the matrix $\Phi_{u,N}$ is the regressor matrix for the finite impulse response system (3.2). Hence, we can immediately establish some results concerning persistency for the more general model (3.17).

Proposition 3.4.1. If Φ_N given by (3.18) has full row rank, then $u \in \mathbb{R}^m$ has a degree of persistency ℓ which is greater than n.

Proof. Since Φ_N has full row rank, both $\Phi_{y,N}$ and $\Phi_{u,N}$ have full row rank. Hence, from Theorem 3.3.1, since $\Phi_{u,N}$ has full row rank, then $\ell > n$. $\qquad \square$

Next, note that when the degree n of (A, B) is unknown, we cannot exactly construct the regressor matrix Φ_N in (3.18). Instead we use an estimate $\hat{n}$ of n, which may bear no resemblance to n. Specifically, let $\hat{\Phi}_N$ denote the regressor matrix (3.18) where n is replaced by $\hat{n}$. Then we have the following theorem:

71

Theorem 3.4.1. Consider the system (3.17), where (A, B) has a degree of n, and the estimate of the degree of (A, B) is $\hat{n}$. Furthermore, let $u \in \mathbb{R}^m$ have a degree of persistency of ℓ, where $C_0, \ldots, C_\ell \in \mathbb{R}^{m \times m}$ are not all zero and

$$C_0 u(k + \ell) + \cdots + C_\ell u(k) = 0_{m \times 1},$$

for all $k = 1, \ldots, N - \ell$. If C_0 is nonsingular, then

$$m \cdot \min(\ell, \hat{n} + 1) \leq \text{rank}\big[\hat{\Phi}_N\big] \leq m \cdot \min(\ell, \hat{n} + 1) + p \cdot \min(\hat{n}, n), \qquad (3.21)$$

where $\hat{\Phi}_N$ is given by (3.18) with n replaced by $\hat{n}$.

Proof. First, let $\hat{\Phi}_{u,N}$ denote the matrix containing the first $m(\hat{n}+1)$ rows of $\hat{\Phi}_N$. Then $\text{rank}\big[\hat{\Phi}_{u,N}\big] \leq \text{rank}\big[\hat{\Phi}_N\big]$, and from Theorem 3.3.1, $m \cdot \min(\ell, \hat{n}+1) \leq \text{rank}\big[\hat{\Phi}_N\big]$. Next, suppose that $n < \hat{n}$. Also, let

$$\vec{\phi}_{u,N} \triangleq \Big[\; u(n+1), \; \cdots, \; u(N) \; \Big],$$
$$\vec{\phi}_{y,N} \triangleq \Big[\; y(n+1), \; \cdots, \; y(N) \; \Big],$$

where $\mathbf{r}^i \vec{\phi}_{u,N}$ and $\mathbf{r}^i \vec{\phi}_{y,N}$ are the ith block-rows of $\hat{\Phi}_{u,N}$ and $\hat{\Phi}_{y,N}$, respectively. Then for every $i \in [0, \hat{n} - n]$, we have that

$$\mathbf{r}^i \vec{\phi}_{y,N} = -\sum_{j=1}^{n} A_j \big[\mathbf{r}^{i+j} \vec{\phi}_{y,N}\big] + \sum_{j=0}^{n} B_j \big[\mathbf{r}^{i+j} \vec{\phi}_{u,N}\big].$$

Therefore, at most pn rows of $\hat{\Phi}_{y,N}$ are linearly independent of $\hat{\Phi}_{u,N}$, and hence it follows that $\text{rank}\big[\hat{\Phi}_N\big] \leq \text{rank}\big[\hat{\Phi}_{u,N}\big] + pn$. Furthermore, since C_0 is nonsingular, then from Theorem 3.3.1, $\text{rank}\big[\hat{\Phi}_N\big] \leq m \cdot \min(\ell, \hat{n} + 1) + pn$.

Finally, if $\hat{n} \leq n$, then

$$\text{rank}[\hat{\Phi}_N] \leq \text{rank}[\hat{\Phi}_{u,N}] + \text{rank}[\hat{\Phi}_{y,N}],$$
$$= m \cdot \min(\ell, \hat{n} + 1) + \text{rank}[\hat{\Phi}_{y,N}],$$
$$\leq m \cdot \min(\ell, \hat{n} + 1) + p\hat{n}.$$

$\square$

Numerical testing suggests that, for SISO systems $\text{rank}[\hat{\Phi}_N] = \min(\ell, \hat{n} + 1) + \min(\hat{n}, n)$ for almost all initial conditions of y. However, the following example demonstrates a specific case in which $\text{rank}[\hat{\Phi}_N] < \min(\ell, \hat{n} + 1) + \min(\hat{n}, n)$.

Example 3.4.1. Consider the SISO system

$$(1 - a\mathbf{r})\, y(k) = u(k), \tag{3.22}$$

where $u(k) = q^k$, and $q \neq 0$. Then $n = 1$, and since u satisfies $u(k + 1) = qu(k)$, its degree of persistency ℓ is 1. Hence letting $\hat{n} \geq 1$ and

$$\alpha \triangleq \frac{q^2}{q - a}, \quad y(1) \triangleq \alpha q, \tag{3.23}$$

it follows that $y(k) = \alpha u(k)$. Therefore $\text{rank}[\hat{\Phi}_N] = 1 < \min(\hat{n}, n) + \min(\hat{n} + 1, \ell)$. However, for all other values of $y(1)$, $\text{rank}[\hat{\Phi}_N] = 2 = \min(\hat{n}, n) + \min(\hat{n} + 1, \ell)$. $\square$

The usefulness of Theorem 3.4.1 is due to the fact that the degree of persistency ℓ of the input can be computed separately from the rank of the regressor matrix $\hat{\Phi}_N$. Hence when $\hat{n} > n$ and the rank equality holds, that is, $\text{rank}[\hat{\Phi}_N] = m \cdot \min(\ell, \hat{n} + 1) + p \cdot \min(\hat{n}, n)$, then

$$n = \frac{1}{p}\left[\text{rank}[\hat{\Phi}_N] - m \cdot \min(\ell, \hat{n} + 1)\right]. \tag{3.24}$$

The following examples demonstrate this technique.

Example 3.4.2. Consider the linearized longitudinal model of the T-2 aircraft (1.1) given by

$$\left(1 - 1.862\mathbf{r} + 0.8798\mathbf{r}^2\right) y(k) = \left(-0.009767\mathbf{r} - 0.006026\mathbf{r}^2\right) u(k), \tag{3.25}$$

where $k \geq 1$, $y(2) = y(1) = 0$, and

$$u(k) = \cos(k/10), \quad k = 1, \ldots, 1000. \tag{3.26}$$

Also, let $\hat{n} = 6$. Then $n = 2$, $\ell = 2$, and from (3.21), we expect

$$\mathrm{rank}\left[\hat{\Phi}_N\right] = \min(\hat{n}, n) + \min(\hat{n} + 1, \ell)$$

$$= 2 + 2 = 4.$$

Finally, Figure 3.5 displays the normalized singular values ($\bar{\sigma}_i \triangleq \sigma_i/\sigma_{\max}$) of the regressor matrix $\hat{\Phi}_N$. From Figure 3.5, we can see that indeed $\mathrm{rank}\left[\hat{\Phi}_N\right] = 4$. □

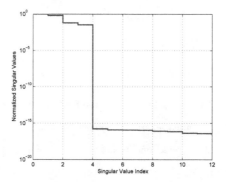

Figure 3.5: Normalized singular values of the regressor matrix $\hat{\Phi}_N$ for the system (3.25), where u is given by (3.26) and $\hat{n} = 6$.

Example 3.4.3. Consider the linearized longitudinal model of the T-2 aircraft (1.1) given by (3.25), where $k \geq 1$, $y(2) = y(1) = 0$, and

$$
u(k) = \begin{cases} 0, & k = 1, \ldots, 10, \\ \cos\left([k-11]/10\right), & 11 \leq k \leq 1000. \end{cases} \tag{3.27}
$$

Also, let $\hat{n} = 6$. Then $n = 2$, $\ell = 12$, and from (3.21), we expect

$$
\begin{aligned}
\text{rank}\big[\hat{\Phi}_N\big] &= \min(\hat{n}, n) + \min(\hat{n}+1, \ell) \\
&= 2 + 7 = 9,
\end{aligned}
$$

Finally, Figure 3.6 displays the normalized singular values ($\bar{\sigma}_i \triangleq \sigma_i/\sigma_{\max}$) of the regressor matrix $\hat{\Phi}_N$. From Figure 3.6, we can see that indeed $\text{rank}\big[\hat{\Phi}_N\big] = 9$. $\square$

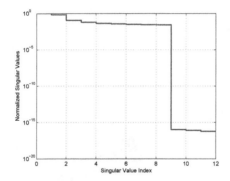

Figure 3.6: Normalized singular values of the regressor matrix $\hat{\Phi}_N$ for the system (3.25), where u is given by (3.27) and $\hat{n} = 6$.

3.5 Conclusions

We have considered a new notion of persistency within a deterministic, finite-data context. Furthermore, we have introduced a degree estimation technique that was

75

demonstrated with illustrative examples.

CHAPTER IV

Zero Buffering

In this chapter, we introduce the technique of *zero buffering*, in which the input signal begins with a sequence of zeros. Furthermore, we show that zero-buffering increases the degree of persistency of a general signal. We then demonstrate the effectiveness of zero-buffering in increasing the numerical degree of persistency of a Schröder-phased signal, which, without zero buffering, yields a poorly conditioned regressor matrix. Finally, we show the importance of good numerical persistency in identification with an example.

4.1 Introduction

In Chapter III, we introduced the notion of persistency within a deterministic, finite-data context. Specifically, we examined persistency from a regression point of view, analyzing the numerical persistency of several signals, defining the degree of persistency, and proving its relation to the rank of the regressor matrix. Furthermore, we provided conditions on the degree of persistency of the input such that the regressor matrix has full rank, and introduced a degree-estimation technique. In addition, while Chapter III addresses how to analyze previously collected data sets, this chapter examines a simple technique for choosing (or augmenting) the input before the data is collected so that the input is strongly persistent, and thus the data are more informative.

The novel contribution of this chapter is the technique of *zero buffering*, in which a signal is preceded by a sequence of zeros. Furthermore, we show that the degree of persistency of a signal is increased by zero buffering, In particular, we demonstrate the effectiveness of zero buffering in increasing the degree of persistency of a Schröder-phased signal [37], which, without zero buffering, yields a poorly conditioned regressor matrix. Thus, without zero buffering, the Schröder-phased signal has limited value in time-domain least-squares identification.

The contents of this chapter are as follows. In Section 4.2, we introduce zero buffering and show that it can increase the persistency of a signal. Then in Section 4.3, we give a numerical example in which a Schröder-phased signal is zero-buffered, show that zero buffering improves the conditioning of the regressor matrix, and show that the zero-buffered signal dramatically improves the quality of the estimation results in a numerical example. Finally we end with conclusions in Section 4.4.

4.2 Zero Buffering

The structure of the regressor matrix Φ_N due to the shifted impulse (3.12) suggests an advantage in starting the input signal with a sequence of zeros. We call this procedure *zero buffering*. With zero buffering, the regressor matrix of the FIR model (3.2) has the form

$$
\Phi_N = \begin{bmatrix} u(1) & \cdots & \cdots & u(n+1) & \cdots & u(N) \\ 0_{m\times 1} & \ddots & & \vdots & & \vdots \\ \vdots & \ddots & \ddots & \vdots & & \vdots \\ 0_{m\times 1} & \cdots & 0_{m\times 1} & u(1) & \cdots & u(N-n) \end{bmatrix}. \tag{4.1}
$$

Hence we have the following lemma:

78

Lemma 4.2.1. Consider the system

$$y(k+n) = B_0 u(k+n) + \cdots + B_n u(k).$$

where $B_0, \ldots, B_n \in \mathbb{R}^{p \times 1}$ and $u \in \mathbb{R}$ is sampled for $k = 1, \ldots, N$. If there exists $j \in [1, N-n]$ such that $u(j)$ is nonzero, and

$$u_{\mathrm{zb},n}(k) \triangleq \begin{cases} 0, & k = 1, \ldots, n, \\ u(k-n), & k > n, \end{cases}$$

then the degree of persistency of the zero-buffered signal $u_{\mathrm{zb},n}$ is greater than n.

Proof.   Since u is nonzero for some $j \in [1, N-n]$, then by inspection, the regressor matrix (4.1) has full row rank. Hence from Theorem 3.3.1, the degree of persistency of the zero-buffered signal $u_{\mathrm{zb},n}$ is greater than n. $\square$

Specifically, we have the more general theorem regarding zero buffering:

Theorem 4.2.1. Let $u \in \mathbb{R}^m$ have a degree of persistency of $\ell \geq 1$, where $C_0, \ldots, C_\ell \in \mathbb{R}^{m \times m}$ are not all zero and

$$C_0 u(k+\ell) + \cdots + C_\ell u(k) = 0_{m \times 1}, \tag{4.2}$$

for all $k = 1, \ldots, N - \ell$. Also, let $\ell_c \leq \ell$ be the smallest positive integer such that

$$C_0 u(\ell_c + 1) + \cdots + C_{\ell_c} u(1) = 0_{m \times 1}. \tag{4.3}$$

Then for every nonnegative integer r, the degree of persistency of the zero-buffered

79

signal

$$u_{\mathrm{zb},r}(k) = \begin{cases} 0_{m\times 1}, & k = 1,\ldots,r, \\ u(k - r + 1), & k > r. \end{cases} \tag{4.4}$$

is $\ell + \tilde{\ell}$, where $\tilde{\ell} \triangleq \min(r + \ell_c - \ell, 0)$.

Proof. Suppose $r + \ell_c \leq \ell$. Then (4.2) still holds. Hence the degree of persistency

of $u_{\mathrm{zb},r}$ is ℓ.

Finally, suppose that $r + \ell_c > \ell$ and there exist $E_0, \ldots, E_{\ell+\tilde{\ell}-1} \in \mathbb{R}^{m\times m}$ which are

not all zero and satisfy

$$E_0 u_{\mathrm{zb},r}(k + \ell + \tilde{\ell} - 1) + \cdots + E_{\ell+\tilde{\ell}-1} u_{\mathrm{zb},r}(k) = 0_{m\times 1},$$

for all $k = 1, \ldots, N - \ell - \tilde{\ell} + 1$. Then

$$E_0 u(\ell_c) + \cdots + E_{\ell_c-1} u(1) = 0_{m\times 1},$$

which is a contradiction. □

Remark 4.2.1. One interpretation of why the technique of zero buffering is so effective is that it reveals the initial condition of the system. For instance, if we were going to identify a system such as the T-2 aircraft (1.1) with a multisine u, the technique of zero buffering suggests that we wait, observe the output y (that is, set $u = 0$ while we are observing y), and then actuate the system with the multisine u we were going to use for identification. This process of observing the output while not actuating the input allows us to observe the free response of the system. □

Remark 4.2.2. Typically, $\ell_c = \ell$, and hence the the degree of persistency of the zero-buffered signal $u_{\mathrm{zb},r}$ is $\ell + r$. However, for signals where zeros would have naturally proceeded u, then $\ell_c < \ell$. □

Next, we demonstrate a signal whose degree of persistency is not increased by zero buffering.

Example 4.2.1. Consider the binary signal

$$u(k) = \begin{cases} 1, & \mod(k-1,4) \leq 1, \\ 0, & \mod(k-1,4) > 1, \end{cases}$$

that is, $u = \{1, 1, 0, 0, 1, 1, 0, 0, \ldots\}$. Then for $k = 1, 2, \ldots$,

$$u(k+3) - u(k+2) + u(k+1) - u(k) = 0, \tag{4.5}$$

and hence u has a degree of persistency of 3. Also, from Theorem 4.2.1, $\ell_c = 1$. Thus $u_{\mathrm{zb},2}(k) = \{0, 0, u(k)\}$ has a degree of persistency of 3 as well. Specifically, $u_{\mathrm{zb},2}$ also satisfies (4.5). □

4.3 Identification in the Presence of Noise

In this section, we introduce Schröder-phased signals, which are multi-sine signals commonly used for identification [37–40]. We show that Schröder-phased signals have poor numerical persistency, although the persistency can be substantially increased via zero-buffering. We also consider a Schröder-phased signal and a zero-buffered Schröder-phased signal for identifying a system in the presence of output measurement noise, demonstrating that poor numerical persistency significantly degrades identification accuracy.

4.3.1 Schröder-Phased Signals

Schröder-phased signals minimize the peak-to-peak amplitude of multi-sine signals through judicious phasing [37, 38]. Specifically, a Schröder-phased signal with flat power spectrum has the form

$$u_S(k) = \sum_{i=1}^{n_s} \cos\left(\left[\frac{2\pi i}{T}\right]k - \frac{\pi i^2}{n_s}\right). \tag{4.6}$$

Unfortunately, as we demonstrate with the following example, the Schröder-phased signal (4.6) has poor numerical persistency, like the other multi-sine signals considered in Example 3.3.1.

Example 4.3.1. Consider a Schröder-phased signal with $n_s = 20$ and $T = 200$ for $k = 1, \ldots, 2T$. Also, consider the zero-buffered Schröder-phased signal

$$u_{\mathrm{zb},40}(k) = \begin{cases} 0, & k = 1, \ldots, 40, \\ u_S(k-39), & 40 < k \leq 2T. \end{cases} \tag{4.7}$$

Then letting $n = 40$ in the regressor matrix (3.5), Figure 4.1 displays the normalized singular values ($\bar{\sigma}_i \triangleq \sigma_i/\sigma_{\max}$) of the regressor matrix (3.5) for both the Schröder-phased and zero-buffered Schröder-phased signal. From Figure 4.1, we can see that the regressor matrix with the Schröder-phased signal is poorly conditioned, whereas with the zero-buffered signal, the regressor matrix has a good condition number and thus full row rank. □

4.3.2 Schröder-Phased Signals in Identification

Here we consider two different input signals, namely the Schröder-phased and zero-buffered Schröder-phased signals, for identification in the presence of output measurement noise. Specifically, we compare the ensemble average of the error in the impulse response of the estimated system when zero-mean Gaussian white noise is superimposed on the output y with a specified signal-to-noise ratio (SNRs), where the SNR is taken to be the RMS value of the true signal divided by the RMS value of the noise superimposed on that signal.

82

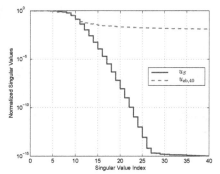

Figure 4.1: Normalized singular values of the regressor matrix (3.5) with $n = 40$ and the Schröder-phased and zero-buffered Schröder-phased signals (4.6) and (4.7), respectively.

In this setting, we show that signals which have poor numerical persistency, such as the Schröder-phased signal, yield poor identification results in the presence of noise. Note that we compare the impulse response of the estimated system as opposed to the model coefficients directly since small deviations in parameter coefficients can have a large effect on the system dynamics, while the impulse response is an invariant system property which reflects the system behavior.

Example 4.3.2. Consider again the Schröder-phased signal (4.6) and zero-buffered Schröder-phased signal (4.7), where $n_s = 20$ and $T = 200$ for $k = 1, \ldots, 2T$. Also, consider again the linearized longitudinal model of the T-2 aircraft (1.1) given by

$$\left(1 - 1.862\mathbf{r} + 0.8798\mathbf{r}^2\right) y(k) = \left(-0.009767\mathbf{r} - 0.006026\mathbf{r}^2\right) u(k), \qquad (4.8)$$

where $y(2) = y(1) = 0$. Then the first $\mu \triangleq 10$ impulse response coefficients of (4.8) are given by

$$\Theta_H \triangleq \left[\begin{array}{ccc} H_0, & \cdots, & H_{\mu-1} \end{array} \right]$$

$$= -10^{-2} \times \left[\begin{array}{cccccccccc} 0, & 0.977, & 2.42, & 3.65, & 4.66, & 5.47, & 6.09, & 6.52, & 6.79, & 6.90 \end{array} \right].$$

Furthermore, let z denote the measurement of y, where

$$z(k) = y(k) + w(k),$$

and w is a realization of an independent and identically distributed, zero-mean, Gaussian noise process $\mathcal{W}$ with unit variance.

Finally, let $\hat{n} = 10$, let

$$\Phi_N = \left[\begin{array}{ccc} u(\hat{n}+1) & \cdots & u(N) \\ \vdots & & \vdots \\ u(1) & \cdots & u(N-\hat{n}) \\ z(\hat{n}) & \cdots & z(N-1) \\ \vdots & & \vdots \\ z(1) & \cdots & z(N-\hat{n}) \end{array} \right],$$

$$Z_N \triangleq \left[\begin{array}{ccc} z(\hat{n}+1), & \cdots, & z(N) \end{array} \right],$$

$$\Theta \triangleq \left[\begin{array}{cccccc} B_0, & \cdots, & B_{\hat{n}}, & -A_0, & \cdots, & -A_{\hat{n}-1} \end{array} \right],$$

and consider the least-squares estimate $\hat{\Theta}$ of Θ given by

$$\hat{\Theta} = \arg\min_{\hat{\Theta}} \left\| Z_N - \hat{\Theta}\Phi_N \right\|_{\mathrm{F}}.$$

Then estimating $\hat{\Theta}$ for $M \triangleq 1000$ realizations of the random process $\mathcal{W}$, and letting $\hat{\Theta}_H(j)$ denote the impulse response of the estimated system $\hat{\Theta}$ for each realization

$j \in [1, M]$, Figure 4.2 displays the ensemble average of the estimated impulse response error given by

$$\varepsilon \triangleq \frac{1}{\mu M \left\| \Theta_H \right\|_2} \sum_{j=1}^{M} \left\| \Theta_H - \hat{\Theta}_H(j) \right\|_2, \tag{4.9}$$

for several SNRs. From Figure 4.2, we can see that the Schröder-phased signal is worse than the zero-buffered signal for identifying the model (4.8) according to the performance metric ε. Also, note that although the input portion of the regressor matrix Φ_N has full row rank for the Schröder-phased signal, it is poorly conditioned and hence poor estimates are obtained. □

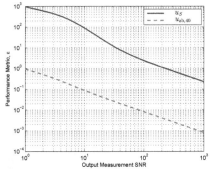

Figure 4.2: Comparison of the ensemble average of the error in the estimated impulse response of (4.8) when zero-mean Gaussian white noise is superimposed on the output y with a specified signal-to-noise ratio (SNR), and the inputs are taken to be the Schröder-phased signal (4.6) and the zero-buffered Schröder-phased signal (4.7), where $n_s = 20$ and $T = 200$ for $k = 1, \ldots, 2T$.

4.4 Conclusions

We have introduced the technique of zero buffering, where the input signal begins with a sequence of zeros. We showed that this technique increases the richness of the input, the condition number of the regressor matrix, and the accuracy of the least-squares estimates of a system.

CHAPTER V

Deterministic Noise

.

In this chapter, we address the issue of identification in the presence of deterministic process or measurement noise. Specifically, we study how deterministic signals propagate through polynomial matrix models. We also show that both the system and deterministic noise can be identified exactly via overparameterization using ordinary least-squares, and then decoupled using one of the many matrix fraction decomposition techniques available in the literature.

5.1 Introduction

In the previous chapters, we showed how regressor matrices are constructed for models in arbitrary operators. We also introduced the notion of persistency within a deterministic, finite-data context. Here we introduce a complementary definition called the *full degree of persistency*, and show that this notion is useful for understanding how deterministic signals propagate through polynomial matrix models. Furthermore, we show that both the system and deterministic noise can be identified exactly via overparameterization using ordinary least-squares. Specifically, by combining the noise and system model, we arrive at a single polynomial matrix model, which can be identified reliably using computationally efficient techniques. Furthermore, the system and noise process can be decoupled using one of the many matrix fraction decomposition techniques available in the literature [41–43].

The contents of this chapter are as follows. In Section 5.2, we define the *full degree of persistency*, and show how this concept is related to how signals propagate through polynomial matrix models. In Section 5.3, we show that, by combining the system and noise model, then via overparameterization we can identify the coupled model reliably using ordinary least-squares, followed by conclusions in Section 5.4.

5.2   Deterministic Signals

In previous chapters, we introduced the concept of the degree of persistency. Specifically, we said that the degree of persistency of the signal $u \in \mathbb{R}^m$ is the smallest nonnegative integer ℓ such that there exist $C_0, \ldots, C_\ell \in \mathbb{R}^{m \times m}$ which are not all zero and satisfy

$$C_0 u(k + \ell) + \cdots + C_\ell u(k) = 0_{m \times 1},$$

for all $k = 1, \ldots, N - \ell$. Here, we introduce a new concept called the *full degree of persistency*, which bounds the degree of persistency from above. We then use this definition to show how signals propagate through systems. Specifically, we have the following definition:

Definition 5.2.1. Let $u \in \mathbb{R}^m$. Then the *full degree of persistency of u* is the smallest nonnegative integer ℓ such that there exist $\alpha_0, \ldots, \alpha_\ell \in \mathbb{R}$ which are not all zero and satisfy

$$\alpha_0 u(k + \ell) + \cdots + \alpha_\ell u(k) = 0_{m \times 1},$$

for all $k = 1, \ldots, N - \ell$.

Remark 5.2.1. The only difference between the degree of persistency and the full degree of persistency, is the requirement that the coefficients be scalar. Note that when u is scalar, the degree of persistency and full degree of persistency are equal. Otherwise, the full degree of persistency is an upper bound on the degree of persistency. □

Next, we introduce the following theorem which shows how deterministic signals propagate through polynomial matrix models:

Theorem 5.2.1. Consider the system

$$A(\mathbf{r})y(k) = B(\mathbf{r})u(k), \tag{5.1}$$

where $A \in \mathbb{R}^{p \times p}[\mathbf{r}]$, $B \in \mathbb{R}^{p \times m}[\mathbf{r}]$, $A(\mathbf{r})$ has a degree of n, $y \in \mathbb{R}^p$, and $u \in \mathbb{R}^m$. Also, let u have a full degree of persistency of ℓ, where $\alpha_0, \ldots, \alpha_\ell \in \mathbb{R}$ are not all zero and

$$\alpha_0 u(k+\ell) + \cdots + \alpha_\ell u(k) = 0_{m \times 1},$$

for all $k = 1, \ldots, N - \ell$. Then the degree of persistency of y is less than or equal $n + \ell$. Furthermore, if $A(\mathbf{r})$ has full normal rank and the degree of $\det \big[A(\mathbf{r}) \big]$ is n_A, then the full degree of persistency of y is less than or equal $n_A + \ell$.

Proof. Letting

$$\alpha(\mathbf{r}) \triangleq \alpha_0 + \alpha_1 \mathbf{r} + \cdots + \alpha_\ell \mathbf{r}^\ell,$$

it follows that

$$\alpha(\mathbf{r})A(\mathbf{r})y(k) = \alpha(\mathbf{r})B(\mathbf{r})u(k) = B(\mathbf{r})\big[\alpha(\mathbf{r})u(k)\big] = B(\mathbf{r})\big[0_{m \times 1}\big] = 0_{p \times 1},$$

for all $k = 1, \ldots, N - n - \ell$. Hence the degree of persistency of y is less than or equal $n + \ell$.

Finally, let $A(\mathbf{r})$ have full normal rank and let $E(\mathbf{r}) \triangleq \operatorname{adj}[A(\mathbf{r})]$. Then

$$\alpha(\mathbf{r}) \det [A(\mathbf{r})] y(k) = \alpha(\mathbf{r}) E(\mathbf{r}) A(\mathbf{r}) y(k) = \alpha(\mathbf{r}) E(\mathbf{r}) B(\mathbf{r}) u(k),$$

$$= E(\mathbf{r}) B(\mathbf{r}) [\alpha(\mathbf{r}) u(k)] = 0_{p \times 1},$$

and hence the full degree of persistency of y is less than or equal $n_A + \ell$. $\qquad \square$

5.3 Identification of Coupled Models

In Chapter III, we studied persistency as if no noise were present. Here we allow for an additional deterministic process noise signal w, which is unknown, or equivalently, unmeasured. Specifically, consider the model

$$A(\mathbf{r}) y(k) = B(\mathbf{r}) u(k) + C(\mathbf{r}) w(k), \tag{5.2}$$

where $A \in \mathbb{R}^{p \times p}[\mathbf{r}]$, $B \in \mathbb{R}^{p \times m}[\mathbf{r}]$, $C \in \mathbb{R}^{p \times l}[\mathbf{r}]$, $y \in \mathbb{R}^p$ is known, $u \in \mathbb{R}^m$ is known, and $w \in \mathbb{R}^l$ is unknown.

Remark 5.3.1. Note that the process noise model (5.2) can capture a wide variety of noise sources. For instance, consider the system

$$A(\mathbf{r}) y_0(k) = B(\mathbf{r}) u_0(k),$$

where u_0 and y_0 are measured with the additive deterministic noise processes w_u and w_y, respectively, that is,

$$u(k) = u_0(k) + w_u(k),$$

$$y(k) = y_0(k) + w_y(k).$$

90

Then

$$A(\mathbf{r})y(k) = B(\mathbf{r})u(k) + \begin{bmatrix} -B(\mathbf{r}), & A(\mathbf{r}) \end{bmatrix} \begin{bmatrix} w_u(k) \\ w_y(k) \end{bmatrix},$$

which is of the form (5.2).   □

Next, since w is a deterministic process, let w have a finite full degree of persistency, that is, let $\alpha(\mathbf{r})w(k) = 0_{l \times 1}$, where $\alpha \in \mathbb{R}^{l \times l}[\mathbf{r}]$ is nonzero and quasi-scalar. Then from (5.2), we have that

$$\alpha(\mathbf{r})A(\mathbf{r})y(k) = \alpha(\mathbf{r})B(\mathbf{r})u(k).$$

Hence, letting

$$\Phi_{\hat{n},N} \triangleq \begin{bmatrix} u(\hat{n}+1) & \cdots & u(N) \\ \vdots & & \vdots \\ u(1) & \cdots & u(N-\hat{n}) \\ y(\hat{n}) & \cdots & y(N-1) \\ \vdots & & \vdots \\ y(1) & \cdots & y(N-\hat{n}) \end{bmatrix}, \tag{5.3}$$

$$Y_{\hat{n},N} \triangleq \begin{bmatrix} y(\hat{n}+1), & \cdots, & y(N) \end{bmatrix}, \tag{5.4}$$

we have the following theorem:

Theorem 5.3.1. Consider the system (5.2), where $A(\mathbf{r})$ has full normal rank and (A, B) is left coprime, causal, and has a degree of n. Also, let ℓ_w denote the full degree of persistency of $w \in \mathbb{R}^l$, where $\alpha_0, \ldots, \alpha_{\ell_w} \in \mathbb{R}$ are not all zero and

$$\alpha_0 w(k + \ell_w) + \cdots + \alpha_{\ell_w} w(k) = 0_{l \times 1},$$

91

for all $k = 1, \ldots, N - \ell_w$. Finally, let $\hat{n} \triangleq n + \ell_w$, let

$$\alpha(\mathbf{r}) \triangleq \alpha_0 + \alpha_1 \mathbf{r} + \cdots + \alpha_{\ell_w} \mathbf{r}^{\ell_w},$$

$$A'(\mathbf{r}) \triangleq \alpha(\mathbf{r}) A(\mathbf{r}) = A'_0 + A'_1 \mathbf{r} + \cdots + A'_{\hat{n}} \mathbf{r}^{\hat{n}},$$

$$B'(\mathbf{r}) \triangleq \alpha(\mathbf{r}) B(\mathbf{r}) = B'_0 + B'_1 \mathbf{r} + \cdots + B'_{\hat{n}} \mathbf{r}^{\hat{n}},$$

$$A''(\mathbf{r}) \triangleq \left(A'_0 \right)^+ A'(\mathbf{r}) = A''_0 + A''_1 \mathbf{r} + \cdots + A''_{\hat{n}} \mathbf{r}^{\hat{n}},$$

$$B''(\mathbf{r}) \triangleq \left(A'_0 \right)^+ B'(\mathbf{r}) = B''_0 + B''_1 \mathbf{r} + \cdots + B''_{\hat{n}} \mathbf{r}^{\hat{n}},$$

and let $\hat{\Theta}_{\hat{n}}$ be a solution of

$$\hat{\Theta}_{\hat{n}} \Phi_{\hat{n},N} = Y_{\hat{n},N},$$

where $(\cdot)^+$ denotes the Moore-Penrose psuedo-inverse of $(\cdot)$, and $\Phi_{\hat{n},N}$ and $Y_{\hat{n},N}$ are given by (5.3) and (5.4), respectively. If $\Phi_{\hat{n},N}$ has full row rank, then

$$\hat{\Theta}_{\hat{n}} = \left[\ B''_0, \ \cdots, \ B''_{\hat{n}}, \ A''_1, \ \cdots, \ A''_{\hat{n}} \ \right]. \tag{5.5}$$

Proof. Since

$$A(\mathbf{r}) y(k) = B(\mathbf{r}) u(k) + C(\mathbf{r}) w(k),$$

and $\alpha(\mathbf{r}) w(k) = 0_{l \times 1}$, it follows that

$$\alpha(\mathbf{r}) A(\mathbf{r}) y(k) = \alpha(\mathbf{r}) B(\mathbf{r}) u(k).$$

Furthermore, from Fact 2.2.10, A_0 is nonsingular, and from Fact 3.3.1, α_0 is nonzero. Hence A'_0 is nonsingular.

92

Finally, note that

$$A''(\mathbf{r})y(k) = B''(\mathbf{r})u(k),$$

where (A'', B'') has a degree of $\hat{n}$. Furthermore, since $\Phi_{\hat{n},N}$ has full row rank it follows that there only exists one comonic solution (A''', B''') of $A'''(\mathbf{r})y(k) = B'''(\mathbf{r})u(k)$, namely $A''(\mathbf{r})y(k) = B''(\mathbf{r})u(k)$. Hence (5.5). $\qquad\square$

Next, we show that if only an upper bound $\hat{n}$ of $n + \ell_w$ is known, then every solution $\hat{\Theta}_{\hat{n}}$ of $\hat{\Theta}_{\hat{n}}\Phi_{\hat{n},N} = Y_{\hat{n},N}$ yields a comonic multiple (A'', B'') of (A', B').

Corollary 5.3.1. Consider the system (5.2), where $A(\mathbf{r})$ has full normal rank and (A, B) is left coprime, causal, and has a degree of n. Also, let ℓ_w denote the full degree of persistency of $w \in \mathbb{R}^l$, where $\alpha_0, \ldots, \alpha_{\ell_w} \in \mathbb{R}$ are not all zero and

$$\alpha_0 w(k + \ell_w) + \cdots + \alpha_{\ell_w} w(k) = 0_{l \times 1},$$

for all $k = 1, \ldots, N - \ell_w$. Finally, let

$$\alpha(\mathbf{r}) \triangleq \alpha_0 + \alpha_1 \mathbf{r} + \cdots + \alpha_{\ell_w} \mathbf{r}^{\ell_w},$$

$$A'(\mathbf{r}) \triangleq \alpha(\mathbf{r})A(\mathbf{r}) = A'_0 + A'_1 \mathbf{r} + \cdots + A'_{n+\ell_w} \mathbf{r}^{n+\ell_w},$$

$$B'(\mathbf{r}) \triangleq \alpha(\mathbf{r})B(\mathbf{r}) = B'_0 + B'_1 \mathbf{r} + \cdots + B'_{n+\ell_w} \mathbf{r}^{n+\ell_w},$$

and let $\Phi_{\hat{n},N}$ and $Y_{\hat{n},N}$ be given by (5.3) and (5.4), respectively.

If $\Phi_{n+\ell_w,N}$ has full row rank, $\hat{n} \geq n + \ell_w$, $\ell > \hat{n}$, $\hat{\Theta}_{\hat{n}}$ is a solution of

$$\hat{\Theta}_{\hat{n}}\Phi_{\hat{n},N} = Y_{\hat{n},N},$$

and $A'' \in \mathbb{R}^{p \times p}[\mathbf{r}]$ and $B'' \in \mathbb{R}^{p \times m}[\mathbf{r}]$ are given by

$$A''(\mathbf{r}) \triangleq I_p + \hat{\Theta}_{\hat{n}} \begin{bmatrix} 0_{p \times m(\hat{n}+1)}, & I_p \mathbf{r}, & \cdots, & I_p \mathbf{r}^{\hat{n}} \end{bmatrix}^T,$$

$$B''(\mathbf{r}) \triangleq \hat{\Theta}_{\hat{n}} \begin{bmatrix} I_m, & I_m \mathbf{r}, & \cdots, & I_m \mathbf{r}^{\hat{n}}, & 0_{m \times p \hat{n}} \end{bmatrix}^T.$$

then (A'', B'') is a comonic multiple of (A', B').

Proof. First, since $\Phi_{n+\ell_w, N}$ has full row rank, then from Theorem 5.3.1 it follows that $A'(\mathbf{r})y(k) = B'(\mathbf{r})u(k)$. Furthermore, from Fact 2.2.10, A_0 is nonsingular, and from Fact 3.3.1, α_0 is nonzero. Hence A'_0 is nonsingular.

Next, if $\hat{n} > n + \ell_w$, then there exists multiple solutions $\hat{\Theta}_{\hat{n}}$ of $\hat{\Theta}_{\hat{n}} \Phi_{\hat{n},N} = Y_{\hat{n},N}$. Furthermore, for each solution, we have that $A''(\mathbf{r})y(k) = B''(\mathbf{r})u(k)$.

Finally, let $\hat{n} > n + \ell_w$ and $\ell > \hat{n}$. Then a basis for the left nullspace of $\Phi_{\hat{n},N}$ is given by

$$V \triangleq \begin{bmatrix} B'_0 & \cdots & B'_{n+\ell_w} & 0 & \cdots & 0 & A'_0 & \cdots & A'_{n+\ell_w} & 0 & \cdots & 0 \\ 0 & \ddots & & \ddots & \ddots & \vdots & 0 & \ddots & & \ddots & \ddots & \vdots \\ \vdots & \ddots & \ddots & & \ddots & 0 & \vdots & \ddots & \ddots & & \ddots & 0 \\ 0 & \cdots & 0 & B'_0 & \cdots & B'_{n+\ell_w} & 0 & \cdots & 0 & A'_0 & \cdots & A'_{n+\ell_w} \end{bmatrix},$$

where $V \in \mathbb{R}^{p(\hat{n}-n-\ell_w) \times [m(\hat{n}+1)+p\hat{n}]}$ has full row rank since A'_0 is nonsingular. Hence there exists $\Theta_L \in \mathbb{R}^{p \times p(\hat{n}-n-\ell_w)}$ such that

$$\begin{bmatrix} B'_0, & \cdots, & B'_{n+\ell_w}, & 0_{p \times m(\hat{n}-n-\ell_w)}, & A'_0, & \cdots, & A'_{n+\ell_w-1}, & 0_{p \times p(\hat{n}-n-\ell_w)} \end{bmatrix} + \Theta_L V = \hat{\Theta}_{\hat{n}},$$

and therefore letting

$$L(\mathbf{r}) \triangleq I_p + \Theta_L \begin{bmatrix} I_p \mathbf{r}, & \cdots, & I_p \mathbf{r}^{\hat{n}-n-\ell_w} \end{bmatrix}^T,$$

94

it follows that $(A'', B'') = (LA', LB')$. $\qquad\qquad\qquad\qquad\qquad\qquad\qquad\Box$

Remark 5.3.2. Corollary 5.3.1 showed us that $n + \ell_w$ did not need to be known exactly. Specifically, if only an upper bound $\hat{n}$ of $n + \ell_w$ is known, then every solution $\hat{\Theta}_{\hat{n}}$ of $\hat{\Theta}_{\hat{n}} \Phi_{\hat{n},N} = Y_{\hat{n},N}$ yields a comonic multiple (A'', B'') of (A', B'). Fortunately, there are many matrix fraction decomposition techniques available in the literature to decouple the system (A, B) from the noise model [41–43]. Specifically, if (A, B) is left coprime, and $L(\mathbf{r})$ and $\alpha(\mathbf{r})$ are given by Corollary 5.3.1, then a matrix fraction decomposition will yield $A(\mathbf{r})$, $B(\mathbf{r})$, and the product $L(\mathbf{r})\alpha(\mathbf{r})$, given $A''(\mathbf{r})$ and $B''(\mathbf{r})$. Furthermore, note that once (A, B) has been decoupled from (A'', B''), then the noise process $C(\mathbf{r})w(k)$ is simply given by

$$C(\mathbf{r})w(k) = A(\mathbf{r})y(k) - B(\mathbf{r})u(k),$$

where $A(\mathbf{r})$, $B(\mathbf{r})$, y, and u are known. $\qquad\qquad\qquad\qquad\qquad\qquad\Box$

Remark 5.3.3. In the SISO case, the assumption that (A, B) is left coprime is equivalent to saying that $A(\mathbf{r})$ and $B(\mathbf{r})$ have no common zeros. Hence the matrix fraction decomposition of (A'', B'') simply removes the common zeros of $A''(\mathbf{r})$ and $B''(\mathbf{r})$ to yield $A(\mathbf{r})$ and $B(\mathbf{r})$. $\qquad\qquad\qquad\qquad\Box$

Example 5.3.1. Consider again the Schröder-phased signal

$$u(k) = \sum_{i=1}^{n_s} \cos\left(\left[\frac{2\pi i}{T}\right] k - \frac{\pi i^2}{n_s}\right), \qquad (5.6)$$

where $n_s = 20$ and $T = 200$ for $k = 1, \ldots, 2T$. Also, consider the linearized longitudinal model of the T-2 aircraft (1.1), where now we have an additional deterministic noise component, that is,

$$A(\mathbf{r})y(k) = B(\mathbf{r})u(k) + A(\mathbf{r})w(k),$$

where $y(2) = y(1) = 0$ and

$$A(\mathbf{r}) \triangleq 1 - 1.862\mathbf{r} + 0.8798\mathbf{r}^2,$$

$$B(\mathbf{r}) \triangleq -0.009767\mathbf{r} - 0.006026\mathbf{r}^2.$$

Furthermore, let w be the binary sequence from Example 4.2.1, that is,

$$w(k) = \begin{cases} 1, & \mod(k-1, 4) \leq 1, \\ 0, & \mod(k-1, 4) > 1. \end{cases}$$

Finally, note that $\alpha(\mathbf{r})w(k) = 0$, where

$$\alpha(\mathbf{r}) \triangleq 1 - \mathbf{r} + \mathbf{r}^2 - \mathbf{r}^3.$$

Hence $n + \ell_w = 2 + 3 = 5$.

Then letting $\hat{n} = 5$, we have that $\Phi_{\hat{n},N}$ given by (5.3) has full row rank. Furthermore, $A''(\mathbf{r})$ and $B''(\mathbf{r})$ given by Corollary 5.3.1 are

$$A''(\mathbf{r}) = 1 - 2.862\mathbf{r} + 3.7418\mathbf{r}^2 - 3.7418\mathbf{r}^3 + 2.7418\mathbf{r}^4 - 0.8798\mathbf{r}^5,$$

$$B''(\mathbf{r}) = -0.009767\mathbf{r} + 0.003741\mathbf{r}^2 - 0.003741\mathbf{r}^3 + 0.003741\mathbf{r}^4 + 0.006026\mathbf{r}^5,$$

where $A''(\mathbf{r}) = \alpha(\mathbf{r})A(\mathbf{r})$ and $B''(\mathbf{r}) = \alpha(\mathbf{r})B(\mathbf{r})$. Hence (A'', B'') is a multiple of (A', B').

Finally, we let $\hat{n} > n + \ell_w$. Specifically, we let $\hat{n} = 7$, and consider the solution $\hat{\Theta}_{\hat{n}}$ of $\hat{\Theta}_{\hat{n}}\Phi_{\hat{n},N} = Y_{\hat{n},N}$ which yields

$$A''(\mathbf{r}) = 1 - 1.783\mathbf{r} + 1\mathbf{r}^2 - 0.69539\mathbf{r}^3 + 0.78303\mathbf{r}^5 - 0.30461\mathbf{r}^7,$$

$$B''(\mathbf{r}) = 10^{-3} \times \left(-9.767\mathbf{r} - 6.797\mathbf{r}^2 - 3.086\mathbf{r}^3 + 0.9998\mathbf{r}^4 + 8.767\mathbf{r}^5 + 7.797\mathbf{r}^6 + 2.086\mathbf{r}^7\right),$$

96

which have the roots

$$\lambda[A''] = \begin{bmatrix} 1, & \pm i, & -0.53949 \pm 0.2349i, & 0.9310 \pm 0.1142i \end{bmatrix}, \tag{5.7}$$

$$\lambda[B''] = \begin{bmatrix} 1, & \pm i, & -0.53949 \pm 0.2349i, & -0.6170, & -2.44 \times 10^{12} \end{bmatrix}. \tag{5.8}$$

Then the first three roots of $A''(\mathbf{r})$ and $B''(\mathbf{r})$ listed in (5.7) and (5.8) are the roots due to $\alpha(\mathbf{r})$, and the final two roots are those due to $A(\mathbf{r})$ and $B(\mathbf{r})$, respectively. Thus letting

$$L(\mathbf{r}) \triangleq \Big(1 - \mathbf{r}[0.53949 - 0.2349i]\Big)\Big(1 - \mathbf{r}[0.53949 + 0.2349i]\Big),$$

it follows that $(A'', B'') = (LA', LB')$. Note that the spurious root in $B''(\mathbf{r})$ is due to the fact that the trailing coefficient of $B''(\mathbf{r})$ is approximately zero.

Hence in the the SISO case, (A, B) can be separated from the overparameterized solution (A'', B'') simply by looking for the common roots of (A'', B''), as noted in Remark 5.3.3. $\qquad\square$

5.4 Conclusions

In this chapter, we addressed the issue of identification in the presence of deterministic process or measurement noise. Specifically, we studied how deterministic signals propagate through polynomial matrix models. We also showed that both the system and deterministic noise could be identified exactly via overparameterization using ordinary least-squares, and then decoupled using one of the many matrix fraction decomposition techniques available in the literature.

CHAPTER VI

Consistency and Semi-Consistency

In this chapter, we address the issue of identification in the presence of random noise. Specifically, we study the consistency of the estimates in two scenarios, namely, the equation-error framework and the case where the input and input noise are white. In the latter case, we present an approach based on using least-squares with a μ-Markov model. Finally, we introduce the concept of semi-consistency and show how, using the techniques developed in Chapter II, one can obtain semi-consistent linear system estimates from semi-consistent Markov parameter estimates.

6.1   Introduction

In the previous chapters, we developed a framework for handling linear deterministic processes in identification. In this chapter, we allow for random noise processes, and examine the effect of the noise on least-squares estimates. Specifically, we consider the identification of polynomial matrix models in the presence of input and output measurement noise, a longstanding problem in system identification known as errors-in-variables identification [2,44,45]. A challenging aspect of this problem is to obtain consistent parameter estimates, that is, parameter estimates that converge to the true values with probability 1 as the amount of data increases without bound. When the autocorrelation function of the noise on the input and output is known to within a scaling, consistent parameter estimation is possible by using the Koopman-Levins algorithm [11]. This approach has been revisited and refined over the years; numerous references are given in [10].

When the noise properties are unknown, instrumental variables techniques can be applied, and consistency is achievable under specific assumptions [46, 47]. Another approach is to use prediction error methods, which depend on the ability to compute the global minimizer of a nonconvex function [6]. The frequency domain approach given in [48] also yields consistency, although the model order is required to increase rapidly as the amount of data increases.

The approach that we consider in this chapter is based on the μ-Markov model, which is a μ-step prediction model that has the property that μ coefficients of the numerator polynomial are Markov parameters of the system [49]. The usefulness of this model structure is the fact that, under arbitrary output noise and with an input signal that is a realization of a white stochastic process, least-squares estimates of the Markov parameters are consistent. This result is noted without proof in [50], and a related result is given in [51], although the proof given in [51] is incomplete.

Interest in consistent estimates of the Markov parameters stems from the fact that the Markov parameters can be used to construct a consistent state-space model by using the Ho-Kalman algorithm [1], or to construct a consistent polynomial matrix model using the algorithms developed in Chapter II. In this chapter we consider a least-squares technique for extracting polynomial matrices from Markov parameters, which is based on the results of Chapter II. Furthermore, we show that, given consistent Markov parameter estimates, the polynomial matrix estimates are also consistent. Several methods for estimating Markov parameters are compared in [52].

The first goal of this chapter is to provide an extension and complete proof of the result mentioned above, namely, that the μ Markov parameters of a μ-Markov model can be estimated consistently when the input is a realization of a white noise

99

process and the outputs are corrupted by noise with arbitrary unknown statistics and spectrum. Since the proof is formulated in a MIMO setting using polynomial matrices, this result extends the results of [50, 51]. The second goal of this chapter is to prove that the Markov parameters can be estimated consistently to within an unknown scale factor when the input is a realization of a white noise process and the inputs are corrupted by a white noise process independent of the input, in which case we say that the Markov parameters estimates are *semi-consistent*. Furthermore, we show that *semi-consistent* polynomial matrix estimates are obtainable from *semi-consistent* Markov parameter estimates.

The contents of the chapter are as follows. In Section 6.2, we present preliminaries concerning the μ-Markov model and convergence with probability one. Then in Section 6.3 we present the problem statement. In Section 6.4 we show two circumstances in which either the system coefficients or Markov parameters can be identified consistently. Finally, in Section 6.5 we show how to obtain semi-consistent linear system estimates from semi-consistent Markov parameter estimates, followed by conclusions in Section 6.6.

6.2 Preliminaries

Here we present the necessary preliminaries concerning the μ-Markov multiple and convergence with probability one that will be used throughout the chapter.

6.2.1 The μ-Markov Model

In this section, we introduce the μ-Markov multiple, which explicitly displays μ Markov parameters. Since μ Markov parameters are explicitly displayed in the numerator polynomial, we will see later that the μ-Markov multiple is useful for identifying the Markov parameters of a linear system under certain assumptions.

Proposition 6.2.1. Let $C \in \mathbb{R}^{p \times p}[\mathbf{r}]$ have full normal rank, let $D \in \mathbb{R}^{p \times m}[\mathbf{r}]$, and

100

let (C, D) be left coprime, causal, and have a degree of s. Also, let $H \in \mathbb{R}_\infty^{p \times m}[\mathbf{r}]$ be the Markov parameter polynomial of (C, D), and let $C(\mathbf{r})$ and $E \in \mathbb{R}^{p \times p}[\mathbf{r}]$ be given by

$$
\begin{aligned}
C(\mathbf{r}) &\triangleq C_0 + C_1 \mathbf{r} + \cdots + C_s \mathbf{r}^s, \\
E(\mathbf{r}) &\triangleq C_0^+ + E_1 \mathbf{r} + \cdots + E_{\mu-1} \mathbf{r}^{\mu-1},
\end{aligned}
$$

where $\mu \geq 1$, $(\cdot)^+$ denotes the Moore-Penrose psuedo-inverse of $(\cdot)$, and for $i \in [1, \mu - 1]$,

$$
E_i \triangleq - \left(\sum_{j=1}^{\min(i,s)} E_{i-j} C_j \right) C_0^+.
$$

Then the first μ coefficients of $C^\mu(\mathbf{r}) \triangleq E(\mathbf{r})C(\mathbf{r})$ and $D^\mu(\mathbf{r}) \triangleq E(\mathbf{r})D(\mathbf{r})$ are given by

$$
\begin{aligned}
\theta_{\mu-1} \left(C^\mu \right) &= \theta_{\mu-1} \left(E \right) \mathcal{T}_{\mu-1} \left(C \right), \\
&= \left[\begin{array}{cc} I_p, & 0_{p \times p(\mu-1)} \end{array} \right], \\
\theta_{\mu-1} \left(D^\mu \right) &= \theta_{\mu-1} \left(E \right) \mathcal{T}_{\mu-1} \left(D \right), \\
&= \theta_{\mu-1} \left(E \right) \mathcal{T}_{\mu-1} \left(C \right) \mathcal{T}_{\mu-1} \left(H \right), \\
&= \left[\begin{array}{cc} I_p, & 0_{p \times p(\mu-1)} \end{array} \right] \mathcal{T}_{\mu-1} \left(H \right), \\
&= \theta_{\mu-1} \left(H \right),
\end{aligned}
$$

where $\theta_{\mu-1}(\cdot)$ and $\mathcal{T}_{\mu-1}(\cdot)$ are defined in Definition 2.5.1. Thus $C^\mu(\mathbf{r})$ and $D^\mu(\mathbf{r})$ are of the form

$$
\begin{aligned}
C^{\mu}(\mathbf{r}) &= I_p &+ C^{\mu}_{\mu}\mathbf{r}^{\mu} &+ \cdots &+ C^{\mu}_{\mu+s-1}\mathbf{r}^{\mu+s-1}, \\
D^{\mu}(\mathbf{r}) &= H_0 &+ H_1\mathbf{r} &+ \cdots &+ H_{\mu-1}\mathbf{r}^{\mu-1} \\
& & + D^{\mu}_{\mu}\mathbf{r}^{\mu} &+ \cdots &+ D^{\mu}_{\mu+s-1}\mathbf{r}^{\mu+s-1}.
\end{aligned}
\tag{6.1}
$$

We call (C^{μ}, D^{μ}) the μ-*Markov multiple of* (C, D) since μ Markov parameters of (C, D) appear explicitly in $D^{\mu}(\mathbf{r})$.

Proof. Since $C(\mathbf{r})$ has full normal rank and (C, D) is left coprime and causal, then from Fact 2.2.10, C_0 is nonsingular. Furthermore, since $H(\mathbf{r})$ is the Markov parameter polynomial of (C, D), $C(\mathbf{r})H(\mathbf{r}) = D(\mathbf{r})$, and hence

$$
\mathcal{T}_{\mu-1}(C)\,\mathcal{T}_{\mu-1}(H) = \mathcal{T}_{\mu-1}(D).
$$

$\square$

Remark 6.2.1. The μ-Markov multiple (C^{μ}, D^{μ}) of (C, D) is derived without mention of a system or a model. However, given the system

$$
C(\mathbf{r})y(k) = D(\mathbf{r})u(k),
\tag{6.2}
$$

where $u \in \mathbb{R}^m$ and $y \in \mathbb{R}^p$, we say that

$$
C^{\mu}(\mathbf{r})y(k) = E(\mathbf{r})C(\mathbf{r})y(k) = E(\mathbf{r})D(\mathbf{r})u(k) = D^{\mu}(\mathbf{r})u(k),
\tag{6.3}
$$

is the μ-Markov *model* of (6.2). $\square$

Remark 6.2.2. For every comonic multiple (C', D') of (C, D), one can also construct the μ-Markov multiple of (C', D') using the above procedure. $\square$

6.2.2 Convergence With Probability One

Here we introduce convergence with probability one (w.p.1) and give examples of sequences which converge in this manner.

Definition 6.2.1. Let $X_1, X_2, \ldots \in \mathbb{R}^{m \times p}$ and $X \in \mathbb{R}^{m \times p}$. Then X_N *converges with probability one (or almost surely) to* X *if*

$$P\left(\lim_{N \to \infty} X_N = X\right) = 1,$$

where $P(\cdot)$ denotes the probability of $(\cdot)$. Specifically, we write

$$X_N \xrightarrow[N \to \infty]{\text{w.p.1}} X.$$

Fact 6.2.1. Let $Y_1, Y_2, \ldots \in \mathbb{R}$, $Z_1, Z_2, \ldots \in \mathbb{R}$, $Y_N \xrightarrow[N \to \infty]{\text{w.p.1}} Y$, and $Z_N \xrightarrow[N \to \infty]{\text{w.p.1}} Z$. Then

$$Y_N + Z_N \xrightarrow[N \to \infty]{\text{w.p.1}} Y + Z,$$

$$Y_N Z_N \xrightarrow[N \to \infty]{\text{w.p.1}} YZ.$$

Furthermore, if $Z \neq 0$ and $f : \mathbb{R} \to \mathbb{R}$, then

$$Y_N / Z_N \xrightarrow[N \to \infty]{\text{w.p.1}} Y/Z,$$

$$f(Y_N) \xrightarrow[N \to \infty]{\text{w.p.1}} f(Y).$$

Proof. See [71]. □

Fact 6.2.2. Let $R_1, R_2, \ldots \in \mathbb{R}^{m \times m}$ and $S_1, S_2, \ldots \in \mathbb{R}^{m \times p}$, where

$$R_N \xrightarrow[N \to \infty]{\text{w.p.1}} R, \qquad S_N \xrightarrow[N \to \infty]{\text{w.p.1}} S,$$

and R is nonsingular. Then

$$R_N^{-1} S_N \xrightarrow[N \to \infty]{\text{w.p.1}} R^{-1} S.$$

Proof. Let $\alpha \triangleq \det[R]$ and $\alpha_N \triangleq \det[R_N]$. Then since α_N is the finite product and sum of entries of R_N, where each of the entries converges w.p.1, from Fact 6.2.1 we have that $\alpha_N \xrightarrow[N \to \infty]{\text{w.p.1}} \alpha$. Similarly, letting $T \triangleq \text{adj}[R]$ and $T_N \triangleq \text{adj}[R_N]$, we have that $T_N \xrightarrow[N \to \infty]{\text{w.p.1}} T$. Finally, since R is nonsingular, $\alpha \neq 0$. Hence from Fact 6.2.1,

$$\frac{1}{\alpha_N} T_N S_N \xrightarrow[N \to \infty]{\text{w.p.1}} \frac{1}{\alpha} T S = R^{-1} S.$$

$\square$

Fact 6.2.3. Let $C \in \mathbb{R}^{p \times p}[\mathbf{r}]$, $D \in \mathbb{R}^{p \times m}[\mathbf{r}]$, and

$$C(\mathbf{r}) y(k) = D(\mathbf{r}) u(k),$$

where $u \in \mathbb{R}^m$, $y \in \mathbb{R}^p$, $k \geq 1$, and (C, D) is causal and asymptotically stable. Also, let $H \in \mathbb{R}^{p \times m}[\mathbf{r}]$ be the Markov parameter polynomial of (C, D), and let $u = \{u_1, \ldots, u_m\} \in \mathbb{R}^m$ and $v = \{v_1, \ldots, v_m\} \in \mathbb{R}^m$ be realizations of the independent and identically distributed random processes $\mathcal{U}$ and $\mathcal{V}$, respectively, where $\mathcal{U}$ and $\mathcal{V}$ are mutually independent white processes with bounded second and fourth moments, that is, for all, $i, j, k, \ell \in [1, m]$,

$$\mathbb{E}[\mathcal{U}_i \mathcal{U}_j] < \infty, \qquad \mathbb{E}[\mathcal{V}_i \mathcal{V}_j] < \infty,$$
$$\mathbb{E}[\mathcal{U}_i \mathcal{U}_j \mathcal{U}_k \mathcal{U}_\ell] < \infty, \qquad \mathbb{E}[\mathcal{V}_i \mathcal{V}_j \mathcal{V}_k \mathcal{V}_\ell] < \infty.$$

Then for all $i \in \mathbb{Z}$,

$$\frac{1}{N} \sum_{k=1}^{N} y(k+i) y^T(k) \xrightarrow[N \to \infty]{\text{w.p.1}} \sum_{j=0}^{\infty} H_{j+i} R H_j,$$

$$\frac{1}{N} \sum_{k=1}^{N} y(k+i) u^T(k) \xrightarrow[N \to \infty]{\text{w.p.1}} H_i R,$$

$$\frac{1}{N} \sum_{k=1}^{N} y(k+i) v^T(k) \xrightarrow[N \to \infty]{\text{w.p.1}} 0_{p \times m},$$

$$\frac{1}{N} \sum_{k=1}^{N} u(k+i) v^T(k) \xrightarrow[N \to \infty]{\text{w.p.1}} 0_{m \times m},$$

where $R \in \mathbb{R}^{m \times m}$ is the covariance matrix of $\mathcal{U}$, that is,

$$R \triangleq \mathbb{E}\left[\mathcal{U}(k) \mathcal{U}^T(k) \right].$$

Proof. See [5,6]. $\qquad\qquad\qquad\qquad\qquad\qquad\qquad\qquad\qquad\qquad\qquad$ $\square$

6.3   Problem Statement

Consider the system

$$A(\mathbf{r}) y(k) = B(\mathbf{r}) u(k), \tag{6.4}$$

where $k \geq 1$, $u \in \mathbb{R}^m$, $y \in \mathbb{R}^p$, $A \in \mathbb{R}^{p \times p}[\mathbf{r}]$ is comonic with $A_0 = I_p$, $B \in \mathbb{R}^{p \times m}[\mathbf{r}]$, and (A, B) is left coprime, causal, and has a degree of n. Furthermore, consider the case where the measurement x of u is corrupted by an additive noise signal v, and the measurement z of y is corrupted by an additive noise signal w, that is,

$$\begin{aligned} x(k) &= u(k) + v(k), \\ z(k) &= y(k) + w(k). \end{aligned} \tag{6.5}$$

as shown in Figure 6.1.

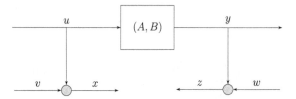

Figure 6.1: Measurements of the input and output of a linear system in the presence of the measurement noise processes v and w.

Throughout the chapter, we attempt to identify the system (A, B) given only the signals x and z. The identification setup is shown in Figure 6.2.

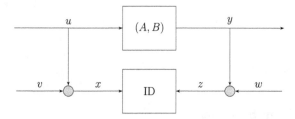

Figure 6.2: Identification of a linear system in the presence of the measurement noise processes v and w.

6.4 Least-Squares Identification

Here we analyze least-squares estimates in the presence of random noise. We begin by introducing the concept of consistency and semi-consistency as well as the regression notation that we will use henceforth for least-squares identification.

Definition 6.4.1. For all $N \geq 1$ and $i \in [1, s]$, let $\hat{X}_{i,N} \in \mathbb{R}^{m \times p}$ be an estimate of

$X_i \in \mathbb{R}^{m \times p}$. Also, let

$$\hat{\Theta}_N \triangleq \left[\hat{X}_{1,N}, \cdots, \hat{X}_{s,N} \right] \in \mathbb{R}^{m \times ps},$$

$$\Theta \triangleq \left[X_1, \cdots, X_s \right] \in \mathbb{R}^{m \times ps}.$$

Then we say that $\hat{\Theta}_N$ *is a strongly consistent estimate of* Θ if

$$\hat{\Theta}_N \xrightarrow[N \to \infty]{\text{w.p.1}} \Theta,$$

(see [2]). Furthermore, we say that $\hat{\Theta}_N$ *is a semi-consistent estimate of* Θ if there exists a nonsingular $R \in \mathbb{R}^{p \times p}$ such that

$$\hat{\Theta}_N \xrightarrow[N \to \infty]{\text{w.p.1}} \Theta \left(I_s \otimes R \right).$$

In this case, for all $i \in [1, s]$,

$$\hat{X}_{i,N} \xrightarrow[N \to \infty]{\text{w.p.1}} X_i R.$$

Remark 6.4.1. Let $B \in \mathbb{R}^{p \times m}[\mathbf{r}]$, let $R \in \mathbb{R}^{m \times m}$ be nonsingular, and let $\widehat{\theta(B)}_N$ be a semi-consistent estimate of $\theta(B)$, where $B(\mathbf{r})$ has a degree of n and

$$\widehat{\theta(B)}_N \xrightarrow[N \to \infty]{\text{w.p.1}} \theta(B) \left(I_{n+1} \otimes R \right).$$

Then reconstructing $\hat{B}_N(\mathbf{r})$ from its coefficient matrix $\widehat{\theta(B)}_N$, we have that

$$\hat{B}_N(\mathbf{r}) \xrightarrow[N \to \infty]{\text{w.p.1}} B(\mathbf{r}) R.$$

However, while this may not seem useful, note that the zeros of $B(\mathbf{r})$ and the zeros of $B(\mathbf{r})R$ are the same (Appendix A). Hence semi-consistent polynomial matrix estimates preserve the zero-structure. □

Notation 6.4.1. Let $N \geq 1$ and let $x(k) \in \mathbb{R}^m$ for all $k \in [1, N]$. Then for $s \in [1, N]$ and $\mu \in [1, N - s]$, we employ the notation

$$\Psi_{x,s,\mu,N} \triangleq \begin{bmatrix} x(s+\mu) & \cdots & x(N) \\ \vdots & & \vdots \\ x(s+1) & \cdots & z(N-\mu+1) \end{bmatrix},$$

$$\Lambda_{x,s,\mu,N} \triangleq \begin{bmatrix} x(s) & \cdots & x(N-\mu) \\ \vdots & & \vdots \\ x(1) & \cdots & x(N-s-\mu+1) \end{bmatrix},$$

$$\Omega_{x,s,\mu,N} \triangleq \begin{bmatrix} \Psi_{x,s,\mu,N} \\ \Lambda_{x,s,\mu,N} \end{bmatrix},$$

$$\Gamma_{x,s,\mu,N} \triangleq \begin{bmatrix} x(s+\mu), & \cdots, & x(N) \end{bmatrix}.$$

Notation 6.4.2. Let $D \in \mathbb{R}^{p \times m}[\mathbf{r}]$ be given by

$$D(\mathbf{r}) \triangleq D_0 + D_1\mathbf{r} + \cdots + D_s\mathbf{r}^s.$$

Then for $\beta \geq 0$ and $\eta \geq 0$, we employ the notation

$$\theta'(D) \triangleq \begin{bmatrix} D_1, & \cdots, & D_s \end{bmatrix} \in \mathbb{R}^{p \times sm},$$

$$\theta_{\beta,\eta}(D) \triangleq \begin{bmatrix} D_\beta, & \cdots, & D_{\beta+\eta-1} \end{bmatrix} \in \mathbb{R}^{p \times \eta m},$$

where $D_j = 0_{p \times m}$ for $j > s$.

6.4.1 Equation Error Model

A common estimation framework is the equation error approach. Specifically, in the context of the additive measurement noise model (6.5), let the following additional assumption hold:

Assumption 6.4.1. $v(k) = 0_{m \times 1}$ for all $k \geq 1$.

Assumption 6.4.2. There exists a comonic $L \in \mathbb{R}^{p \times p}[\mathbf{r}]$ such that, for all $k \geq 1$,

$$L(\mathbf{r})A(\mathbf{r})w(k) = w'(k),$$

where $w' \in \mathbb{R}^p$ is a realization of the independent and identically distributed, zero-mean, random process $\mathcal{W}'$ with finite covariance. Furthermore, $L_0 = I_p$.

Then from (6.4)-(6.5) and Assumptions 6.4.1-6.4.2, we have the equation error model of (6.4) given by

$$L(\mathbf{r})A(\mathbf{r})z(k) = L(\mathbf{r})B(\mathbf{r})u(k) + w'(k). \tag{6.6}$$

Hence, letting

$$C(\mathbf{r}) \triangleq L(\mathbf{r})A(\mathbf{r}),$$

$$D(\mathbf{r}) \triangleq L(\mathbf{r})B(\mathbf{r}),$$

$$\Theta \triangleq \left[\ \theta(D), \ \theta'(C) \ \right],$$

$$\Phi_N \triangleq \begin{bmatrix} \Omega_{x,s,1,N} \\ -\Lambda_{z,s,1,N} \end{bmatrix},$$

$$Z_N \triangleq \Gamma_{z,s,1,N},$$

$$W'_N \triangleq \Gamma_{w,s,1,N},$$

and letting s denote the degree of (C, D), it follows that

$$Z_N = \Theta \Phi_N + (L_0 A_0)^+ W_N'. \tag{6.7}$$

Next, consider the least-squares estimate $\hat{\Theta}_N$ of Θ given by

$$\hat{\Theta}_N = \arg\min_{\hat{\Theta}_N} \left\| Z_n - \hat{\Theta}_N \Phi_N \right\|_{\mathrm{F}}.$$

Furthermore, let the following assumptions also hold:

Assumption 6.4.3. For all $k \geq 1$ one of the following holds

i) $u(k)$ is deterministic and bounded.

ii) $u \in \mathbb{R}^m$ is a realization of the random process $\mathcal{U}$, where $\mathcal{U}$ has finite mean and variance.

Assumption 6.4.4. For all $k \geq 1$ and nonnegative i,

$$\mathbb{E}\left[\mathcal{W}'(k+i)\mathcal{U}^T(k) \right] = 0_{p \times m}.$$

Assumption 6.4.5. $(1/N)\Phi_N \Phi_N^T \xrightarrow[N \to \infty]{\text{w.p.1}} \chi$, where $\chi \in \mathbb{R}^{(m[s+1]+ps) \times (m[s+1]+ps)}$ is nonsingular.

Assumption 6.4.6. (C, D) is asymptotically stable.

Fact 6.4.1. Let Assumptions 6.4.1-6.4.6 hold. Then $\hat{\Theta}_N$ is a strongly consistent estimate of Θ.

Proof. First, note that the least-squares estimate $\hat{\Theta}_N$ of Θ satisfies

$$\hat{\Theta}_N \Phi_N \Phi_N^T = Z_N \Phi_N^T.$$

110

Next, from Assumptions 6.4.1 and 6.4.2, we have (6.7) and hence

$$\hat{\Theta}_N \Phi_N \Phi_N^T = \Theta \Phi_N \Phi_N^T + W_N' \Phi_N^T.$$

Furthermore, from Assumptions 6.4.3-6.4.6 and Fact 6.2.3, we have that

$$\frac{1}{N} W_N' \Omega_{x,s,1,N}^T$$
$$= \frac{1}{N} \sum_{k=1}^{N-s} \left[\; w'(k+s)x^T(k+s) \;\; \cdots \;\; w'(k+s)x^T(k) \; \right],$$
$$\xrightarrow[N \to \infty]{\text{w.p.1}} 0_{p \times m(s+1)}.$$

Finally, from (6.6), Assumptions 6.4.3-6.4.6, and Fact 6.2.3, note that

$$\frac{1}{N} W_N' \Lambda_{z,s,1,N}^T$$
$$= \frac{1}{N} \sum_{k=1}^{N-s} \left[\; w'(k+s)z^T(k+s-1) \;\; \cdots \;\; w'(k+s)z^T(k) \; \right],$$
$$\xrightarrow[N \to \infty]{\text{w.p.1}} 0_{p \times ps}.$$

Hence

$$\frac{1}{N} W_N' \Phi_N^T \xrightarrow[N \to \infty]{\text{w.p.1}} 0_{p \times (sp+m[s+1])},$$

and thus, from Assumption 6.4.5,

$$\hat{\Theta}_N \xrightarrow[N \to \infty]{\text{w.p.1}} \Theta \Phi_N \Phi_N^T \left(\Phi_N \Phi_N^T \right)^{-1} = \Theta.$$

$\square$

6.4.2 μ-Markov-Based Least-Squares Estimates of Markov Parameters

Here we show that when the input u and input noise v are white, the Markov parameters can be estimated semi-consistently under fairly general conditions using least-squares and the μ-Markov model.

Consider again the system (6.4) and measurement noise equations (6.5). Also, let

$$\Phi_{s,\mu,N} \triangleq \begin{bmatrix} \Omega_{x,s,\mu,N} \\ -\Lambda_{z,s,\mu,N} \end{bmatrix}, \tag{6.8}$$

$$\tilde{\Phi}_{s,\mu,N} \triangleq \mathbf{r}^{n-s} \begin{bmatrix} \Omega_{u,n,\mu,N+n-s} \\ -\Lambda_{y,n,\mu,N+n-s} \end{bmatrix}, \tag{6.9}$$

$$\Theta_\mu \triangleq \begin{bmatrix} \theta_{\mu-1}(H), & \theta_{\mu,n}(B^\mu), & \theta_{\mu,n}(A^\mu) \end{bmatrix}. \tag{6.10}$$

Next, consider the least-squares estimate

$$\hat{\Theta}_{s,\mu,N} \triangleq \begin{bmatrix} \widehat{\theta_{\mu-1}(H)}, & \widehat{\theta_{\mu,s}(B^\mu)}, & \widehat{\theta_{\mu,s}(A^\mu)} \end{bmatrix},$$

given by

$$\hat{\Theta}_{s,\mu,N} = \arg\min_{\hat{\Theta}_{s,\mu,N}} \left\| \Gamma_{z,s,\mu,N} - \hat{\Theta}_{s,\mu,N} \Phi_{s,\mu,N} \right\|_2^2. \tag{6.11}$$

Also, consider the following assumptions:

Assumption 6.4.7. $u \in \mathbb{R}^m$ and $v \in \mathbb{R}^m$ are realizations of the independent and identically distributed processes $\mathcal{U}$ and $\mathcal{V}$, respectively. Furthermore, for all $k \geq 1$, $\mathcal{X}(k) \triangleq \mathcal{U}(k) + \mathcal{V}(k)$.

Assumption 6.4.8. For all $k \geq 1$ and nonnegative p, the means and covariances of $\mathcal{U}(k)$, $\mathcal{X}(k)$, $\mathcal{U}(k+p)\mathcal{X}^T(k)$, and $\mathcal{X}(k+p)\mathcal{X}^T(k)$ are finite. Furthermore, $R \in \mathbb{R}^{m \times m}$

and $S \in \mathbb{R}^{m \times m}$ given by

$$R \triangleq \mathbb{E}\Big[\mathcal{X}(k)\mathcal{X}^T(k)\Big], \qquad (6.12)$$

$$S \triangleq \mathbb{E}\Big[\mathcal{U}(k)\mathcal{X}^T(k)\Big], \qquad (6.13)$$

are nonsingular.

Assumption 6.4.9. $w \in \mathbb{R}^p$ is a realization of the stationary, colored random process $\mathcal{W}$ with finite mean and autocorrelation function, that is, for all $j, k \geq 1$ and nonnegative i,

$$\mathbb{E}\Big[\mathcal{W}(k)\Big] = \mathbb{E}\Big[\mathcal{W}(j)\Big] < \infty,$$

$$\mathbb{E}\Big[\mathcal{W}(k+i)\mathcal{W}^T(k)\Big] = \mathbb{E}\Big[\mathcal{W}(j+i)\mathcal{W}^T(j)\Big] < \infty.$$

Assumption 6.4.10. The random processes $\mathcal{U}$, $\mathcal{V}$, and $\mathcal{W}$ are independent of each other.

Fact 6.4.2. Let Assumptions 6.4.6-6.4.10 hold. Furthermore, let $s \geq 0$ and $\mu \geq 1$. Then $\widehat{\theta_{\mu-1}(H)}$ is a semi-consistent estimate of $\theta_{\mu-1}(H)$. Specifically,

$$\widehat{\theta_{\mu-1}(H)} \xrightarrow[N \to \infty]{\text{w.p.1}} \theta_{\mu-1}(H)\Big(I_\mu \otimes SR^{-1}\Big),$$

where R and S are given by (6.12) and (6.13), respectively, and $\widehat{\theta_{\mu-1}(H)}$ is the Markov parameter portion of the least-squares estimate $\hat{\Theta}_{s,\mu,N}$.

Proof. First, note that the least-squares estimate $\hat{\Theta}_{s,\mu,N}$ satisfies

$$\left(\Gamma_{z,s,\mu,N} - \hat{\Theta}_{s,\mu,N}\Phi_{s,\mu,N}\right)\Phi^T_{s,\mu,N}$$

$$= \left(\Gamma_{z,s,\mu,N} - \hat{\Theta}_{s,\mu,N}\Phi_{s,\mu,N}\right)\begin{bmatrix} \Omega_{x,s,\mu,N} \\ -\Lambda_{z,s,\mu,N} \end{bmatrix}^T$$

$$= \left(\Gamma_{z,s,\mu,N} - \hat{\Theta}_{s,\mu,N}\Phi_{s,\mu,N}\right)\begin{bmatrix} \Psi_{x,s,\mu,N} \\ \Lambda_{x,s,\mu,N} \\ -\Lambda_{z,s,\mu,N} \end{bmatrix}^T$$

$$= 0_{p\times(m[\mu+s]+ps)}.$$

Next, we examine the subset of previous equations given by

$$\left(\Gamma_{z,s,\mu,N} - \hat{\Theta}_{s,\mu,N}\Phi_{s,\mu,N}\right)\Psi^T_{x,s,\mu,N} = 0_{p\times m\mu},$$

where, from (6.4)-(6.5) and (6.8)-(6.10), we have that

$$\left(\Theta_\mu\tilde{\Phi}_{s,\mu,N} + W_N - \hat{\Theta}_{s,\mu,N}\Phi_{s,\mu,N}\right)\Psi^T_{x,s,\mu,N} = 0_{p\times m\mu}.$$

Next, from Assumptions 6.4.6-6.4.10 and Fact 6.2.3, we have that

$$\frac{1}{N}\tilde{\Phi}_{s,\mu,N}\Psi^T_{x,s,\mu,N} \xrightarrow[N\to\infty]{\text{w.p.1}} \begin{bmatrix} I_\mu \otimes S \\ 0_{n(m+p)\times m\mu} \end{bmatrix},$$

$$\frac{1}{N}W_{s,\mu,N}\Psi^T_{x,s,\mu,N} \xrightarrow[N\to\infty]{\text{w.p.1}} 0_{p\times m\mu},$$

$$\frac{1}{N}\Phi_{s,\mu,N}\Psi^T_{x,s,\mu,N} \xrightarrow[N\to\infty]{\text{w.p.1}} \begin{bmatrix} I_\mu \otimes R \\ 0_{s(m+p)\times m\mu} \end{bmatrix}.$$

Thus

$$\theta_{\mu-1}(H)\left(I_\mu \otimes S\right) - \widehat{\theta_{\mu-1}(H)}\left(I_\mu \otimes R\right) \xrightarrow[N\to\infty]{\text{w.p.1}} 0_{p \times m\mu},$$

and hence from Assumption 6.4.8, it follows that

$$\widehat{\theta_{\mu-1}(H)} \xrightarrow[N\to\infty]{\text{w.p.1}} \theta_{\mu-1}(H)\left(I_\mu \otimes SR^{-1}\right).$$

$\square$

Corollary 6.4.1. Let Assumptions 6.4.1 and 6.4.6-6.4.10 hold. Furthermore, let $s \geq 0$ and $\mu \geq 1$. Then $\widehat{\theta_{\mu-1}(H)}$ is a strongly consistent estimate of $\theta_{\mu-1}(H)$, where $\widehat{\theta_{\mu-1}(H)}$ is the Markov parameter portion of the least-squares estimate $\hat{\Theta}_{s,\mu,N}$.

Proof. From Assumption 6.4.1, $v(k) = 0_{m \times 1}$. Thus letting R and S be given by (6.12) and (6.13), respectively, it follows that $R = S$. Finally, from Fact 6.4.2 it follows that $\widehat{\theta_{\mu-1}(H)} \xrightarrow[N\to\infty]{\text{w.p.1}} \theta_{\mu-1}(H)$. $\square$

Remark 6.4.2. In the μ-Markov-based Markov parameter estimates, we need to choose a model degree s as well as the number of Markov parameters μ we would like explicitly displayed in the model (6.1). Furthermore, from Fact 6.4.2, the degree s of the model does not depend on the degree n of (A, B) in (6.4). In what follows, we refer to s as the model degree which is used in (6.1) and Fact 6.4.2. $\square$

Example 6.4.1. Consider the linearized longitudinal model of the T-2 aircraft (1.1) given by

$$\left(1 - 1.862\mathbf{r} + 0.8798\mathbf{r}^2\right)y(k) = \left(-0.009767\mathbf{r} - 0.006026\mathbf{r}^2\right)u(k), \qquad (6.14)$$

115

where $y(2) = y(1) = 0$. Then letting $\mu \triangleq 10$, we have that

$$\theta_{\mu-1}(H) = \begin{bmatrix} H_0, & \cdots, & H_{\mu-1} \end{bmatrix}$$

$$= -10^{-2} \times \begin{bmatrix} 0, & 0.977, & 2.42, & 3.65, & 4.66, & 5.47, & 6.09, & 6.52, & 6.79, & 6.90 \end{bmatrix}.$$

Furthermore, let u, v, and w_w be realizations of the independent and identically distributed Gaussian processes $\mathcal{U}$, $\mathcal{V}$, and $\mathcal{W}_w$, respectively, where $\mathcal{U}$, $\mathcal{V}$, and $\mathcal{W}_w$ are all zero mean, independent of each other, and have unit variance. Also, let

$$w(k) = 4w_w(k) + 3w_w(k-1) + 2w_w(k-2) + 1w_w(k-3), \tag{6.15}$$

and consider the additive measurement noise model (6.5). Then from (6.12), $R = 2$, and from (6.13), $S = 1$.

Finally, we let $s = 6$ and estimate $\hat{\Theta}_{s,\mu,N}$ via (6.11) for $M \triangleq 1000$ realizations of the random processes $\mathcal{V}$ and $\mathcal{W}_w$. Then letting $\widehat{\theta^j_{\mu-1}(H)}$ denote the Markov parameter portion of $\hat{\Theta}_{s,\mu,N}$ for each realization $j \in [1, M]$, Figure 6.3 displays the ensemble average of the estimated Markov parameter error given by

$$\varepsilon \triangleq \frac{1}{\mu M \left\| \theta_{\mu-1}(H) \right\|_2} \sum_{j=1}^{M} \left\| \widehat{\theta^j_{\mu-1}(H)} - \theta_{\mu-1}(H) \right\|_2, \tag{6.16}$$

for several values of N. Specifically, Figure 6.3 displays two cases: the case where the input measurement noise v is zero, and the case where v is a realization of the zero-mean, unit variance, Gaussian random process $\mathcal{V}$ mentioned previously. In the second case, the estimates are scaled by 2 such that they should in theory be strongly consistent estimates of the true Markov parameters. From Figure 6.3, it appears that the error ε converges to zero in both both cases, suggesting that $\widehat{\theta_{\mu-1}(H)} \xrightarrow[N\to\infty]{\text{w.p.1}} \theta_{\mu-1}(H)$ when $v = 0$, and $\widehat{\theta_{\mu-1}(H)} \xrightarrow[N\to\infty]{\text{w.p.1}} \theta_{\mu-1}(H)\left(I_\mu \otimes SR^{-1} \right) = (1/2)\theta_{\mu-1}(H)$ when v is a realization of the zero-mean, unit variance, Gaussian random process $\mathcal{V}$. Furthermore,

116

from Figure 6.3, it appears that the estimates converge more slowly when $v \neq 0$. □

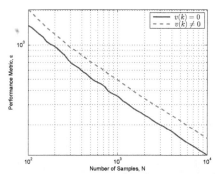

Figure 6.3: Comparison of the ensemble average of the error in the estimated Markov parameters of (6.14) when y is measured with the additive colored noise signal (6.15), and either $v(k) = 0$ or v a realization of a zero-mean, unit variance, Gaussian random variable, where $s = 6$ and $\mu = 10$.

6.5 Recovering the Linear System from Markov Parameters

Here we show how to obtain semi-consistent system estimates from semi-consistent Markov parameter estimates.

Fact 6.5.1. Consider the system (6.4), where $H \in \mathbb{R}^{p \times m}[\mathbf{r}]$ is the Markov parameter polynomial of (A, B). Also, let n^* be the degree of the quasi-scalar multiple of (A, B) given by Proposition 2.2.1, and let $\bar{n} \geq n^*$, let $R \in \mathbb{R}^{m \times m}$ be nonsingular, and let $\hat{H}_{0,N}, \ldots, \hat{H}_{2\bar{n},N} \in \mathbb{R}^{p \times m}$ be semi-consistent estimates of $H_0, \ldots, H_{2\bar{n}}$, respectively. Specifically, for all $i \in [0, 2\bar{n}]$, let

$$\hat{H}_{i,N} \xrightarrow[N \to \infty]{\text{w.p.1}} H_i R.$$

Finally, let

$$\hat{H}_N(\mathbf{r}) \triangleq \sum_{i=0}^{2s} \hat{H}_{i,N}\mathbf{r}^i,$$

$$\hat{\theta}_{C,N} \triangleq \left[\hat{C}_{1,N}, \cdots, \hat{C}_{\bar{n},N} \right],$$

$$\hat{\theta}_{D,N} \triangleq \left[\hat{D}_{0,N}, \cdots, \hat{D}_{\bar{n},N} \right],$$

where $\hat{\theta}_{C,N}$ and $\hat{\theta}_{D,N}$ minimize

$$J_N = \left\| \theta_{2\bar{n}}(\hat{H}_N) - \left[\hat{\theta}_{C,N}, \hat{\theta}_{D,N} \right] \overline{\mathcal{K}}_{\bar{n},\bar{n}}(\hat{H}_N) \right\|_F, \qquad (6.17)$$

and where $\overline{\mathcal{K}}_{\bar{n},\bar{n}}(\hat{H}_N)$ is given by Definition 2.5.1. If $\hat{C}_N \in \mathbb{R}^{p \times p}[\mathbf{r}]$ and $\hat{D}_N \in \mathbb{R}^{p \times m}[\mathbf{r}]$ are given by

$$\hat{C}_N(\mathbf{r}) \triangleq I_p + \hat{C}_{1,N}\mathbf{r} + \cdots + \hat{C}_{\bar{n},N}\mathbf{r}^{\bar{n}},$$

$$\hat{D}_N(\mathbf{r}) \triangleq \hat{D}_{0,N} + \hat{D}_{1,N}\mathbf{r} + \cdots + \hat{D}_{\bar{n},N}\mathbf{r}^{\bar{n}},$$

the $\left(\hat{C}_N, \hat{D}_N \right)$ converges with probability one to a multiple of (A, BR).

Proof. Since R is nonsingular and $\hat{H}_{i,N} \xrightarrow[N\to\infty]{\text{w.p.1}} H_i R$ for all $i \in [0, 2\bar{n}]$,

$$\overline{\mathcal{K}}_{\bar{n},\bar{n}}(\hat{H}_N) \xrightarrow[N\to\infty]{\text{w.p.1}} \overline{\mathcal{K}}_{\bar{n},\bar{n}}(HR).$$

Hence

$$\left[\theta\left(\hat{C}_N\right), \ \theta\left(\hat{D}_N\right) \right] \overline{\mathcal{K}}_{\bar{n},\bar{n}}(\hat{H}_N) \xrightarrow[N\to\infty]{\text{w.p.1}} 0_{p \times m(2\bar{n}+1)},$$

and therefore, from Proposition 2.7.1,

$$\hat{C}_N(\mathbf{r})H(\mathbf{r})R - \hat{D}_N(\mathbf{r}) \xrightarrow[N\to\infty]{\text{w.p.1}} 0_{p\times m}.$$

Finally, since $\hat{C}_N(\mathbf{r})$ is comonic, $C(\mathbf{r})$ has full normal rank, and thus from Theorem 2.4.2, $(\hat{C}_N, \hat{D}_N)$ converges with probability one to a multiple of (A, BR). □

Remark 6.5.1. There may exist multiple minimizers $\hat{\theta}_{C,N}$ and $\hat{\theta}_{D,N}$ of (6.17), even if $\bar{n} = n$. This is due to the fact that in MIMO polynomial matrix models, there may exist more than one parameterization of the same system. However, every solution will still be a multiple of (A, BR). □

Remark 6.5.2. Note that if R is nonsingular, then the zeros of $B(\mathbf{r})R$ are the same as the zeros of $B(\mathbf{r})$ (see Appendix A). □

Example 6.5.1. Consider the linearized longitudinal model of the T-2 aircraft (1.1) in Example 6.4.1, where

$$\left(1 - 1.862\mathbf{r} + 0.8798\mathbf{r}^2\right) y(k) = \left(-0.009767\mathbf{r} - 0.006026\mathbf{r}^2\right) u(k).$$

Furthermore, let $y(2) = y(1) = 0$, and let u, v, and w_w be realizations of the independent and identically distributed Gaussian processes $\mathcal{U}$, $\mathcal{V}$, and $\mathcal{W}_w$, respectively, where $\mathcal{U}$, $\mathcal{V}$, and $\mathcal{W}_w$ are all zero mean and independent of each other. However, now let the variances of $\mathcal{U}$, $\mathcal{V}$, and $\mathcal{W}_w$ be 1, $1/20$, and $1/10000$, respectively. Also, let

$$w(k) = 4w_w(k) + 3w_w(k - 1) + 2w_w(k - 2) + 1w_w(k - 3),$$

and consider the additive measurement noise model (6.5). Then the signal to noise ratios of x and z are both approximately 5.

Finally, let $s = 6$, $\mu = 10$, and let $\widehat{\theta_{\mu-1}(H)}$ be the Markov parameter portion of the least-squares estimate $\hat{\Theta}_{s,\mu,N}$ given by (6.11). Furthermore, let $\bar{n} = 3$ and let the

119

Markov parameters estimates in $\widehat{\theta_{\mu-1}(H)}$) be used to estimate $\hat{C}_N(\mathbf{r})$ and $\hat{D}_N(\mathbf{r})$ in Fact 6.5.1. Then Figure 6.4 displays the estimates of the coefficients of $\hat{C}_N(\mathbf{r})$ given by Fact 6.5.1 along with their limiting values

$$\hat{C}_N(\mathbf{r}) \xrightarrow[N\to\infty]{\text{w.p.1}} 1 - 1.862\mathbf{r} + 0.8798\mathbf{r}^2,$$

for $N = 10^2, \ldots, 10^4$ and a sample realization of $\mathcal{U}$, $\mathcal{V}$, and $\mathcal{W}_w$. Figure 6.5 displays the estimates the coefficients of $\hat{D}_N(\mathbf{r})$ given by Fact 6.5.1 along with their limiting values

$$\hat{D}_N(\mathbf{r}) \xrightarrow[N\to\infty]{\text{w.p.1}} \left[\frac{20}{21}\right] \left(-0.009767\mathbf{r} - 0.006026\mathbf{r}^2\right),$$

for $N = 10^2, \ldots, 10^4$ and the same realization of $\mathcal{U}$, $\mathcal{V}$, and $\mathcal{W}_w$. Note that the scaling $20/21$ in the coefficients of $\hat{D}_N(\mathbf{r})$ reflects the fact that the input variance is $1/20$.
□

6.6 Conclusions

We addressed the issue of identification in the presence of random noise. Specifically, we studied the consistency of the estimates in two scenarios, namely, the equation-error framework and the case where the input and input noise were white. In the latter case, we presented an approach based on using least-squares with a μ-Markov model. Finally, we introduced the concept of semi-consistency and showed how, using the techniques developed in Chapter II, one could obtain semi-consistent linear system estimates from semi-consistent Markov parameter estimates.

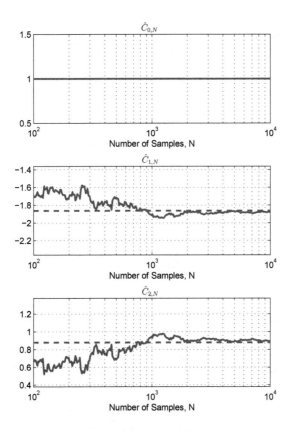

Figure 6.4: Comparison of the coefficients of $\hat{C}_N(\mathbf{r})$ (solid line) along with their limiting values (dashed line) as N increases, where $\hat{C}_N(\mathbf{r})$ is given by Fact 6.5.1.

121

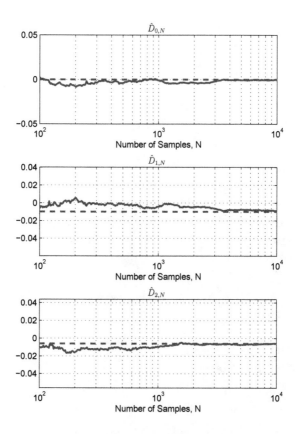

Figure 6.5: Comparison of the coefficients of $\hat{D}_N(\mathbf{r})$ (solid line) along with their limiting values (dashed line) as N increases, where $\hat{D}_N(\mathbf{r})$ is given by Fact 6.5.1.

CHAPTER VII

Parametric and Nonparametric Hammerstein

System Identification

We explore the role of ersatz nonlinearities in parametric and nonparametric MIMO Hammerstein system identification. In parametric identification, where a linear-in-the-parameters structure for the Hammerstein nonlinearity is known, we show that via overparameterization, the fundamentally bilinear optimization problem can be recast as a linear optimization problem, and then decoupled using the singular value decomposition. In nonparametric identification, we revisit correlation-based Markov parameter estimation techniques, and show that the Markov parameters can be estimated semi-consistently using general ersatz nonlinearities in addition to the linear element. We also introduce the method of μ-Markov-based Markov parameter estimation with an ersatz nonlinearity, and show that numerically this method yields Markov parameter estimates with a lower variance than the correlation-based estimates.

7.1 Introduction

Hammerstein system identification is a block-structured method of nonlinear system identification, which parameterizes the system as a static nonlinearity, followed by a linear dynamic system. Hammerstein models are widely used in the literature because of their ability to capture a wider variety of phenomenon than linear dynamic systems alone, and the relative ease with which they can be identified. Indeed, several prominent methods are available for Hammerstein system identification such as [53–65]. However, at their core, there are essentially two main competing methods:

1. Methods that parameterize the Hammerstein nonlinearity, then solve a least-squares-type optimization problem using zig-zag optimization.

2. Methods that employ separable inputs such that identification of the linear system and Hammerstein nonlinearity become decoupled.

The primary purpose of the chapter is to demonstrate that ersatz nonlinearities are ubiquitous in Hammerstein system identification. Furthermore, we present a method for identifying the linear system with no knowledge of the Hammerstein nonlinearity. This method is based on identifying the Markov parameters in the μ-Markov model. We then show numerically that for finite data, this method yields Markov parameter estimates with a lower variance than correlation-based methods. We also show that this method is capable of producing accurate estimates for unstable systems, while the correlation-based method yields estimates with an unacceptably large variance.

The contents of the chapter are as follows: In Section 7.2, we present the problem statement. In Section 7.3, we show that when a parametric form for the Hammerstein is known, identification of the Hammerstein nonlinearity and linear system can be formed as a linear optimization problem via overparameterization. In Section 7.4, we then show how to decouple the Hammerstein nonlinearity and linear system. Finally, in Section 7.5 we establish conditions under which the Markov parameters of the linear system can be identified with no knowledge of the Hammerstein nonlinearity using correlation-type methods, followed by conclusions in Section 7.6.

7.2   Problem Statement

Consider the Hammerstein system

$$A(\mathbf{r})y(k) = B(\mathbf{r})\mathcal{H}\big[u(k)\big], \qquad (7.1)$$

where $k \geq 1$, $u \in \mathbb{R}^m$, $y \in \mathbb{R}^p$, $A \in \mathbb{R}^{p \times p}[\mathbf{r}]$ is comonic with $A_0 = I_p$, $B \in \mathbb{R}^{p \times m}[\mathbf{r}]$, $\mathcal{H} : \mathbb{R}^m \to \mathbb{R}^m$ is a static nonlinearity, and (A, B) is left coprime, causal, and has a degree of n. Furthermore, consider the case where the measurement x of u is corrupted by an additive noise signal v, and the measurement z of y is corrupted by an additive noise signal w, that is,

$$
\begin{aligned}
x(k) &= u(k) + v(k), \\
z(k) &= y(k) + w(k).
\end{aligned}
\qquad (7.2)
$$

as shown in Figure 7.1.

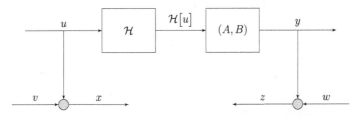

Figure 7.1: Measurements of the input and output of a Hammerstein system in the presence of the measurement noise processes v and w.

Throughout the chapter, we attempt to identify the system G and nonlinearity $\mathcal{H}$ given only the signals x and z. Specifically, we employ an ersatz nonlinearity $\mathcal{E} : \mathbb{R}^m \to \mathbb{R}^m$, even though $\mathcal{E}$ may bear little resemblance to $\mathcal{H}$. The identification setup is shown in Figure 7.2.

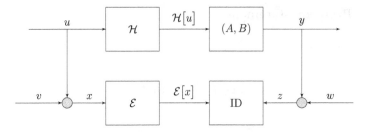

Figure 7.2: Identification of a Hammerstein system using the ersatz nonlinearity $\mathcal{E}$.

7.3 Parametric Hammerstein System Estimation

When there exists a known parametric form for the Hammerstein nonlinearity $\mathcal{H}$, then concurrent identification of both the Hammerstein nonlinearity $\mathcal{H}$ as well as the linear system G can be posed as a straight-forward bilinear optimization problem as in [54, 56, 61, 63]. Here we show that via overparameterization, the problem can be posed as a linear optimization problem. First, we introduce the assumption:

Assumption 7.3.1. $\mathcal{H}$ is of the form

$$\mathcal{H}[x] = \sum_{i=0}^{d-1} E_i \cdot F_i[x],$$

where $E_0, \ldots, E_{d-1} \in \mathbb{R}^{m \times m}$ are unknown coefficient matrices and $F_0, \ldots, F_{d-1}$ are known functions which map $\mathbb{R}^m \to \mathbb{R}^m$.

7.3.1 Deterministic Output Measurement Noise

We now consider the case where the output measurement noise w is deterministic, and the input measurement noise v is zero. In this case, we show that deterministic noise components can be handled exactly via overparameterization. Specifically, in the context of the additive measurement noise model (7.2), let the following assumptions hold:

126

Assumption 7.3.2. $v(k) = 0_{m \times 1}$ for all $k \geq 1$.

Assumption 7.3.3. There exists a comonic $L \in \mathbb{R}^{p \times p}[\mathbf{r}]$ such that, for all $k \geq 1$,

$$L(\mathbf{r})A(\mathbf{r})w(k) = 0_{p \times 1}.$$

Furthermore, $L_0 = I_p$.

Remark 7.3.1. Assumption 7.3.3 holds when w is the sum of sinusoids, ramps, constants, damped exponentials, etc, as in Chapter V. $\square$

Then from (7.1)-(7.2) and Assumptions 7.3.1-7.3.3, we have that

$$L(\mathbf{r})A(\mathbf{r})z(k) = L(\mathbf{r})B(\mathbf{r}) \sum_{i=0}^{d-1} E_i \cdot F_i\big[u(k)\big]. \tag{7.3}$$

Hence, letting

$$C(\mathbf{r}) \triangleq L(\mathbf{r})A(\mathbf{r}),$$

$$D(\mathbf{r}) \triangleq L(\mathbf{r})B(\mathbf{r}),$$

$$\vec{F}[x] \triangleq \left[\ F_0^T[x], \ \cdots, \ F_{d-1}^T[x] \ \right]^T,$$

$$\theta(E) \triangleq \left[\ E_0, \ \cdots, \ E_{d-1} \ \right],$$

$$\Theta \triangleq \left[\ D_0 \cdot \theta(E), \ \cdots, \ D_s \cdot \theta(E), \ \theta'(C) \ \right],$$

$$\Phi_N \triangleq \left[\begin{array}{c} \Omega_{\vec{F}[x],s,1,N} \\ -\Lambda_{z,s,1,N} \end{array} \right],$$

$$Z_N \triangleq \Gamma_{z,s,1,N},$$

and letting s denote the degree of (C, D), it follows that

$$Z_N = \Theta \Phi_N. \tag{7.4}$$

Next, consider the least-squares estimate $\hat{\Theta}_N$ of Θ given by

$$\hat{\Theta}_N = \arg\min_{\hat{\Theta}_N} \left\| Z_n - \hat{\Theta}_N \Phi_N \right\|_F ,$$

and consider the following assumption:

Assumption 7.3.4. There exists a finite positive integer N' such that Φ_N has full rank for all $N \geq N'$.

Then we have the following fact:

Fact 7.3.1. Let Assumptions 7.3.1 - 7.3.4 hold. If $N \geq N'$, then $\hat{\Theta}_N = \Theta$.

Proof. First, note that the least-squares estimate $\hat{\Theta}_N$ of Θ satisfies

$$\hat{\Theta}_N \Phi_N \Phi_N^T = Z_N \Phi_N^T .$$

Next, from Assumptions 7.3.1-7.3.3, we have (7.4). Hence it follows that

$$\hat{\Theta}_N \Phi_N \Phi_N^T = \Theta \Phi_N \Phi_N^T ,$$

and from Assumption 7.3.4,

$$\hat{\Theta}_N = \Theta \Phi_N \Phi_N^T \left(\Phi_N \Phi_N^T \right)^{-1} = \Theta .$$

$\square$

Remark 7.3.2. Two difficulties are presented in the above analysis. First, the degree s of (C, D) was used in constructing the regressor Φ_N in the least-squares estimate. However, in lieu of this information, one can simply overestimate the degree sufficiently, or use a rank estimation technique such as that presented in Chapter III. Unfortunately, there is also a second difficulty, namely, even when s is known

128

exactly, Φ_N may be rank deficient (a violation of Assumption 7.3.4), regardless of the input. This is simply due to the fact that in MIMO polynomial matrix models (unlike scalar systems), there may not exist a unique comonic parameterization of degree s (see Chapter II). In both of these cases, one could simply choose a single parameterization, such as

$$\hat{\Theta}_N = Z_N \Phi_N^+,$$

where $(\cdot)^+$ denotes the Moore-Penrose psuedo-inverse of $(\cdot)$. Then for all γ,

$$\hat{\Theta}_N^\gamma = Z_N \Phi_N^+ + \mathcal{N}(\Phi_N)\gamma,$$

is also an equally valid representation of Θ, where $\mathcal{N}(\cdot)$ denotes a basis for the nullspace of $(\cdot)$. Thus without imposing addition constraints on the estimated model or placing assumptions on the form of the original system, sometimes the best one can due (using these techniques) is obtain a multiple of the original linear system (A, B). Refer to Theorem 5.3.1 and Corollary 5.3.1. □

7.3.2 Equation Error Model

Another common estimation framework is to consider the equation error approach. Specifically, in the context of the additive measurement noise model (7.2), let the following additional assumption hold:

Assumption 7.3.5. There exists a comonic $L \in \mathbb{R}^{p \times p}[\mathbf{r}]$ such that, for all $k \geq 1$,

$$L(\mathbf{r})A(\mathbf{r})w(k) = w'(k),$$

where $w' \in \mathbb{R}^p$ is a realization of the independent and identically distributed, zero-mean, random process $\mathcal{W}'$ with finite covariance. Furthermore, $L_0 = I_p$.

Then from (7.1)-(7.2) and Assumptions 7.3.1, 7.3.2, and 7.3.5, we have the equation error model of (7.1) given by

$$C(\mathbf{r})z(k) = D(\mathbf{r})\sum_{i=0}^{d-1} E_i \cdot F_i\big[x(k)\big] + w'(k). \tag{7.5}$$

Furthermore, letting

$$W'_N \triangleq \Gamma_{w,s,1,N},$$

and letting Z_N, Θ, and Φ_N be defined as before, it follows that

$$Z_N = \Theta\Phi_N + W'_N. \tag{7.6}$$

Next, consider the least-squares estimate $\hat{\Theta}_N$ of Θ given by

$$\hat{\Theta}_N = \underset{\hat{\Theta}_N}{\arg\min} \left\| Z_n - \hat{\Theta}_N\Phi_N \right\|_{\mathrm{F}}.$$

Furthermore, let the following assumptions also hold:

Assumption 7.3.6. For all $k \geq 1$ and $j \in [0, d-1]$, one of the following holds

i) $F_j\big[u(k)\big]$ is deterministic and bounded.

ii) $u \in \mathbb{R}^m$ is a realization of the random process $\mathcal{U}$, where $F_j\big[\mathcal{U}(k)\big]$ has finite mean and variance.

Assumption 7.3.7. For all $k \geq 1$, $j \in [0, d-1]$, and nonnegative i,

$$\mathbb{E}\left[\mathcal{W}'(k+i)F_j^T\big[\mathcal{U}(k)\big]\right] = 0_{p\times m}.$$

Assumption 7.3.8. $(1/N)\Phi_N\Phi_N^T \xrightarrow[N\to\infty]{\mathrm{w.p.1}} \chi$, where $\chi \in \mathbb{R}^{(dm[s+1]+ps)\times(dm[s+1]+ps)}$ is nonsingular.

130

Assumption 7.3.9. (C, D) is asymptotically stable.

Fact 7.3.2. Let Assumptions 7.3.1-7.3.2 and 7.3.5-7.3.9 hold. Then $\hat{\Theta}_N$ is a strongly consistent estimate of Θ.

Proof. First, note that the least-squares estimate $\hat{\Theta}_N$ of Θ satisfies

$$\hat{\Theta}_N \Phi_N \Phi_N^T = Z_N \Phi_N^T.$$

Next, from Assumptions 7.3.1, 7.3.2, and 7.3.5, we have (7.6) and hence

$$\hat{\Theta}_N \Phi_N \Phi_N^T = \Theta \Phi_N \Phi_N^T + W_N' \Phi_N^T.$$

Furthermore, from Assumptions 7.3.6-7.3.9 and Fact 6.2.3, we have that

$$\frac{1}{N} W_N' \Omega_{\vec{F}[x], s, 1, N}^T$$
$$= \frac{1}{N} \sum_{k=1}^{N-s} \left[\ w'(k+s)\vec{F}^T\big[x(k+s)\big] \ \cdots \ w'(k+s)\vec{F}^T\big[x(k)\big] \ \right],$$
$$\xrightarrow[N \to \infty]{\text{w.p.1}} 0_{p \times dm(s+1)}.$$

Finally, from (7.5), Assumptions 7.3.6-7.3.9, and Fact 6.2.3, note that

$$\frac{1}{N} W_N' \Lambda_{z, s, 1, N}^T$$
$$= \frac{1}{N} \sum_{k=1}^{N-s} \left[\ w'(k+s)z^T(k+s-1) \ \cdots \ w'(k+s)z^T(k) \ \right],$$
$$\xrightarrow[N \to \infty]{\text{w.p.1}} 0_{p \times ps}.$$

Hence

$$\frac{1}{N} W_N' \Phi_N^T \xrightarrow[N \to \infty]{\text{w.p.1}} 0_{p \times (sp + dm[s+1])},$$

131

and thus, from Assumption 7.3.8,

$$\hat{\Theta}_N \xrightarrow[N\to\infty]{\text{w.p.1}} \Theta\Phi_N\Phi_N^T \left(\Phi_N\Phi_N^T\right)^{-1} = \Theta.$$

$\square$

7.4 Decoupling Parametric Estimates

In the previous section, we showed several cases in which the least-squares estimate $\hat{\Theta}_N$ is a strongly consistent estimate of Θ. In this way, the bilinear least-squares problem was cast as a linear least-squares problem via overparameterization. However, now we would like to separate the components. Here we show that this can be done with the singular value decomposition.

Consider the least-squares estimate $\hat{\Theta}_N$ of Θ. Then in the previous section, we showed several cases in which

$$\hat{\Theta}_N \xrightarrow[N\to\infty]{\text{w.p.1}} \Theta,$$

and hence for all $i \in [0, s]$,

$$\widehat{\theta_{1,s}(C)} \xrightarrow[N\to\infty]{\text{w.p.1}} \theta_{1,s}(C), \tag{7.7}$$

$$\widehat{D_i\theta(E)} \xrightarrow[N\to\infty]{\text{w.p.1}} D_i\theta(E). \tag{7.8}$$

However, now we would like to decouple the estimates, that is, we would like to obtain estimates $\hat{D}_0, \ldots, \hat{D}_s$ and $\hat{E}_0, \ldots, \hat{E}_{d-1}$ from the strongly consistent estimates $\widehat{D_0\theta(E)}, \ldots, \widehat{D_s\theta(E)}$.

Algorithm 7.4.1. Let $\widehat{D_0\theta(E)}, \ldots, \widehat{D_s\theta(E)}$ be strongly consistent estimates of $D_0\theta(E), \ldots, D_s\theta(E)$. Then the following algorithm yields estimates $\hat{D}_0, \ldots, \hat{D}_s$ and

132

$\hat{E}_0, \ldots, \hat{E}_{d-1}$ of $D_0, \ldots, D_s$ and $E_0, \ldots, E_{d-1}$, respectively.

1) Let $\widehat{\mathcal{K}_{D,E}} \triangleq \begin{bmatrix} \widehat{D_0\theta(E)} \\ \vdots \\ \widehat{D_s\theta(E)} \end{bmatrix} \in \mathbb{R}^{p(s+1) \times dm}$.

2) Let $\eta \triangleq \min(m, p(s+1))$.

3) Note that $\widehat{\mathcal{K}_{D,E}} \xrightarrow[N \to \infty]{\text{w.p.1}} \mathcal{K}_{D,E} = \left[\theta(D^T)\right]^T \cdot \theta(E)$. Hence

$$\text{rank}\left[\mathcal{K}_{D,E}\right] \leq \min\left(\text{rank}\left[\theta(D^T)\right], \text{rank}\left[\theta(E)\right]\right),$$

$$\leq \min\left(m, p(s+1)\right),$$

$$= \eta.$$

4) Compute the singular value decomposition of $\widehat{\mathcal{K}_{D,E}}$, that is,

$$\widehat{\mathcal{K}_{D,E}} = \begin{bmatrix} U, & U' \end{bmatrix} \begin{bmatrix} S & 0 \\ 0 & S' \end{bmatrix} \begin{bmatrix} V \\ V' \end{bmatrix},$$

where $U \in \mathbb{R}^{p(s+1) \times \eta}$, $S \in \mathbb{R}^{\eta \times \eta}$, $V \in \mathbb{R}^{\eta \times dm}$, $U^T U' = 0$, $U^T U = I_\eta$, $V' V^T = 0$, and $VV^T = I_\eta$.

5) $\widehat{\theta(D^T)} \triangleq \begin{bmatrix} S^T U^T \\ 0_{(m-\eta) \times p(s+1)} \end{bmatrix}$.

6) $\widehat{\theta(E)} \triangleq \begin{bmatrix} V \\ 0_{(m-\eta) \times dm} \end{bmatrix}$.

Remark 7.4.1. From the previous algorithm, it should be apparent that the decomposition of $\widehat{\mathcal{K}_{D,E}}$ into $\widehat{\theta(D^T)}$ and $\widehat{\theta(E)}$ is not unique. For instance,

$$\widehat{\theta(D^T)} \triangleq \begin{bmatrix} U^T \\ 0_{(m-\eta) \times p(s+1)} \end{bmatrix},$$

$$\widehat{\theta(E)} \triangleq \begin{bmatrix} SV \\ 0_{(m-\eta) \times dm} \end{bmatrix},$$

is an equally valid choice. Hence, even though

$$\widehat{\mathcal{K}_{D,E}} \xrightarrow[N \to \infty]{\text{w.p.1}} \mathcal{K}_{D,E},$$

it is impossible to make statements such as

$$\widehat{\theta(D^T)} \xrightarrow[N \to \infty]{\text{w.p.1}} \theta(D^T),$$

since there will always be at least a matrix scale factor ambiguity in between $\widehat{\theta(D^T)}$ and $\widehat{\theta(E)}$. □

7.5 Nonparametric Hammerstein System Estimation

There are several methods of nonparametric Hammerstein system identification, most of which use separable inputs to decouple the identification of Hammerstein nonlinearity and linear system [53, 59, 60, 72]. Here we present two methods for identifying the linear system, namely, a correlation-based approach already well-known in the literature [59] (based on the generalized Bussgang theorem [59, 73]), and a novel μ-Markov-based least-squares approach. Furthermore, we show via numerical examples, that the μ-Markov-based approach yields estimates with a lower variance, and hence, is preferable. We also show that the μ-Markov-based approach works well in the case of unstable system identification.

134

7.5.1 Correlation-Based Markov Parameter Estimation

The correlation-based Markov parameter estimation technique we present here is based upon the generalized Bussgang theorem [59, 73]. However, while the ersatz nonlinearity is almost always taken to be the linear or absolute value function in the literature [60], here we generalize to allow for an arbitrary ersatz nonlinearity.

Let the following assumptions hold:

Assumption 7.5.1. $u \in \mathbb{R}^m$ and $v \in \mathbb{R}^m$ are realizations of the independent and identically distributed processes $\mathcal{U}$ and $\mathcal{V}$, respectively. Furthermore, for all $k \geq 1$,

$$u_{\mathcal{H}}(k) \triangleq \mathcal{H}\Big[u(k)\Big], \quad x_{\mathcal{E}}(k) \triangleq \mathcal{E}\Big[u(k) + v(k)\Big],$$
$$\mathcal{U}_{\mathcal{H}}(k) \triangleq \mathcal{H}\Big[\mathcal{U}(k)\Big], \quad \mathcal{X}_{\mathcal{E}}(k) \triangleq \mathcal{E}\Big[\mathcal{U}(k) + \mathcal{V}(k)\Big],$$

Assumption 7.5.2. For all $k \geq 1$ and nonnegative p, the means and covariances of $\mathcal{U}_{\mathcal{H}}(k)$, $\mathcal{X}_{\mathcal{E}}(k)$, $\mathcal{U}_{\mathcal{H}}(k+p)\mathcal{X}_{\mathcal{E}}^T(k)$, and $\mathcal{X}_{\mathcal{E}}(k+p)\mathcal{X}_{\mathcal{E}}^T(k)$ are finite. Furthermore, $R \in \mathbb{R}^{m \times m}$ and $S \in \mathbb{R}^{m \times m}$ given by

$$R \triangleq \mathbb{E}\Big[\mathcal{X}_{\mathcal{E}}(k)\mathcal{X}_{\mathcal{E}}^T(k)\Big], \tag{7.9}$$
$$S \triangleq \mathbb{E}\Big[\mathcal{U}_{\mathcal{H}}(k)\mathcal{X}_{\mathcal{E}}^T(k)\Big], \tag{7.10}$$

are nonsingular.

Assumption 7.5.3. $w \in \mathbb{R}^p$ is a realization of the stationary, colored random process $\mathcal{W}$ with finite mean and autocorrelation function, that is, for all $j, k \geq 1$ and nonnegative i,

$$\mathbb{E}\Big[\mathcal{W}(k)\Big] = \mathbb{E}\Big[\mathcal{W}(j)\Big] < \infty,$$
$$\mathbb{E}\Big[\mathcal{W}(k+i)\mathcal{W}^T(k)\Big] = \mathbb{E}\Big[\mathcal{W}(j+i)\mathcal{W}^T(j)\Big] < \infty.$$

135

Assumption 7.5.4. The random processes $\mathcal{U}$, $\mathcal{V}$, and $\mathcal{W}$ are independent of each other.

Assumption 7.5.5. The ersatz nonlinearity $\mathcal{E}$ satisfies

$$\mathbb{E}[\mathcal{X}_{\mathcal{E}}] = 0_m.$$

Remark 7.5.1. When the distribution of $\mathcal{X}$ is known, we can always choose an ersatz nonlinearity which satisfies Assumption 7.5.5. Specifically, suppose our first choice of ersatz nonlinearity $\mathcal{E}$, does not satisfy Assumption 7.5.5. Then choosing

$$\mathcal{E}'(\cdot) = \mathcal{E}(\cdot) - \mathbb{E}[\mathcal{X}_{\mathcal{E}}], \tag{7.11}$$

yields an ersatz nonlinearity $\mathcal{E}'$ which does satisfy Assumption 7.5.5. Furthermore, when the distribution of $\mathcal{X}$ is unknown, we can simply replace $\mathbb{E}[\mathcal{X}_{\mathcal{E}}]$ with its sample mean in (7.11) since x is measured. $\square$

Fact 7.5.1. Let Assumptions 7.5.1-7.5.5 hold. Furthermore, for all $i \geq 0$, let

$$\hat{H}_i \triangleq \frac{1}{N} \sum_{k=1}^{N-i} z(k+i)x_{\mathcal{E}}(k). \tag{7.12}$$

Then $\hat{H}_i$ is a semi-consistent estimate of H_i. Specifically,

$$\hat{H}_i \xrightarrow[N\to\infty]{\text{w.p.1}} H_i S,$$

where $S \in \mathbb{R}^{m \times m}$ is given by (7.10) and is nonsingular.

Proof. From (7.2), for all $i \geq 0$, it follows that

$$\hat{H}_i = \frac{1}{N} \sum_{k=1}^{N-i} z(k+i)x_{\mathcal{E}}(k),$$

$$= \frac{1}{N} \sum_{k=1}^{N-i} \Big[y(k+i) + w(k+i) \Big] x_{\mathcal{E}}(k).$$

Hence, from Assumptions 7.5.1-7.5.5 and Fact 6.2.3, it follows that

$$\frac{1}{N} \sum_{k=1}^{N-i} y(k+i)x_{\mathcal{E}}^T(k) \xrightarrow[N\to\infty]{\text{w.p.1}} H_i S,$$

$$\frac{1}{N} \sum_{k=1}^{N-i} w(k+i)x_{\mathcal{E}}^T(k) \xrightarrow[N\to\infty]{\text{w.p.1}} 0_{p\times m},$$

and therefore

$$\hat{H}_i \xrightarrow[N\to\infty]{\text{w.p.1}} H_i S,$$

where S is nonsingular from Assumption 7.5.2. $\qquad\qquad\square$

Remark 7.5.2. Satisfying the condition that S is nonsingular in Assumption 7.5.2 is typically the most difficult assumption to satisfy *a priori* since the signal $u_{\mathcal{H}}$ is not measured. In practice, however, there are some non-rigorous tests we can apply. For example, when S is singular in the SISO case, then

$$\widehat{\theta_{\mu-1}(H)} = \Big[\hat{H}_0, \ \cdots, \ \hat{H}_{\mu-1} \Big] \xrightarrow[N\to\infty]{\text{w.p.1}} 0_{1\times\mu}.$$

Although, it is impossible to determine whether this is due to the fact that $S = 0$, $\theta_{\mu-1}(H) = 0_{1\times\mu}$, or both, in this case, one can simply test several choices of $\mathcal{E}$; these choices including strictly odd, strictly odd, and combination ersatz nonlinearities. If $\widehat{\theta_{\mu-1}(H)}$ appears to be the zero vector for all of the choices of $\mathcal{E}$, then it is reasonable to assume that $\theta_{\mu-1}(H) = 0_{1\times\mu}$. $\qquad\qquad\square$

7.5.2 μ-Markov-Based Least-Squares Estimates of Markov Parameters

Here we show that when the input and input noise are white, the Markov parameters can be estimated semi-consistently under fairly general conditions using least-squares and the μ-Markov model.

Consider again the system (7.1) and measurement noise equations (7.2), where we have no knowledge of the form of the Hammerstein nonlinearity $\mathcal{H}$. Also, let

$$\Phi_{s,\mu,N} \triangleq \begin{bmatrix} \Omega_{\mathcal{E}[x],s,\mu,N} \\ -\Lambda_{z,s,\mu,N} \end{bmatrix}, \tag{7.13}$$

$$\tilde{\Phi}_{s,\mu,N} \triangleq \mathbf{r}^{n-s} \begin{bmatrix} \Omega_{\mathcal{H}[u],n,\mu,N+n-s} \\ -\Lambda_{y,n,\mu,N+n-s} \end{bmatrix}, \tag{7.14}$$

$$\Theta_\mu \triangleq \begin{bmatrix} \theta_{\mu-1}(H), & \theta_{\mu,n}(B^\mu), & \theta_{\mu,n}(A^\mu) \end{bmatrix}. \tag{7.15}$$

Next, consider the least-squares estimate

$$\hat{\Theta}_{s,\mu,N} \triangleq \begin{bmatrix} \widehat{\theta_{\mu-1}(H)}, & \widehat{\theta_{\mu,s}(B^\mu)}, & \widehat{\theta_{\mu,s}(A^\mu)} \end{bmatrix},$$

given by

$$\hat{\Theta}_{s,\mu,N} = \arg\min_{\hat{\Theta}_{s,\mu,N}} \left\| \Gamma_{z,s,\mu,N} - \hat{\Theta}_{s,\mu,N} \Phi_{s,\mu,N} \right\|_2^2.$$

Then we have the following fact:

Fact 7.5.2. Let Assumptions 7.5.1-7.5.5 hold. Furthermore, let $s \geq 0$ and $\mu \geq 1$. Then $\widehat{\theta_{\mu-1}(H)}$ is a semi-consistent estimate of $\theta_{\mu-1}(H)$. Specifically,

$$\widehat{\theta_{\mu-1}(H)} \xrightarrow[N\to\infty]{\text{w.p.1}} \theta_{\mu-1}(H)\left(I_\mu \otimes SR^{-1}\right),$$

where R and S are given by (7.9) and (7.10), respectively, and $\widehat{\theta_{\mu-1}(H)}$ is the Markov

138

parameter portion of the least-squares estimate $\hat{\Theta}_{s,\mu,N}$.

Proof. First, note that the least-squares estimate $\hat{\Theta}_{s,\mu,N}$ satisfies

$$\left(\Gamma_{z,s,\mu,N} - \hat{\Theta}_{s,\mu,N}\Phi_{s,\mu,N}\right)\Phi_{s,\mu,N}^T$$

$$= \left(\Gamma_{z,s,\mu,N} - \hat{\Theta}_{s,\mu,N}\Phi_{s,\mu,N}\right)\begin{bmatrix} \Omega_{\mathcal{E}[x],s,\mu,N} \\ -\Lambda_{z,s,\mu,N} \end{bmatrix}^T$$

$$= \left(\Gamma_{z,s,\mu,N} - \hat{\Theta}_{s,\mu,N}\Phi_{s,\mu,N}\right)\begin{bmatrix} \Psi_{\mathcal{E}[x],s,\mu,N} \\ \Lambda_{\mathcal{E}[x],s,\mu,N} \\ -\Lambda_{z,s,\mu,N} \end{bmatrix}^T$$

$$= 0_{p\times(m[\mu+s]+ps)}.$$

Next, we examine the subset of previous equations given by

$$\left(\Gamma_{z,s,\mu,N} - \hat{\Theta}_{s,\mu,N}\Phi_{s,\mu,N}\right)\Psi_{\mathcal{E}[x],s,\mu,N}^T = 0_{p\times m\mu},$$

where, from (7.1)-(7.2) and (7.13)-(7.15), we have that

$$\left(\Theta_\mu\tilde{\Phi}_{s,\mu,N} + W_N - \hat{\Theta}_{s,\mu,N}\Phi_{s,\mu,N}\right)\Psi_{\mathcal{E}[x],s,\mu,N}^T = 0_{p\times m\mu}.$$

Next, from Assumptions 7.5.1-7.5.5 and Fact 6.2.3, we have that

$$\frac{1}{N}\tilde{\Phi}_{s,\mu,N}\Psi_{\mathcal{E}[x],s,\mu,N}^T \xrightarrow[N\to\infty]{\text{w.p.1}} \begin{bmatrix} I_\mu \otimes S \\ 0_{n(m+p)\times m\mu} \end{bmatrix},$$

$$\frac{1}{N}W_{s,\mu,N}\Psi_{\mathcal{E}[x],s,\mu,N}^T \xrightarrow[N\to\infty]{\text{w.p.1}} 0_{p\times m\mu},$$

$$\frac{1}{N}\Phi_{s,\mu,N}\Psi_{\mathcal{E}[x],s,\mu,N}^T \xrightarrow[N\to\infty]{\text{w.p.1}} \begin{bmatrix} I_\mu \otimes R \\ 0_{s(m+p)\times m\mu} \end{bmatrix}.$$

139

Thus

$$\theta_{\mu-1}(H)\left(I_\mu \otimes S\right) - \widehat{\theta_{\mu-1}(H)}\left(I_\mu \otimes R\right) \xrightarrow[N\to\infty]{\text{w.p.1}} 0_{p\times m\mu},$$

and hence from Assumptions 7.5.2 it follows that

$$\widehat{\theta_{\mu-1}(H)} \xrightarrow[N\to\infty]{\text{w.p.1}} \theta_{\mu-1}(H)\left(I_\mu \otimes SR^{-1}\right),$$

where the product SR^{-1} is nonsingular from Assumption 7.5.2. $\qquad\square$

7.5.3   Numerical Comparison

Here we compare the correlation-based Markov parameter estimation approach with the μ-Markov-based least-squares approach. Specifically, we examine the bias and variance of the estimates for finite data with Monte Carlo simulations.

Remark 7.5.3. In the μ-Markov-based Markov parameter estimates, we need to choose a model degree s as well as the number of Markov parameters μ we would like explicitly displayed in the model (6.1). Furthermore, from Fact 7.5.2, the degree s of the model does not depend on the degree n of (A, B) in (7.1). In what follows, we refer to s as the model degree which is used in (6.1) and Fact 7.5.2. $\qquad\square$

Example 7.5.1. Consider the linearized longitudinal model of the T-2 aircraft (1.1) in the presence of a Hammerstein nonlinearity as in (7.1), where for all $k \geq 1$, $\mathcal{U}$ is an independent and identically distributed Gaussian random variable with zero mean and unit variance, and

$$A(\mathbf{r}) \triangleq 1 - 1.862\mathbf{r} + 0.8798\mathbf{r}^2,$$

$$B(\mathbf{r}) \triangleq -0.009767\mathbf{r} - 0.006026\mathbf{r}^2,$$

$$v(k) \triangleq 0,$$

$$w(k) \triangleq 0, \tag{7.16}$$

$$\mathcal{H}\big[x(k)\big] \triangleq x(k)^3/10 + 1,$$

$$\mathcal{E}\big[x(k)\big] \triangleq \exp\big[x(k)/2 + 2\big]/10 - 0.83729,$$

that is, the input and output measurement noise are zero so that estimation errors are attributable solely to the fact that the Hammerstein nonlinearity is not known. Furthermore, the initial conditions are taken to be zero, that is,

$$u(2) = u(1) = y(2) = y(1) = 0.$$

Figure 7.3 displays the Hammerstein and ersatz nonlinearities, as well as the probability density function of $\mathcal{U}$ over the range $[-2, 2]$ which contains the significant portion of the input distribution space. Note that the ersatz nonlinearity bears no resemblance to the Hammerstein nonlinearity over this range. Furthermore, neither the ersatz nor the Hammerstein nonlinearity is strictly even or odd.

Next, let $\hat{H}_i^{\mathrm{CO}}$ and $\hat{H}_i^{\mathrm{LS}}$ denote the correlation-based and μ-Markov-based least-squares estimates, respectively, of the ith Markov parameter. Then numerically evaluating R and S given by (7.9)-(7.10), we find that

$$R = \mathbb{E}\Big[\mathcal{E}^2\big[x(k)\big]\Big] = +0.19912,$$

$$S = \mathbb{E}\Big[\mathcal{H}\big[u(k)\big]\mathcal{E}\big[x(k)\big]\Big] = -0.13606.$$

141

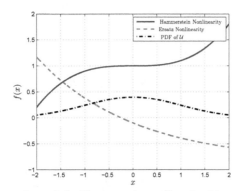

Figure 7.3: Comparison of the Hammerstein nonlinearity $\mathcal{H}$, ersatz nonlinearity $\mathcal{E}$, and probability density function of $\mathcal{U}$.

Hence, from Fact 7.5.1 and Fact 7.5.2, for all $i \geq 0$ it follows that

$$\hat{H}_i^{CO} S^{-1} \xrightarrow[N \to \infty]{\text{w.p.1}} H_i,$$

$$\hat{H}_i^{LS} RS^{-1} \xrightarrow[N \to \infty]{\text{w.p.1}} H_i.$$

Next, we examine the mean and variance of the scaled version of both estimates using Monte Carlo simulations. Specifically, let $\mu = 10$, $s = 6$, $N = 100$, and consider 5,000 independent realizations of $\mathcal{U}$. Then Figure 7.4 shows the scatter of the scaled correlation-based and μ-Markov based estimates of the first ten Markov parameters, the true Markov parameters, and the mean of the estimates. From Figure 7.4, we can see that for the chosen set of parameters, the correlation-based approach yields estimates with a higher degree of scatter than the μ-Markov-based estimates. Furthermore, it appears that both estimates are unbiased. Figure 7.5 then shows the histogram of the error of the tenth Markov parameter estimates over the 5,000 trials. Figure 7.5, like Figure 7.4, shows that the μ-Markov based estimates have less scatter than the correlation-based estimates. Figure 7.5 also confirms that both methods appear to be unbiased. $\square$

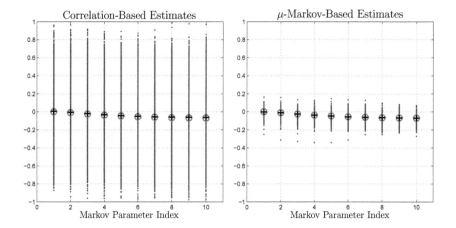

Figure 7.4: Comparison of the scaled correlation-based and μ-Markov-based Markov parameter estimates for the first ten Markov parameters over 5,000 trials when $\mu = 10$, $s = 6$, $N = 100$, $\mathcal{E}[x] \triangleq \exp[x/2 + 2]/10 - 0.83729$, and the system is stable. The red ○ denotes the true Markov parameter, the black + denotes the mean of the estimates over the trials (as an indication of biasedness), and the blue • denotes the estimate for each trial.

Next, we show a case in which the Hammerstein nonlinearity is known fairly well. In this case, as in section 7.3, as long as an upper bound for the degree of (A, B) is known, we can exactly identify the Markov parameters using the μ-Markov-based least-squares approach. However, the correlation-based estimates will still only converge in the limit. We demonstrate this with the following example:

Example 7.5.2. Consider the Hammerstein system (7.1), where for all $k \geq 1$, $\mathcal{U}$ is an independent and identically distributed Gaussian random variable with zero mean and unit variance. Furthermore, we have the same conditions (7.17) as in the previous example, except that now the ersatz nonlinearity is given by

$$\mathcal{E}[x(k)] \triangleq x^3(k).$$

143

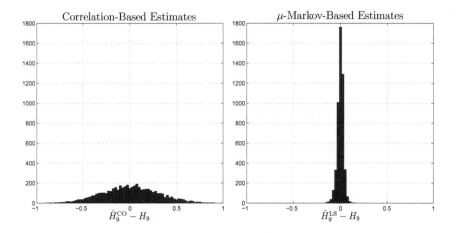

Figure 7.5: Histogram of the error in the scaled correlation-based and μ-Markov-based Markov parameter estimates of the tenth Markov parameter over 5,000 trials when $\mu = 10$, $s = 6$, $N = 100$, $\mathcal{E}[x] \triangleq \exp[x/2 + 2]/10 - 0.83729$, and the system is stable.

Then numerically evaluating R and S given by (7.9)-(7.10), we find that

$$R = 1.5, \quad S = 15.$$

Finally, letting $\mu = 10$, $s = 6$, $N = 100$, and considering 5,000 independent realizations of $\mathcal{U}$, Figure 7.6 shows the scatter of the scaled correlation-based and μ-Markov-based estimates of the first ten Markov parameters, the true Markov parameters, and the mean of the estimates. From Figure 7.6, we can see that the μ-Markov-based estimates are exact, although the correlation-based estimates are not. In fact, it appears that the correlation-based estimates have approximately the same degree of scatter as in Example 7.5.1, where we used an ersatz nonlinearity that bore no resemblance to the Hammerstein nonlinearity. Figure 7.7 shows a very similar histogram for the correlation-based estimates as Figure 7.5, while the μ-Markov-based estimates are now exact. □

144

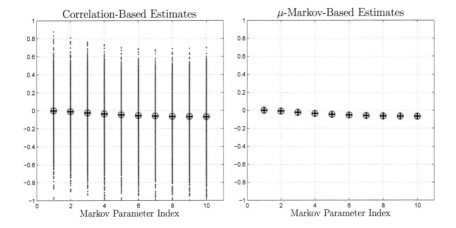

Figure 7.6: Comparison of the scaled correlation-based and μ-Markov-based Markov parameter estimates for the first ten Markov parameters over 5,000 trials when $\mu = 10$, $s = 6$, $N = 100$, $\mathcal{E}[x] \triangleq x^3$, and the system is stable. The red ∘ denotes the true Markov parameter, the black + denotes the mean of the estimates over the trials (as an indication of biasedness), and the blue • denotes the estimate for each trial.

Finally, as a point of comparison, we examine the effect of choosing the ersatz nonlinearity to be the linear function, as is common throughout the literature [59].

Example 7.5.3. Consider the Hammerstein system (7.1), where for all $k \geq 1$, $\mathcal{U}$ is an independent and identically distributed Gaussian random variable with zero mean and unit variance. Furthermore, we have the same conditions (7.17) as in the previous example, except that now the ersatz nonlinearity is given by

$$\mathcal{E}\big[x(k)\big] \triangleq x(k).$$

Then numerically evaluating R and S given by (7.9)-(7.10), we find that

$$R = 1.0, \quad S = 0.3.$$

145

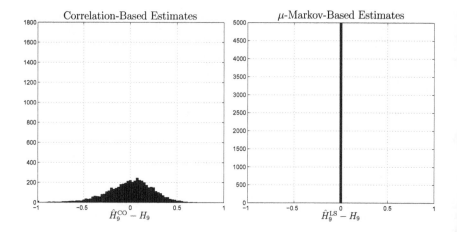

Figure 7.7: Histogram of the error in the scaled correlation-based and μ-Markov-based Markov parameter estimates of the tenth Markov parameter over 5,000 trials when $\mu = 10$, $s = 6$, $N = 100$, $\mathcal{E}[x] \triangleq x^3$, and the system is stable.

Finally, letting $\mu = 10$, $s = 6$, $N = 100$, and considering 5,000 independent realizations of $\mathcal{U}$, Figure 7.8 shows the scatter of the scaled correlation-based and μ-Markov based estimates of the first ten Markov parameters, the true Markov parameters, and the mean of the estimates. From Figure 7.8, we can see that the μ-Markov-based estimates still appear to have less scatter than the correlation-based estimates. Furthermore, comparing Figure 7.8 and Figure 7.4, it appears that taking the ersatz nonlinearity to be linear yields approximately the same quality of estimates as in Example 7.5.1. However, comparing Figure 7.9 with Figure 7.5, it is apparent that in general, taking the ersatz nonlinearity to be linear does not yield better estimates than our choice in Example 7.5.1. □

Remark 7.5.4. The previous examples appear to show that it is always beneficial to use the μ-Markov-based least-squares estimates of the Markov parameters over the correlation-based estimates. However, it turns out that proving this is very difficult. Although it is easy to verify that the correlation-based estimates are unbiased, this

146

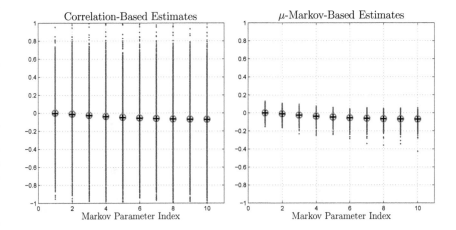

Figure 7.8: Comparison of the scaled correlation-based and μ-Markov-based Markov parameter estimates for the first ten Markov parameters over 5,000 trials when $\mu = 10$, $s = 6$, $N = 100$, $\mathcal{E}[x] \triangleq x$, and the system is stable. The red ○ denotes the true Markov parameter, the black + denotes the mean of the estimates over the trials (as an indication of biasedness), and the blue ● denotes the estimate for each trial.

is not easily accomplished for the μ-Markov model, the difficulty being that consistency is an asymptotic result. Some results can be found on establishing confidence ellipsoids for least-squares estimates in the finite data context (and in the presence of no Hammerstein nonlinearity), although these results require simplifications, such as the need that the input be Gaussian [74]. Furthermore, as the authors note, these bounds tend to be vastly overconservative. □

7.5.4 Unstable Systems

In the previous sections, we showed conditions under which the correlation-based and μ-Markov-based estimates were semi-consistent. However, both methods required the assumption that the system was asymptotically stable. Here we show that, even when the system is unstable, numerically it appears that we can still obtain unbiased estimates

147

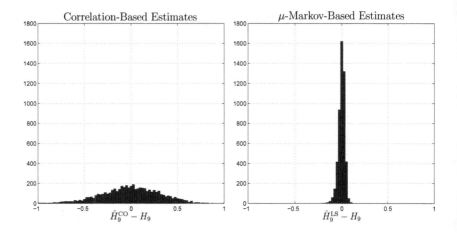

Figure 7.9: Histogram of the error in the scaled correlation-based and μ-Markov-based Markov parameter estimates of the tenth Markov parameter over 5,000 trials when $\mu = 10$, $s = 6$, $N = 100$, $\mathcal{E}[x] \triangleq x$, and the system is stable.

Example 7.5.4. Consider the Hammerstein system (7.1), where for all $k \geq 1$, $\mathcal{U}$ is an independent and identically distributed Gaussian random variable with zero mean and unit variance, and

$$A(\mathbf{r}) \triangleq 1 - 1.862\mathbf{r} + 1.001\mathbf{r}^2,$$

$$B(\mathbf{r}) \triangleq -0.009767\mathbf{r} - 0.006026\mathbf{r}^2,$$

$$v(k) \triangleq 0,$$

$$w(k) \triangleq 0, \tag{7.17}$$

$$\mathcal{H}\big[x(k)\big] \triangleq x(k)^3/10 + 1,$$

$$\mathcal{E}\big[x(k)\big] \triangleq \exp\big[x(k)/2 + 2\big]/10 - 0.83729,$$

that is, the input and output measurement noise are zero so that errors are attributable solely to the fact that the Hammerstein nonlinearity is not known. Furthermore, the initial conditions are taken to be nonzero, specifically

$$u(2) = u(1) = y(2) = y(1) = 5,$$

and R and S are given in Example 7.5.1. Also, note that $A(\mathbf{r})$ is unstable, specifically, the roots of $A(\mathbf{r})$ are now $0.931 \pm 0.3664i$, where $0.931^2 + 0.3664^2 = 1.001$.

Next, letting $\mu = 10$, $s = 6$, $N = 100$, and considering 5,000 independent realizations of $\mathcal{U}$, Figure 7.10 shows the scatter of the scaled correlation-based and μ-Markov based estimates of the first ten Markov parameters, the true Markov parameters, and the mean of the estimates. From Figure 7.10, we can see that the μ-Markov-based estimates are fairly accurate compared to Figures 7.4 and 7.8. Also, from Figure 7.10, we can see that the correlation-based estimates are much less accurate compared to the same figures. In fact, we had to scale the axis differently in Figure 7.10 to be able to capture all of the scatter in the estimates. However, note that a direct comparison with the previous examples is difficult, since the variance of the estimates is directly related to the system parameters, which are different in this example. Figure 7.11 displays the histograms of the errors in the estimates of the tenth Markov parameter.

Finally, note that, unlike the previous examples, where we considered a stable system, the model degree ($s = 6$) was important for capturing the initial condition response in the μ-Markov-based estimates. In fact, Figure 7.12 shows that when $s = 0$, the μ-Markov-based estimates perform just as badly as the correlation-based estimates. $\qquad\square$

Remark 7.5.5. The rule of thumb, when modeling unstable systems, is that the degree s of the μ-Markov model must be greater than or equal the number of unstable modes of the system to allow the model structure to capture the instability. $\qquad\square$

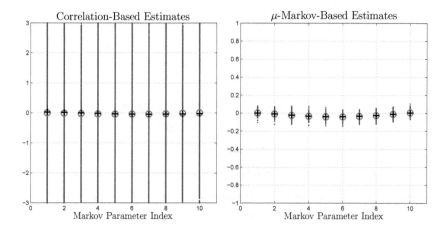

Figure 7.10: Comparison of the scaled correlation-based and μ-Markov-based Markov parameter estimates for the first ten Markov parameters over 5,000 trials when $\mu = 10$, $s = 6$, $N = 100$, $\mathcal{E}[x] \triangleq \exp[x/2 + 2]/10 - 0.83729$, and the system is unstable. The red $\circ$ denotes the true Markov parameter, the black $+$ denotes the mean of the estimates over the trials (as an indication of biasedness), and the blue $\bullet$ denotes the estimate for each trial.

7.6 Conclusions

We considered the use of an ersatz nonlinearity in parametric and nonparametric MIMO Hammerstein system identification. In parametric identification, we recast the problem as a linear optimization problem, after which the estimates were decoupled using the singular value decomposition. In nonparametric identification, we revisited correlation-based Markov parameter estimation techniques and introduced a novel method of μ-Markov-based Markov parameter estimation. Furthermore, we showed numerically that the μ-Markov-based estimation method yields Markov parameter estimates with a lower variance than the correlation-based estimates. We also showed numerically, that the μ-Markov-based method was able to produce reasonable estimates in the unstable case.

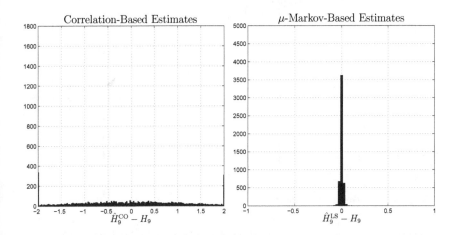

Figure 7.11: Histogram of the error in the scaled correlation-based and μ-Markov-based Markov parameter estimates of the tenth Markov parameter over 5,000 trials when $\mu = 10$, $s = 6$, $N = 100$, $\mathcal{E}[x] \triangleq \exp[x/2 + 2]/10 - 0.83729$, and the system is unstable.

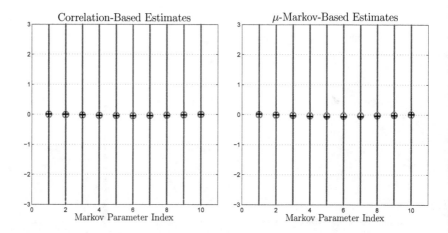

Figure 7.12: Comparison of the scaled correlation-based and μ-Markov-based Markov parameter estimates for the first ten Markov parameters over 5,000 trials when $\mu = 10$, $s = 0$, $N = 100$, $\mathcal{E}[x] \triangleq \exp[x/2 + 2]/10 - 0.83729$, and the system is unstable. The red $\circ$ denotes the true Markov parameter, the black $+$ denotes the mean of the estimates over the trials (as an indication of biasedness), and the blue $\bullet$ denotes the estimate for each trial.

CHAPTER VIII

Nonlinear Least-Squares

In this final chapter, we present an elimination theory-based method for solving equality-constrained multivariate polynomial least-squares problems in system identification. However, while most algorithms in elimination theory rely upon Gröbner bases and symbolic multivariate polynomial division algorithms, we present an algorithm which is based on computing the nullspace of a large sparse matrix and the zeros of a scalar, univariate polynomial.

8.1 Introduction

As system identification stretches the boundaries of optimal estimation toward ever more complicated scenarios, that is, with nonlinearities present and under more difficult noise assumptions, the optimization problems that need be solved also begin to push the boundaries of what is possible. Specifically, system identification is typically concerned with posing an optimization problem and attributing properties such as unbiasedness or consistency to its global minimizer [2, 3, 6]. However, as the identification problems become more difficult, the applicability of advanced system identification theory becomes harder to justify when the global minimizer also becomes increasingly difficult to ascertain. Indeed, many minimization methods guarantee that we find only a local minimizer, while also exhibiting a sometimes severe dependence on the initial guess.

Here we present a method for solving equality-constrained multivariate polynomial least-squares problems in a general manner. Specifically, although this problem has been addressed in algebraic geometry, all of the available literature appears to revolve around Gröbner bases and symbolic multivariate polynomial division algorithms [66, 67]. Here we show how to solve the same problem using linear algebra techniques. Specifically, we show that this problem amounts to nothing more than the computation of the nullspace of a large sparse matrix, and then computing the zeros of a scalar, univariate polynomial. Furthermore, the method we present does not rely on an initial guess, and yields the set of local and global minimizers to equality-constrained multivariate polynomial optimization problems when there exist a finite number of local and global minimizers.

8.2 Preliminaries

There are two types of notation we will interchange between in this chapter, multivariate polynomial notation and Kronecker notation. We use both types for several reasons, namely, to appeal to a wider audience, to relate the present chapter to past results, and finally, to express ideas as concisely as possible, since some ideas may be easier to grasp and explain in one notation. Definition 8.2.1 and 8.2.2 can be found in [66], but are repeated for completeness.

Definition 8.2.1. A **monomial** f in $x_1, \ldots, x_n$ is a product of the form

$$f = x_1^{\alpha_1} \cdot x_2^{\alpha_2} \cdots x_n^{\alpha_n},$$

where $\alpha_1, \ldots, \alpha_n$ are nonnegative integers. Furthermore, the **total degree** of f is the sum $\alpha_1 + \cdots + \alpha_n$. Specifically, we write

154

$$\deg(f) = \alpha_1 + \cdots + \alpha_n.$$

Definition 8.2.2. A **polynomial** g in $x_1, \ldots, x_n$ with coefficients in $\mathbb{R}$ is a finite linear combination (with coefficients in $\mathbb{R}$) of monomials in $x_1, \ldots, x_n$, that is,

$$g = \sum_{i=1}^{k} a_i \cdot f_i,$$

where k is a finite positive integer, $a_1, \ldots, a_k \in \mathbb{R}$ are nonzero, and $f_1, \ldots, f_k$ are monomials in $x_1, \ldots, x_n$. Furthermore, the set of polynomials in $x_1, \ldots, x_n$ with coefficients in $\mathbb{R}$ is denoted $\mathbb{R}[x_1, \ldots, x_n]$, and the **total degree** of g is $\max(\deg(f_1), \ldots, \deg(f_k))$. Specifically we write

$$\deg(g) = \max\left(\deg\left(f_1\right), \ldots, \deg\left(f_k\right)\right).$$

Remark 8.2.1. We primarily consider polynomials in $\mathbb{R}$ here since least-squares problems over complex variables can be recast over real variables, as shown in subsection 8.4.3. $\quad\square$

Definition 8.2.3. Let f_1 and f_2 be monomials in $x_1, \ldots, x_n$ given by

$$f_1 \triangleq x_1^{\alpha_1} \cdots x_n^{\alpha_n}, \quad f_2 \triangleq x_1^{\gamma_1} \cdots x_n^{\gamma_n}.$$

Also, let k be the smallest integer in $[1, n]$ such that $\delta \triangleq \alpha_k - \gamma_k$ is nonzero. Then we say that $f_1 >_{\text{rglex}} f_2$ if either 1) $\deg(f_1) < \deg(f_2)$ or 2) $\deg(f_1) = \deg(f_2)$ and $\delta > 0$, where $(\cdot)_{\text{rglex}}$ denotes a **reverse graded lexicographical ordering**.

Notation 8.2.1. Let $x = (x_1, \ldots, x_n) \in \mathbb{R}^n$ and let t be a nonnegative integer.

Then

$$x^{\otimes t} \triangleq \underset{\substack{\downarrow \\ 1}}{x} \otimes \underset{\substack{\downarrow \\ 2}}{x} \otimes \underset{\substack{\downarrow \\ 3}}{x} \otimes \cdots \otimes \underset{\substack{\downarrow \\ t}}{x},$$

where $\otimes$ represents the Kronecker product, and t x's appear in $x^{\otimes t}$. Furthermore,

$$x^{\otimes \le t} \triangleq \left[\begin{array}{ccccc} 1, & \left(x\right)^T, & \left(x^{\otimes 2}\right)^T, & \cdots, & \left(x^{\otimes t}\right)^T \end{array} \right]^T,$$

and $x^{\otimes \le t}_{\mathrm{rglex}}$ denotes a reduced version of $x^{\otimes \le t}$ where the terms are rglex ordered and the redundant entries are removed.

Remark 8.2.2. If we evaluate $x^{\otimes \le t}_{\mathrm{rglex}}$ at a, then it may happen that some of the entries of $a^{\otimes \le t}_{\mathrm{rglex}}$ are redundant. However these are not removed. For instance. Let $x = (x_1, x_2)$, $t = 2$, and $a = (a_1, a_2) = (1, 1)$. Then

$$
\begin{aligned}
a^{\otimes \le 2}_{\mathrm{rglex}} &= \left[\begin{array}{cccccc} 1, & a_1, & a_2, & a_1^2, & a_1 \cdot a_2, & a_2^2 \end{array} \right]^T, \\
&= \left[\begin{array}{cccccc} 1, & 1, & 1, & 1, & 1, & 1 \end{array} \right]^T.
\end{aligned}
$$

$\square$

Lemma 8.2.1. Let $g \in \mathbb{R}[x_1, \ldots, x_n]$, $\deg(g) = \alpha$, $x = \left[\begin{array}{ccc} x_1 & \cdots & x_n \end{array} \right]^T$, and

$$n_\alpha \triangleq \frac{(n + \alpha)!}{(\alpha)!(n)!}. \tag{8.1}$$

Then there exists $\beta \in \mathbb{R}^{(n+1)^\alpha}$ and $\beta_{\mathrm{rglex}} \in \mathbb{R}^{1 \times n_\alpha}$ such that

$$g = \left[\begin{array}{cc} 1, & x^T \end{array} \right]^{\otimes \alpha} \cdot \beta = \beta_{\mathrm{rglex}} \cdot x^{\otimes \le \alpha}_{\mathrm{rglex}}. \tag{8.2}$$

Proof. Vectors of the form $\left[\begin{array}{cc} 1, & x^T \end{array} \right]^{\otimes \alpha}$ and $x^{\otimes \le \alpha}_{\mathrm{rglex}}$ contain all of the monomials in $x_1, \ldots, x_n$ of total degree less than or equal to α. Since g is defined to be a linear combination of monomials in $x_1, \ldots, x_n$ with total degree less than α, it follows that there exists $\beta \in \mathbb{R}^{(n+1)^\alpha}$ and $\beta_{\mathrm{rglex}} \in \mathbb{R}^{1 \times n_\alpha}$ such that (8.2) holds. $\qquad \square$

Example 8.2.1. Let $x = \begin{bmatrix} x_1, & x_2 \end{bmatrix}^T$ and $t = 2$. Then

$$\begin{bmatrix} 1 \\ x \end{bmatrix}^{\otimes 2} = \begin{bmatrix} 1, & x_1, & x_2, & x_1, & x_1^2, & x_1 \cdot x_2, & x_2, & x_1 \cdot x_2, & x_2^2 \end{bmatrix}^T,$$

$$x_{\mathrm{rglex}}^{\otimes \leq 2} = \begin{bmatrix} 1, & x_1, & x_2, & x_1^2, & x_1 \cdot x_2, & x_2^2 \end{bmatrix}^T.$$

Thus, we can see that the polynomial $g = \begin{bmatrix} 1, & x^T \end{bmatrix}^{\otimes \alpha} \cdot \beta = \beta_{\mathrm{rglex}} \cdot x_{\mathrm{rglex}}^{\otimes \leq 2}$ can contain every monomial in x_1, x_2 of total degree less than or equal 2. $\qquad \square$

8.3 Problem Statement

Consider the equality-constrained multivariate polynomial least-squares problem

$$J = \min_{x \in \mathbb{R}^n} \left\| A \cdot \begin{bmatrix} 1 \\ x \end{bmatrix}^{\otimes s} \right\|_2^2 \quad \text{s.t.} \quad C \cdot \begin{bmatrix} 1 \\ x \end{bmatrix}^{\otimes t} = 0_{m \times 1}, \tag{8.3}$$

where $A \in \mathbb{R}^{k \times (n+1)^s}$, $C \in \mathbb{R}^{m \times (n+1)^t}$, and s and t are nonnegative integers. Then the problem is to determine all of the local and global minimizers of (8.3). In particular, we are interested in the case where there are a finite number of local minimizers of (8.3). Furthermore, (8.3) is equivalently given by

$$J = \min_{x \in \mathbb{R}^n} \left\| A_{\mathrm{rglex}} \cdot x_{\mathrm{rglex}}^{\otimes \leq s} \right\|_2^2 \quad \text{s.t.} \quad C_{\mathrm{rglex}} \cdot x_{\mathrm{rglex}}^{\otimes \leq t} = 0_{m \times 1}, \tag{8.4}$$

where n_s and n_t are given by (8.1), and $A_{\mathrm{rglex}} \in \mathbb{R}^{k \times n_s}$ and $C_{\mathrm{rglex}} \in \mathbb{R}^{m \times n_t}$ are found by combining the columns of A and C respectively to remove redundant terms in the product $\left(\left[\begin{array}{cc} 1, & x^T \end{array}\right]^{\otimes \alpha}\right)^T$.

Remark 8.3.1. Although (8.3) and (8.4) are exactly equivalent, we present them both since most ideas will be easier to express when written in the form (8.3). However, in practice, one should almost always use the form (8.4) since it is a compressed notation for (8.3). $\qquad\square$

Example 8.3.1. Consider the problem (8.3) where $n = 2$, $s = t = 2$, and $A \in \mathbb{R}^{k \times (n+1)^s}$ and $C \in \mathbb{R}^{m \times (n+1)^t}$ are given. Furthermore, let $a_i \in \mathbb{R}^{k \times 1}$ and $c_i \in \mathbb{R}^{m \times 1}$ denote the ith column of A and C, respectively. Then it follows that A_{rglex} and C_{rglex} are given by

$$A_{\text{rglex}} = \left[\begin{array}{cccccc} a_1, & a_2 + a_4, & a_3 + a_7, & a_5, & a_6 + a_8, & a_9 \end{array} \right],$$
$$C_{\text{rglex}} = \left[\begin{array}{cccccc} c_1, & c_2 + c_4, & c_3 + c_7, & c_5, & c_6 + c_8, & c_9 \end{array} \right].$$

$\qquad\square$

Remark 8.3.2. There may exist an infinite number of solutions of (8.4). For instance, let $n = 2$, let $A_{\text{rglex}} = 0_{1 \times n_s}$, and let the constraint $C_{\text{rglex}} \cdot x_{\text{rglex}}^{\otimes \leq t} = 0_{m \times 1}$ reduce to

$$x_1 (x_2 - 1)(x_2 + 1) = 0, \qquad x_1 (x_2 - 1)(x_2 + 2) = 0.$$

Then there are two curves which minimize (8.4), namely,

i) $x_1 = 0$ and $x_2 \in \mathbb{R}$.

ii) $x_1 \in \mathbb{R}$ and $x_2 = 1$.

$\qquad\square$

Remark 8.3.3. There may also be no solution of (8.3). This is typically due to the case where there is no solution which satisfies the constraint equations $C_{\text{rglex}} \cdot x_{\text{rglex}}^{\otimes \leq t} =$

$0_{m \times 1}$. For instance, suppose the constraint $C_{\text{rglex}} \cdot x_{\text{rglex}}^{\otimes \leq t} = 0_{m \times 1}$ reduces to

$$x_1 - 1 = 0, \qquad x_1 - 2 = 0.$$

Then there is no solution of (8.3). $\qquad\qquad\qquad\qquad\qquad\qquad$ □

8.4 Special Cases

Here we present three important commonly encountered special cases of (8.3)-(8.4).

8.4.1 Equality-Constrained Linear Least-Squares

Consider the equality-constrained linear least-squares problem

$$J = \min_{x \in \mathbb{R}^n} \left\| \tilde{A} \cdot x - \tilde{b} \right\|_2^2 \quad \text{s.t.} \quad \tilde{C} \cdot x = \tilde{d}, \tag{8.5}$$

where $\tilde{A} \in \mathbb{R}^{k \times n}$, $\tilde{b} \in \mathbb{R}^k$, $\tilde{C} \in \mathbb{R}^{m \times n}$, and $\tilde{d} \in \mathbb{R}^m$. Then letting

$$A_{\text{rglex}} \triangleq \begin{bmatrix} -\tilde{b}, & \tilde{A} \end{bmatrix}, \quad C_{\text{rglex}} \triangleq \begin{bmatrix} -\tilde{d}, & \tilde{C} \end{bmatrix}, \tag{8.6}$$

we have that (8.5) is equivalently given by (8.4), with $s = t = 1$, and A_{rglex} and C_{rglex} given by (8.6).

8.4.2 Equality-Constrained Bilinear Least-Squares

Consider the equality-constrained bilinear least-squares problem

$$J = \min_{y \in \mathbb{R}^p, z \in \mathbb{R}^q} \left\| A_y \cdot y + A_z \cdot z + A_{yz} \cdot (y \otimes z) - b \right\|_2^2 \tag{8.7}$$

$$\text{s.t.} \quad C_y \cdot y + C_z \cdot z + C_{yz} \cdot (y \otimes z) = d,$$

where $A_y \in \mathbb{R}^{k \times p}$, $A_z \in \mathbb{R}^{k \times q}$, $A_{yz} \in \mathbb{R}^{k \times pq}$, $b \in \mathbb{R}^k$, $C_y \in \mathbb{R}^{\ell \times p}$, $C_z \in \mathbb{R}^{\ell \times q}$, $C_{yz} \in \mathbb{R}^{\ell \times pq}$, $d \in \mathbb{R}^\ell$. Then letting

$$x \triangleq \begin{bmatrix} y^T & z^T \end{bmatrix}^T,$$

$$P \triangleq \begin{bmatrix} I_p, & 0_{p \times q} \end{bmatrix} \otimes \begin{bmatrix} 0_{q \times (p+1)}, & I_q \end{bmatrix},$$

$$A \triangleq \begin{bmatrix} -b, & A_y, & A_z, & A_{yz} \cdot P \end{bmatrix}, \tag{8.8}$$

$$C \triangleq \begin{bmatrix} -d, & C_y, & C_z, & C_{yz} \cdot P \end{bmatrix}, \tag{8.9}$$

we have that (8.7) is equivalently given by (8.3), with $s = t = 2$, $n = p + q$, and A and C given by (8.8) and (8.9), respectively.

8.4.3 Equality-Constrained Multivariate Polynomial Least-Squares over the Complex Domain

Consider the equality-constrained multivariate polynomial least-squares problem over the complex domain,

$$J = \min_{y \in \mathbb{C}^p} \left\| \tilde{A} \cdot \begin{bmatrix} 1 \\ y \end{bmatrix}^{\otimes s} \right\|_F^2 \quad \text{s.t.} \quad \tilde{C} \cdot \begin{bmatrix} 1 \\ y \end{bmatrix}^{\otimes t} = 0_{m \times 1}, \tag{8.10}$$

where $\| \cdot \|_F$ denotes the Frobenius norm of $(\cdot)$, $\tilde{A} \in \mathbb{C}^{k' \times p^s}$, $\tilde{C} \in \mathbb{C}^{m' \times p^t}$, and s and t are nonnegative integers. Then letting

$$\tilde{I}_p \triangleq \begin{bmatrix} 1, & 0_{1 \times p}, & 0_{1 \times p} \\ 0_{p \times 1}, & I_p, & iI_p \end{bmatrix}, \quad x \triangleq \begin{bmatrix} \text{real}(y) \\ \text{imag}(y) \end{bmatrix},$$

$$A \triangleq \begin{bmatrix} \text{real}\left(\tilde{A} \cdot \tilde{I}_p^{\otimes s}\right) \\ \text{imag}\left(\tilde{A} \cdot \tilde{I}_p^{\otimes s}\right) \end{bmatrix}, \quad C \triangleq \begin{bmatrix} \text{real}\left(\tilde{C} \cdot \tilde{I}_p^{\otimes t}\right) \\ \text{imag}\left(\tilde{C} \cdot \tilde{I}_p^{\otimes t}\right) \end{bmatrix}, \tag{8.11}$$

we have that (8.10) is equivalently given by (8.3), with $n = 2p$, $k = 2k'$, $m = 2m'$, and A and C given by (8.11). In this way we have recast (8.10) from a problem over the complex domain to one over the real domain as noted in Remark 8.2.1.

8.5 Necessary Conditions of Optimality

The necessary conditions of optimality that we employ are the standard Lagrangian conditions.

Notation 8.5.1. Let $x = (x_1, \ldots, x_n) \in \mathbb{R}^n$ and let m and p be integers such that $n = m \cdot p$. Then

$$\text{unvec}\,(x, m, p) \triangleq \begin{bmatrix} x_1 & x_{m+1} & \cdots & x_{(p-1)m+1} \\ \vdots & \vdots & & \vdots \\ x_m & x_{2m} & \cdots & x_{pm} \end{bmatrix},$$

$$\text{vec}\big(\text{unvec}\,(x, m, p)\big) \triangleq \begin{bmatrix} x_1, & \cdots, & x_{pm} \end{bmatrix}^T.$$

We will also find the following fact useful [68]:

Fact 8.5.1. Let $x \in \mathbb{R}^n$, $E \in \mathbb{R}^{\ell \times m}$, $F \in \mathbb{R}^{p \times q}$, and $G \in \mathbb{R}^{n \times n}$, where $n = m \cdot p$. Then

$$\left(F^T \otimes E\right) \cdot x = E \cdot \text{unvec}\,(x, m, p) \cdot F.$$

Furthermore,

$$x^T \cdot G \cdot x = (x \otimes x)^T \cdot \text{vec}\,(G).$$

Thus we summarize the necessary conditions of optimality in following lemma:

161

Lemma 8.5.1. Let $\eta \triangleq n + m + 1$, $r \triangleq \max(2s, t+1)$, and

$$
\tilde{A} \triangleq \begin{bmatrix} I_{(n+1)} \\ 0_{m \times (n+1)} \end{bmatrix}^{\otimes 2s} \cdot \mathrm{vec}\left(A^T \cdot A\right),
$$

$$
\tilde{C} \triangleq \left(\begin{bmatrix} I_{(n+1)} \\ 0_{m \times (n+1)} \end{bmatrix}^{\otimes t} \otimes \begin{bmatrix} 0_{(n+1) \times m} \\ I_m \end{bmatrix} \right) \cdot \mathrm{vec}\left(C\right),
$$

$$
\tilde{D} \triangleq \begin{bmatrix} \tilde{A}^T, & 0_{(\eta^r - \eta^{2s}) \times 1} \end{bmatrix}^T + \begin{bmatrix} \tilde{C}^T, & 0_{(\eta^r - \eta^{t+1}) \times 1} \end{bmatrix}^T.
$$

Furthermore, let $\beta \triangleq \eta^{r-1}$ and $p \triangleq n + m$. If $x \in \mathbb{R}^n$ is a minimizer of (8.3), then there exists $\lambda \in \mathbb{R}^m$ such that

$$
D \cdot \left(\begin{bmatrix} 1, & x^T, & \lambda^T \end{bmatrix}^{\otimes(r-1)} \right)^T = 0_{p \times 1}, \tag{8.12}
$$

where $D \in \mathbb{R}^{p \times \beta}$ is given by

$$
D \triangleq \begin{bmatrix} 0_{p \times 1}, & I_p \end{bmatrix} \cdot \sum_{i=1}^{r} \mathrm{unvec}\left(\begin{bmatrix} I_{\eta^{i-1}} \otimes P_{\eta^{r-i}, \eta} \end{bmatrix} \cdot \tilde{D}, \eta, \beta \right), \tag{8.13}
$$

$\lambda = (\lambda_1, \dots, \lambda_m)$ are the Lagrange multipliers, and $P_{\eta^{r-i}, \eta}$ is the Kronecker permutation matrix [68].

Proof. First, due to the constraints, we introduce the Lagrange multipliers $\lambda_1, \dots, \lambda_m$, and let $\lambda \triangleq \begin{bmatrix} \lambda_1 & \cdots & \lambda_m \end{bmatrix}^T$, and $y \triangleq \begin{bmatrix} x^T, & \lambda^T \end{bmatrix}^T$. Hence from Fact 8.5.1, the unconstrained portion of the cost is given by

$$
J_{\mathrm{unc}} = \begin{bmatrix} 1, & x^T \end{bmatrix}^{\otimes 2s} \cdot \mathrm{vec}\left(A^T \cdot A\right) = \begin{bmatrix} 1, & y^T \end{bmatrix}^{\otimes 2s} \cdot \tilde{A},
$$

162

and thus the Lagrange function is given by

$$\Lambda = J_{\text{unc}} + \lambda^T \cdot C \cdot \begin{bmatrix} 1 \\ x \end{bmatrix}^{\otimes t} = J_{\text{unc}} + \begin{bmatrix} 1, & y^T \end{bmatrix}^{\otimes(t+1)} \cdot \tilde{C},$$

or simply $\Lambda = \begin{bmatrix} 1, & y^T \end{bmatrix}^{\otimes r} \cdot \tilde{D}.$

Next, employing the Kronecker permutation matrix [68], for every $i \in [1, r]$, we have that

$$\Lambda = \begin{bmatrix} 1 \\ y \end{bmatrix}^T \cdot \left(\begin{bmatrix} 1 \\ y \end{bmatrix}^{\otimes r-1} \otimes I_\eta \right)^T \cdot \left(I_{\eta^{i-1}} \otimes P_{\eta^{r-i},\eta} \right) \cdot \tilde{D}.$$

Therefore, computing the Jacobian of Λ with respect to y, and setting it equal to zero, we have (8.12). □

Remark 8.5.1. Significant memory and computational savings are possible by saving and computing the necessary conditions of optimality with respect to a rglex ordering. □

8.6 Elimination Theory

Elimination theory deals with eliminating variables from systems of multivariate polynomial equations, such as the equation set (8.12), primarily through the use of Gröbner bases with respect to lexicographic order [66]. However, while the theory is quite powerful, to the knowledge of this author, all of the algorithms available for computing Gröbner bases revolve around symbolic iterative multivariate polynomial division algorithms. Here we will attempt to perform the same basic function of elimination theory (eliminating variables from systems of multivariate polynomial equations) numerically.

163

Definition 8.6.1. Let $g_1, \ldots, g_k \in \mathbb{R}[y_1, \ldots, y_p]$, r be a nonnegative integer, $D \in \mathbb{R}^{k \times (p+1)^r}$, p_r be given by (8.1), $D_{\text{rglex}} \in \mathbb{R}^{k \times p_r}$, and $z = (z_1, \ldots, z_p) \in \mathbb{C}^p$. Then

i) z is a **zero of** $g_1, \ldots, g_k$ if $g_1(z) = \cdots = g_k(z) = 0$.

ii) z is a **zero of** D if $D \cdot \begin{bmatrix} 1 \\ z \end{bmatrix}^{\otimes r} = 0_{k \times 1}$.

iii) z is a **zero of** D_{rglex} if $D_{\text{rglex}} \cdot z_{\text{rglex}}^{\otimes \leq r} = 0_{k \times 1}$,

where p and r in (ii) and (iii) should be clear from context. Furthermore, we say that z_i is a **partial i-zero**.

Theorem 8.6.1. Let $g_1, \ldots, g_k \in \mathbb{R}[y_1, \ldots, y_p]$, let $i \in [1, p]$, and let there exist a finite number of partial i-zeros of $g_1, \ldots, g_k$. Then there exists $h_{i,1} \ldots, h_{i,k} \in \mathbb{R}[y_1, \ldots, y_p]$ and a nonzero $f_i \in \mathbb{R}[y_i]$ such that

$$\sum_{j=1}^{k} h_{i,j} \cdot g_j = f_i. \tag{8.14}$$

Furthermore, if $z_i \in \mathbb{C}$ is a partial i-zero of $g_1, \ldots, g_k$, then $f_i(z_i) = 0$.

Proof. The result (8.14) is a direct result of the Hilbert's well-known Nullstellensatz [66]. □

Corollary 8.6.1. Let $y \in \mathbb{R}^p$, r be a nonnegative integer, p_r be given by (8.1), $D_{\text{rglex}} \in \mathbb{R}^{k \times p_r}$, $i \in [1, p]$, and let there exist a finite number of partial i-zeros of D_{rglex}. Then there exists a nonnegative integer γ_i, $E_{\text{rglex}} \in \mathbb{R}^{p_{\gamma_i} \times k}$, and a nonzero $F_i \in \mathbb{R}^{1 \times p_{(\gamma_i + r)}}$ such that

$$\left(y_{\text{rglex}}^{\otimes \leq \gamma_i} \right)^T \cdot E_{\text{rglex}} \cdot D_{\text{rglex}} \cdot \left(y_{\text{rglex}}^{\otimes \leq r} \right) = F_i \cdot \left(y_i \right)_{\text{rglex}}^{\otimes \leq (\gamma_i + r)}, \tag{8.15}$$

164

where p_{γ_i} and $p_{(\gamma_i+r)}$ are given by (8.1). Furthermore, if $z_i \in \mathbb{C}$ is a partial i-zero of D_{rglex}, then

$$F_i \cdot \left(z_i\right)_{\text{rglex}}^{\otimes \leq (\gamma_i+r)} = 0.$$

Proof. Corollary 8.6.1 is a direct result of Theorem 8.6.1 and Lemma 8.2.1, where the polynomial notation used in Theorem 8.6.1 has been replaced with Kronecker notation using Lemma 8.2.1. □

Remark 8.6.1. From Lemma 8.2.1, one could also recast Corollary 8.6.1 in terms of the vector $\left[\begin{array}{cc} 1, & y^T \end{array}\right]^{\otimes r}$. □

Theorem 8.6.1 and Corollary 8.6.1 show that when there exist a finite number of partial i-zeros, we can always find a nonzero univariate polynomial which is in the range of the original set of multivariate polynomials. This is beneficial since once the equation set is reduced to a univariate polynomial, we can solve for all of the solutions using standard polynomial root solvers, and then determine which combination(s) of partial zeros form a minimizer of our original optimization problem (8.3)-(8.4). Furthermore, recall that some of the unknown variables in the necessary conditions may be Lagrange multipliers. However, we do not need to solve for these to compute the minimizers of (8.3)-(8.4). First, we introduce some notation and elaborate on a numerical algorithm for determining univariate polynomials from a set of multivariate polynomials.

Notation 8.6.1. Let p, r, and γ be nonnegative integers, and let p_r and p_γ be given by (8.1). Then $\Lambda_{p,r,\gamma} \in \mathbb{Z}^{p(r+\gamma) \times p_r p_\gamma}$ is the binary matrix such that for every $y \in \mathbb{C}^p$ and $F \in \mathbb{R}^{p_r p_\gamma \times k}$,

$$\left(y_{\text{rglex}}^{\otimes \leq r} \otimes y_{\text{rglex}}^{\otimes \leq \gamma}\right)^T \cdot F = \left(y_{\text{rglex}}^{\otimes \leq (r+\gamma)}\right)^T \cdot \Lambda_{p,r,\gamma} \cdot F. \tag{8.16}$$

Notation 8.6.2. Let $i \in [1, p]$, let β_i and p be nonnegative integers, and let p_{β_i} be given by (8.1). Then letting

$$\zeta_{i,j} \triangleq \frac{(p+j)!}{(j)!(p)!} - \frac{(p-i+j)!}{(j)!(p-i)!} + 1,$$

for every $j \in [0, \beta_i]$, we take $\Omega_{i,p,\beta_i} \in \mathbb{R}^{(\beta_i+1) \times p_{\beta_i}}$ to be the binary matrix such that the $(j+1)^{th}$ row of Ω_{i,p,β_i} is the $\zeta_{i,j}^{th}$ row of $I_{p_{\beta_i}}$, where I denotes the identity matrix. Furthermore, we take $\Delta_{i,p,\beta_i} \in \mathbb{R}^{(p_{\beta_i}-\beta_i-1) \times p_{\beta_i}}$ to be the p_{β_i} identity matrix $I_{p_{\beta_i}}$, where the rows $\zeta_{i,0}, \ldots, \zeta_{i,\beta_i}$ of $I_{p_{\beta_i}}$ have been removed.

Remark 8.6.2. Let $i \in [1, p]$, let $D_{\text{rglex}} \in \mathbb{R}^{p_{\beta_i} \times 1}$, and let $g \in \mathbb{R}[y_1, \ldots, y_p]$ be given by

$$g \triangleq \left(y_{\text{rglex}}^{\otimes \leq \beta_i} \right)^T \cdot D_{\text{rglex}}.$$

Then Ω_{i,p,β_i} is the binary matrix which returns the monomials in y_i from $y_{\text{rglex}}^{\otimes \leq \beta_i}$, without reordering, that is,

$$\Omega_{i,p,\beta} \cdot y_{\text{rglex}}^{\otimes \leq \beta_i} = \begin{bmatrix} 1, & y_i, & y_i^2, & \cdots, & y_i^{\beta_i} \end{bmatrix}^T.$$

Conversely, Δ_{i,p,β_i} is the binary matrix which removes the monomials in y_i $(1, y_i, y_i^2, \ldots, y_i^{\beta_i}$ from $y_{\text{rglex}}^{\otimes \leq \beta_i}$, without reordering. For instance, letting $y = \begin{bmatrix} y_1, & y_2 \end{bmatrix}^T$, $i = 2$, and $\beta_i = 2$, we have that

$$\Delta_{i,p,\beta_i} \cdot y_{\text{rglex}}^{\otimes \leq \beta_i} = \begin{bmatrix} y_1, & y_1^2, & y_1 \cdot y_2 \end{bmatrix}^T,$$

or more generally,

$$\Delta_{i,p,\beta} \cdot y_{\text{rglex}}^{\otimes \leq \beta_i}$$
$$= \left[y_1, \cdots, y_{i-1}, y_{i+1}, \cdots, y_p, y_1^2, \cdots, (y_{i-1}y_p), (y_iy_{i+1}), \cdots \right]^T.$$

Thus letting $g' \in \mathbb{R}[y_i]$ and $g'' \in \mathbb{R}[y_1, \ldots, y_p]$ be given by

$$g' \triangleq \left(y_{\text{rglex}}^{\otimes \leq \beta_i} \right)^T \cdot \Omega_{i,p,\beta}^T \cdot \Omega_{i,p,\beta} \cdot D_{\text{rglex}},$$
$$g'' \triangleq \left(y_{\text{rglex}}^{\otimes \leq \beta_i} \right)^T \cdot \Delta_{i,p,\beta}^T \cdot \Delta_{i,p,\beta} \cdot D_{\text{rglex}},$$

it follows that $g = g' + g''$, where g' contains all of the monomials in y_i present in g, and g'' contains all of the remaining terms in g. $\qquad \square$

Algorithm 8.6.1. Let r be a nonnegative integer, let p_r be given by (8.1), let $D_{\text{rglex}} \in \mathbb{R}^{k \times p_r}$, and let $i \in [1,p]$. Also, assume that there exist a finite number of partial i-zeros of D_{rglex}. Then the following algorithm yields a set $\mathcal{Z}_i$ which contains the partial i-zeros of D_{rglex}, that is, if $z_i \in \mathbb{C}$ is a partial i-zero of D_{rglex}, then $z_i \in \mathcal{Z}_i$.

1) $\gamma_i = 0$.

2) Increment γ_i by 1.

3) Compute a basis $V \in \mathbb{R}^{kn_{\gamma_i} \times \nu}$ for the nullspace of

$$\Psi_{i,p,r,\gamma_i} \triangleq \left[\Delta_{i,p,r+\gamma_i} \cdot \Lambda_{p,r,\gamma_i} \cdot \left(D_{\text{rglex}}^T \otimes I_{p_{\gamma_i}} \right) \right]. \qquad (8.17)$$

4) If V is empty ($\nu = 0$) or

$$F \triangleq \left[\Omega_{i,p,r+\gamma_i} \cdot \Lambda_{p,r,\gamma_i} \cdot \left(D_{\text{rglex}}^T \otimes I_{p_{\gamma_i}} \right) \cdot V \right],$$

is zero, return to step 2.

5) F is a matrix of coefficients for a set of univariate polynomial equations, that is,

$$(y_i)_{\text{rglex}}^{\otimes \leq (r + \gamma_i)} \cdot F = \begin{bmatrix} f_1, & \cdots, & f_\nu \end{bmatrix}, \qquad (8.18)$$

where $f_1, \ldots, f_\nu \in \mathbb{R}[y_i]$.

6) Compute the set Z_1 of zeros of f_1 using a univariate polynomial root solver.

7) $j = 1$ and $\mathcal{Z}_{i,1} = Z_1$.

8) Increment j by 1.

9) Compute the set Z_j of zeros of f_j using a univariate polynomial root solver.

10) $\mathcal{Z}_{i,j} = \mathcal{Z}_{i,j-1} \cap Z_j$.

11) If $\mathcal{Z}_{i,j} \neq \{\}$ and $j < \nu$, that is, there is at least 1 zero of $f_1, \ldots, f_j$, return to step 8.

12) $\mathcal{Z}_i \triangleq \mathcal{Z}_{i,j}$.

Remark 8.6.3. From Theorem 8.6.1 and Corollary 8.6.1, we are guaranteed that there will exist a nonnegative γ_i and a nonzero F in Algorithm 8.6.1. Furthermore, the nonzero columns of F in step 4 are the the $F_i's$ in Corollary 8.6.1. $\qquad \square$

Remark 8.6.4. Once a nonzero F has been determined in Algorithm 8.6.1, there are several ways of determining the set $\mathcal{Z}_i$. An alternative method is to choose a univariate polynomial f_i in (8.18), compute the zeros of f_i, and choose one of the zeros z_i of f_i. Then $z_i \in \mathcal{Z}_i$ if $f_1(z_i) = \cdots = f_\nu(z_i) = 0$. In this way, looping over all of the zeros of f_i, we could determine the set $\mathcal{Z}_i$. $\qquad \square$

Next, we put together a simple algorithm for determining the all of the local and global minimizers of (8.3)-(8.4).

Algorithm 8.6.2. Let r be a nonnegative integer, p_r be given by (8.1), C_{rglex} be given by (8.4), m denote the number of Lagrange multipliers in Lemma 8.5.1, $n \triangleq p - m$, and let $D_{\text{rglex}} \in \mathbb{R}^{k \times p_r}$ be the rglex reduced version of the necessary condition given in Lemma 8.5.1. Also, assume that there exist a finite number of local minimizers of (8.3)-(8.4). Then the following algorithm yields the set $\mathcal{Z}$ of local minimizers of (8.3)-(8.4).

1) $i = 0$.

2) $i = i + 1$.

3) Apply Algorithm 8.6.1 to D_{rglex}, yielding the set of partial solutions $\mathcal{Z}_i$.

4) Let ξ_i denote the number of elements of $\mathcal{Z}_i$.

5) If $i < n$, return to step 2.

6) Construct the set $\mathcal{P}$ of all of the $\xi_1 \cdots \xi_n$ combinations possible by choosing one element from each $\mathcal{Z}_i$.

7) $j = 0$ and $\mathcal{Z} = \{\}$, the empty set.

8) $j = j + 1$.

9) Choose an element of $y \in \mathcal{P}$ and remove y from $\mathcal{P}$.

10) If y is real and y is a zero of C_{rglex}, add y to the set $\mathcal{Z}$.

11) If $j < \xi_1 \cdots \xi_n$, return to step 8.

8.7 Sparse Nullspace Calculation

In Algorithm 8.6.1, the principal calculation is to compute the nullspace of Ψ_{i,p,r,γ_i} in (8.17), the practicality of which may seem unreasonable since Ψ_{i,p,r,γ_i} is of dimension $\left[p_{(r+\gamma_i)} - r - \gamma_i - 1 \right] \times k p_{\gamma_i}$, which increases rapidly as γ_i is increased (step 2).

169

However, Ψ_{i,p,r,γ_i} also becomes sparse as γ_i increases, as evidenced by the product $D^T_{\text{rglex}} \otimes I_{p_{\gamma_i}}$ in (8.6.2). Hence the practicality of Algorithm 8.6.2, and thus the solvability of the optimization problems (8.3)-(8.4) using the present (non-Gröbner basis based) approach revolves around our ability to compute the nullspace of large space matrices reliably.

However, computation of a nullspace for a large sparse matrix is not a straightforward matter since the most numerically reliable methods, the singular value and QR decomposition, are typically infeasible from a memory and computation point of view. This is primarily because the nullspace in both of these algorithms is necessarily orthogonal, and hence the sparsity of the original matrix is typically not passed along to the nullspace. Hence here we propose an alternative method for computing the nullspace of large sparse matrices. We begin by introducing some necessary facts.

Fact 8.7.1. Let $a = (a_1, \ldots, a_k) \in \mathbb{R}^{1 \times k}$ be nonzero and let $A \in \mathbb{R}^{\ell \times k}$. Also, let

$$c_j \triangleq \max\left(|a_1|, \ldots, |a_k|\right),$$

$$d \triangleq \left[\begin{array}{ccc} (a_1/a_j), & \cdots, & (a_{j-1}/a_j) \end{array} \right] \in \mathbb{R}^{1 \times (j-1)},$$

$$e \triangleq \left[\begin{array}{ccc} (a_{j+1}/a_j), & \cdots, & (a_k/a_j) \end{array} \right] \in \mathbb{R}^{1 \times (k-j)},$$

$$f \triangleq \left[\begin{array}{cc} d, & e \end{array} \right] \in \mathbb{R}^{1 \times (k-1)},$$

$$U \triangleq \left[\begin{array}{cc} I_{(j-1)} & 0_{(j-1) \times (k-j)} \\ -d & -e \\ 0_{(k-j) \times (j-1)} & I_{(k-j)} \end{array} \right] \in \mathbb{R}^{k \times (k-1)},$$

and let $V' \in \mathbb{R}^{(k-1) \times \nu}$ be a basis for the nullspace of $A \cdot U$. Then

i) U is a basis for the nullspace of a.

ii) $V \triangleq U \cdot V'$ is a basis for the nullspace of $A' \triangleq \left[\begin{array}{c} a \\ A \end{array} \right]$.

170

iii) The singular values of U are given by

$$\sigma_1 = \sqrt{1 + f \cdot f^T}, \quad \sigma_2 = \cdots = \sigma_{k-1} = 1.$$

Proof. First, since a is nonzero, the dimension of the nullspace of a is $k - 1$. Furthermore, since rank $[U] = k - 1$ and $a \cdot U = 0_{1 \times (k-1)}$, it follows that U is a basis for the nullspace of a.

Next, suppose that there exists an $y \in \mathbb{R}^k$ in the nullspace of A' which is not in the rangespace of V, that is, suppose V is not a complete basis for the nullspace of A'. Then since $a \cdot y = 0$ and U is a basis for the nullspace of a, there exists $y \in \mathbb{R}^{(k-1)}$ such that $y = U \cdot y$, where y is not in the rangespace of V'. However, since $A \cdot y = A \cdot U \cdot y = 0_{\ell \times 1}$ and V' is a basis for the nullspace of $A \cdot U$, we have a contradiction. Thus V is a basis for the nullspace of A'.

Finally, recall that the singular values of U are the square roots of the eigenvalues of $U^T \cdot U$. We have two cases to consider: First, if f is zero, then

$$\text{rank}\left(U^T \cdot U - I_{(k-1)}\right) = \text{rank}\left(f^T \cdot f\right) = 0, \qquad (8.19)$$

and it follows that $k - 1$ singular values are 1. Second, if f is nonzero, then from (8.19), rank $\left(f^T \cdot f\right) = 1$ and hence $k - 2$ singular values are 1. Furthermore, note that

$$U^T \cdot U - \left(1 - f \cdot f^T\right) \cdot I_{(k-1)} = \left(f \cdot f^T\right) \cdot I_{(k-1)} - f^T \cdot f,$$

and since

$$\left[\left(f \cdot f^T\right) \cdot I_{(k-1)} - f^T \cdot f\right] \cdot f^T = 0_{(k-1) \times 1},$$

171

where we used the fact that $f \cdot f^T$ is scalar and hence commutes, we have that f^T is an eigenvector of $U^T \cdot U$, that is, $1 - f \cdot f^T$ is an eigenvalue of $U^T \cdot U$. $\square$

Remark 8.7.1. If $a = 0_{1 \times k}$, then the nullspace of A is the same as the nullspace of $\begin{bmatrix} a \\ A \end{bmatrix}$ since the nullspace of $0_{1 \times k}$ is the $k \times k$ identity matrix. $\square$

Algorithm 8.7.1. Let $a_1, \ldots, a_\ell \in \mathbb{R}^{1 \times k}$ and

$$A \triangleq \begin{bmatrix} a_1^T & \cdots & a_\ell^T \end{bmatrix}^T.$$

Then the following algorithm, based on Fact 8.7.1, yields a basis V for the nullspace of A.

1) $i = 0$, $V_1 = I_k$, and $\nu_1 = k$.

2) $i = i + 1$.

3) $\begin{bmatrix} b_1 & \cdots & b_{\nu_i} \end{bmatrix} = a_i \cdot V_i$.

4) If $b_1 = \cdots = b_{\nu_i} = 0$, return to step 2.

5) $c_j = \max(|b_1|, \ldots, |b_{\nu_i}|)$.

6) $d = \begin{bmatrix} (b_1/b_j), & \cdots, & (b_{j-1}/b_j) \end{bmatrix}$.

7) $e = \begin{bmatrix} (b_{j+1}/b_j), & \cdots, & (b_{\nu_i}/b_j) \end{bmatrix}$.

8) $U = \begin{bmatrix} I_{(j-1)} & 0_{(j-1) \times (\nu_i - j)} \\ -d & -e \\ 0_{(\nu_i - j) \times (j-1)} & I_{(\nu_i - j)} \end{bmatrix}$.

9) $V_i = V_{i-1} \cdot U$ and $\nu_i = \nu_{i-1} - 1$.

10) If $i < \ell$, return to step 2.

11) $V = V_i$.

Remark 8.7.2. By examining the structure of U in Fact 8.7.1 and Algorithm 8.7.1, we can see that, at each step of Algorithm 8.7.1, the nullspace $V_i \in \mathbb{R}^{k \times \nu_i}$ of $\begin{bmatrix} a_1^T & \cdots & a_i^T \end{bmatrix}^T$ is sparse. In particular, we have that

$$\# \text{ of nonzero entries of } V_i \leq \nu_i \cdot (k - \nu_i + 1),$$

where, in general, the bound is reached only if A is dense. Hence the density of V_i is less than or equal $(k - \nu_i + 1)/k$. $\qquad\square$

8.8 Solution

Here we show that all of the real minimizers will indeed be minimizers in the complex plane.

Fact 8.8.1. Let s and t be nonnegative integers, A and C be given by (8.3), and $y_0 \in \mathbb{R}^p$. Then y_0 is a local minimizer of (8.3) if and only if y_0 is a local minimizer of

$$J = \min_{y \in \mathbb{C}^p} \left\| A \cdot \begin{bmatrix} 1 \\ y \end{bmatrix}^{\otimes s} \right\|_2^2 \quad \text{s.t.} \quad C \cdot \begin{bmatrix} 1 \\ y \end{bmatrix}^{\otimes t} = 0_{m \times 1}. \tag{8.20}$$

Proof. The necessary conditions of optimality given in Lemma 8.5.1 are the same for both (8.3) and (8.20). $\qquad\square$

Remark 8.8.1. As obvious as Fact 8.8.1 may seem, it is important to remember that Algorithm 8.6.1 will yield univariate polynomials, which we will then solve for partial solutions of the necessary conditions of optimality given in Lemma 8.5.1. However, we have taken no effort to ensure that the zeros of the resulting univariate

173

polynomials will be real, which is important since we have posed all of our optimization problems over the real domain. Fortunately, Fact 8.8.1 tells us that this is not an issue, that is, all of the local (and global) minimizers over the real domain will be a subset of the local minimizers over the complex domain. □

8.9   Example

Here we show an example of a system identification problem that can be solved using the current technique.

Example 8.9.1. Consider the discrete-time Wiener system

$$v_k = a_1 \cdot y_{k-1} + b_0 \cdot u_k + b_1 \cdot u_{k-1},$$

$$y_k = c_0 + v_k + v_k^2,$$

for $k = 1, \ldots, 1000$, where $u \in \mathbb{R}$ is the input, $y \in \mathbb{R}$ is the output, and for the current example,

$$c_0 = 0.1, \ a_1 = -0.04, \ b_0 = 0.5, \ b_1 = 0.6,$$

$$u_k = 5 \cdot \exp\left(-0.0007 \cdot k^2\right) + \sin\left(\frac{k}{2}\right) + \sin\left(\frac{k}{3}\right) + \frac{\tan(k)}{20}.$$

Specifically, Figure 8.1 shows the time histories of the input u and output y for the current example.

Next, consider the optimization problem

$$J = \min_{c_0, a_1, b_0, b_1 \in \mathbb{R}} \left\| \sum_{k=1}^{1000} y_k - c_0 - v_k - v_k^2 \right\|_2^2, \tag{8.21}$$

$$\text{s.t.} \quad c_0^2 + a_1^2 + b_0^2 + b_1^2 = 0.6216.$$

174

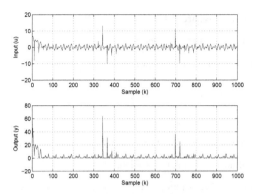

Figure 8.1: Time history of the input u and output y.

Then letting

$$y \triangleq \left[\begin{array}{cccc} c_0, & a_1, & b_0, & b_1 \end{array} \right]^T,$$

$$\tilde{\phi}_{k+1} \triangleq \left[\begin{array}{cccccc} -y_{k+1}, & 1, & y_k, & u_{k+1}, & u_k, & 0_{1\times 4} \end{array} \right],$$

$$\bar{\phi}_{k+1} \triangleq \left[\begin{array}{cccccc} y_k^2, & 2y_k u_{k+1}, & 2y_k u_k, & u_{k+1}^2, & 2u_{k+1}u_k, & u_k^2 \end{array} \right],$$

$$\phi_{k+1} \triangleq \left[\begin{array}{cc} \tilde{\phi}_{k+1}, & \bar{\phi}_{k+1} \end{array} \right],$$

$$\Phi_{k+1} \triangleq \left[\begin{array}{ccc} \phi_1^T, & \cdots, & \phi_{k+1}^T \end{array} \right]^T,$$

$$\Theta \triangleq \left[\begin{array}{ccccccccc} -0.6216, & 0_{1\times 4}, & 1, & 0_{1\times 3}, & 1, & 0_{1\times 2}, & 1, & 0, & 1 \end{array} \right].$$

it follows that (8.21) is equivalently given by

$$J = \min_{y \in \mathbb{R}^6} \left\| \Phi_{1000} \cdot y_{\mathrm{rglex}}^{\otimes \leq 2} \right\|_2^2, \quad \text{s.t.} \quad \Theta \cdot y_{\mathrm{rglex}}^{\otimes \leq 2} = 0.$$

Finally, since the minimizer of the unconstrained portion of (8.21) satisfies the constraint, we set the sole Lagrange multiplier $\lambda_1 = 0$. Hence applying Algorithm 8.6.2 (and using Algorithm 8.7.1 in step 3 of Algorithm 8.6.1), we find that for $\gamma_1 =$

175

$\cdots = \gamma_4 = 5$, we have the partial solutions $\mathcal{Z}_1 = \{0.1\}$, $\mathcal{Z}_2 = \{-0.04\}$, $\mathcal{Z}_3 = \{0.5\}$, and $\mathcal{Z}_4 = \{0.6\}$. Hence in this case Algorithm 8.6.2 yields the solution that we would expect. On the author's laptop, the algorithm ran in 0.8 seconds. □

8.10 Conclusions

We presented an elimination theory-based method for solving equality-constrained multivariate polynomial least-squares problems, that is, for determining all of the local and global minimizers when a finite number of them exist. Furthermore, we showed that this problem amounts to computing the nullspace of a large sparse matrix, and then computing the zeros of a scalar, univariate polynomial.

CHAPTER IX

Conclusions and Future Work

9.1 Conclusions

In this work, we have considered polynomial matrix representations of MIMO discrete-time linear systems and their role in least-squares identification. Since our focus was the identification of polynomial matrices, we began with the necessary background concerning polynomial matrices in Chapter II. Specifically, we considered polynomial matrix representations of MIMO linear systems and their connection to Markov parameters. We also developed theory and numerical algorithms for transforming polynomial matrix models into Markov parameter models, and vice versa.

In Chapter III, we then considered the notion of persistency within a deterministic, finite-data context, namely, in terms of the rank and condition number of the regressor matrix Φ_N, which contains input and output data. We also investigated the feasibility of estimating the degree of a system in terms of the singular values of the regressor matrix by showing that the rank of the regressor matrix Φ_N is related to the degree of persistency of the input, the degree of the model, and the degree of the true system.

In Chapter IV, we introduced the technique of *zero buffering*, in which the input signal begins with a sequence of zeros. Furthermore, we showed that zero-buffering increased the degree of persistency of a general signal. We then demonstrated the effectiveness of zero-buffering in increasing the numerical degree of persistency of a

177

Schröder-phased signal, which, without zero buffering, yielded a poorly conditioned regressor matrix. Finally, we showed the importance of good numerical persistency in identification with an example.

In Chapter V, we addressed the issue of identification in the presence of deterministic process or measurement noise. Specifically, we studied how deterministic signals propagate through polynomial matrix models. We also showed that both the system and deterministic noise could be identified exactly via overparametrization using ordinary least-squares, and then decoupled using one of the many matrix fraction decomposition techniques available in the literature.

In Chapter VI, we addressed the issue of identification in the presence of random noise. Specifically, we studied the consistency of the estimates in two scenarios, namely, the equation-error framework and the case where the input and input noise were white. In the latter case, we presented an approach based on using least-squares with a μ-Markov model. Finally, we introduced the concept of semi-consistency and showed how, using the techniques developed in Chapter II, one could obtain semi-consistent linear system estimates from semi-consistent Markov parameter estimates.

In Chapter VII, we explored the role of ersatz nonlinearities in parametric and nonparametric MIMO Hammerstein system identification. In parametric identification, where a linear-in-the-parameters structure for the Hammerstein nonlinearity was known, we showed that via overparametrization, the fundamentally bilinear optimization problem could be recast as a linear optimization problem, and then decoupled using the singular value decomposition. In nonparametric identification, we revisited correlation-based Markov parameter estimation techniques, and showed that the Markov parameters could be estimated semi-consistently using general ersatz nonlinearities in addition to the linear element. We also introduced the method of μ-Markov-based Markov parameter estimation with an ersatz nonlinearity, and showed that numerically this method yielded Markov parameter estimates with a lower variance than correlation-based estimates.

In the final chapter, we presented an elimination theory-based method for solving equality-constrained multivariate polynomial least-squares problems in system identification. However, while most algorithms in elimination theory rely upon Gröbner bases and symbolic multivariate polynomial division algorithms, we presented an algorithm which is based on computing the nullspace of a large sparse matrix and the zeros of a scalar, univariate polynomial.

9.2 Future Work

This dissertation covers just a small part of the system identification literature. Specifically, we have not touched upon optimal input design, subspace identification, compressed sensing techniques, prediction error methods, maximum likelihood methods, etc. However, despite the narrow focus of this dissertation, the least-squares based methods which we have focused on and developed will continue to play a role in identification in the years to come due to the computational ease of obtaining a solution and the availability of a recursive solution. This is because, as we enter an error pervaded by the massive data sets of bioengineering and financial engineering, there will always be a need for computational efficient solution methods. Thus future work will continue to develop extensions to least-squares methods, such as removing the restriction that the input and input noise are white in Chapters VI and VII.

Finally, at the other end of the spectrum, there will always be a desire to identify increasingly nonlinear systems. Advances in algebraic geometry are indubitably part of the solution, whether taking the approach of Chapter VIII or using another method. In the context of Chapter VIII, there is still much to be done, specifically, exploiting the structure of the problem and coding the algorithm in a more efficient language such as C or FORTRAN.

APPENDICES

APPENDIX A

Zeros of Polynomial Matrices

We present an algorithm for determining the zeros of polynomial matrices of arbitrary degree, normal rank, and dimension. Specifically, we use the singular value decomposition to reduce the problem to an eigenvalue problem.

A.1 Introduction

Polynomials, as the basis for ordinary differential and difference equations, pervade almost every aspect of engineering [3, 75, 76]. Regardless of whether one is working in the continuous-time domain, where one considers polynomials in the differentiation operator, in the discrete-time domain, where one considers polynomials in the backshift operator, or in any other domain, the zeros of a polynomial typify the dynamics and overall stability of the problem at hand [3, 77, 78]. Hence the ability to compute the zeros of a polynomial reliably is of prime importance for practical problems.

When handling scalar polynomials, as is the case for SISO systems, the problem of determining zeros robustly is well understood, and various algorithms are available for computing the zeros of a scalar polynomial [79–82]. However, when dealing with polynomial matrices, the problem is not as clear. Although a theoretical basis for the zeros of a polynomial matrix is provided via the Smith and Hermite forms, or the determinant if the the polynomial matrix is square, their computation is typically carried out symbolically [13, 15, 17], and hence is not amenable to many practical applications. Furthermore, although an extensive treatment of linearizations of polynomial matrices can be found [17, 83–85], much of the attention has been devoted to computing the generalized eigenvalues of polynomial matrix linearizations [17, 86, 87]. However, a simple example (Example A.2.1) we provide in the present chapter shows that the generalized eigenvalues are not necessarily the same as the zeros, even though it appears that this fact is known [17, 85]. In fact, an entire literature has sprung up regarding these "infinite zeros" which are responsible for the difference between the generalized eigenvalues of polynomial matrix linearizations and the zeros of polynomial matrices [88, 89].

Here we present a direct, numerical algorithm for computing the zeros of a polynomial matrix which relies solely on the most basic properties of polynomial matrices and does not encite the need to discuss these "infinite zeros" or other unnecessary facts such as row/column reducedness. The contents of the chapter are as follows. First, we present the necessary preliminaries concerning polynomial matrices, allowing us to build the rest of the chapter from the most basic polynomial matrix facts. Then, after introducing the problem statement, we present our numerical algorithm for computing the zeros of a polynomial matrix. Finally, we present several numerical examples, and conclusions.

A.2   Definitions

In this section, we repeat the definitions of polynomial matrices, normal rank, and zeros. Although many of these definitions can be found in the literature [17], and in previous chapters, we repeat them here for completeness.

Definition A.2.1. Let $C_0, C_1, \ldots, C_n \in \mathbb{R}^{p \times m}$ and

$$C(\mathbf{r}) \triangleq C_n \mathbf{r}^n + \cdots + C_1 \mathbf{r} + C_0. \tag{A.1}$$

Then $C \in \mathbb{R}^{p \times m}[\mathbf{r}]$.

Definition A.2.2. Let $C \in \mathbb{R}^{p \times m}[\mathbf{r}]$ and let n be the smallest nonnegative integer such that $C(\mathbf{r})$ is of the form (A.1). Then the *degree of* $C(\boldsymbol{r})$ is n if $C(\mathbf{r})$ is nonzero, and $-\infty$ if $C(\mathbf{r})$ is zero.

Remark A.2.1. In the literature, (A.1) is sometimes referred to as a matrix pencil, with the common case being the linear (or first-degree) matrix pencil $C(\mathbf{r}) = A - \mathbf{r}B$. □

Definition A.2.3. Let $C \in \mathbb{R}^{p \times m}[\mathbf{r}]$. Then the *normal rank of* $C(\boldsymbol{r})$ is $\max_{z \in \mathbb{C}} \operatorname{rank}\big[C(z)\big]$. Specifically, we write

$$\operatorname{nrank}\big[C(\mathbf{r})\big] \triangleq \max_{z \in \mathbb{C}} \operatorname{rank}\big[C(z)\big].$$

Furthermore, $C(\mathbf{r})$ has *full normal rank* if $m = p$ and $\operatorname{nrank}\big[C(\mathbf{r})\big] = p$.

Definition A.2.4. Let $C \in \mathbb{R}^{p \times m}[\mathbf{r}]$. Then $z \in \mathbb{C}$ is a *zero of* $C(\boldsymbol{r})$ if

$$\operatorname{rank}[C(z)] < \operatorname{nrank}[C(\mathbf{r})].$$

Definition A.2.4 implies that the zero polynomial matrix and all other constant matrices have no zeros. Furthermore, the problem of determining the zeros of a linear matrix pencil with full normal rank is equivalent to the generalized eigenvalue problem. However, when a first-degree polynomial matrix is rectangular or does not have full normal rank, then the generalized eigenvalue problem does not, in general, return the zeros. This is true for generalized eigenvalue solvers that uses the QZ decomposition [80–82], as we demonstrate in the following example.

Example A.2.1. Let

$$C(\mathbf{r}) \triangleq \begin{bmatrix} 0 & 1 \\ 0 & 0 \end{bmatrix} \mathbf{r} - \begin{bmatrix} 0 & \alpha \\ 0 & 0 \end{bmatrix}.$$

Then nrank $[C(\mathbf{r})] = 1$ and the only zero of $C(\mathbf{r})$ is α. However, the QZ-algorithm leaves $C(\mathbf{r})$ unchanged since $C(\mathbf{r})$ is already upper-triangular. Hence generalized eigenvalue solvers that employ the QZ decomposition return, as generalized eigenvalues, the ratios $0/0$ and $0/0$ [80]. □

A.3 Problem Formulation

Given a polynomial matrix $P \in \mathbb{R}^{p \times m}[\mathbf{r}]$, determine all of the zeros of $P(\mathbf{r})$.

A.4 Zeros of a Polynomial Matrix

In this section we present a method for computing the zeros of a polynomial matrix. Although some of these results may again be found in the literature [17], we present them again for completeness with our own proofs, so as to guide the reader in the development of the algorithm.

Lemma A.4.1. Let $A \in \mathbb{C}^{p \times m}$, $B \in \mathbb{C}^{n \times m}$, and

$$C \triangleq \begin{bmatrix} A \\ B \end{bmatrix}.$$

Also, let $V \in \mathbb{C}^{m \times \ell}$ be a basis for the nullspace of B. Then

$$\text{nullity}\,(C) = \text{nullity}\,(AV)\,.\qquad\qquad\text{(A.2)}$$

Proof. Let $T \in \mathbb{C}^{\ell \times k}$ be a basis for the nullspace of AV. Then letting $U \triangleq VT$, it follows that $CU = 0_{(p+n) \times k}$.

Next, suppose that U is not a complete basis for the nullspace of C, that is, suppose there exists an $x \in \mathcal{N}\,(C)$ such that $x \notin \mathcal{R}\,(U)$, where $\mathcal{N}\,(\cdot)$ and $\mathcal{R}\,(\cdot)$ denote the nullspace and rangespace, respectively. Then since $\mathcal{N}\,(C) \subseteq \mathcal{N}\,(B)$, it follows that there exists a $y \in \mathbb{C}^{\ell \times 1}$ such that $x = Vy$ and $y \notin \mathcal{R}\,(T)$. However, since $y \notin \mathcal{R}\,(T)$, it follows that $y \notin \mathcal{N}\,(AV)$, that is, $AVy = Ax \neq 0$, which contradicts the assumption that $x \in \mathcal{N}\,(C)$. Hence U is a complete basis for the nullspace of C.

Finally, since V is a basis, V has full column rank. Hence U has full column rank. Furthermore, since the dimension of the nullspace of C and AV both equal k, we have (A.2). $\qquad\qquad\square$

Fact A.4.1. Let $A \in \mathbb{R}^{p \times m}[\mathbf{r}]$, $B \in \mathbb{R}^{n \times m}$, and

$$C(\mathbf{r}) \triangleq \begin{bmatrix} A(\mathbf{r}) \\ B \end{bmatrix}.$$

Also, let $V \in \mathbb{C}^{m \times \ell}$ be a basis for the nullspace of B. Then $z \in \mathbb{C}$ is a zero of $C(\mathbf{r})$ if and only if z is a zero of $A(\mathbf{r})V$.

Proof. From Lemma A.4.1, for every $x \in \mathbb{C}$, we have that

$$\text{nullity}\big(C(x)\big) = \text{nullity}\big(C(x)V\big) = \text{nullity}\big(A(x)V\big),$$

and hence

$$\text{rank}\big(C(x)\big) = \text{rank}\big(A(x)V\big) + m - \ell.$$

Therefore, $z \in \mathbb{C}$ is a zero of $C(\mathbf{r})$ if and only if z is a zero of $A(\mathbf{r})V$. $\qquad\square$

Fact A.4.2. Let $A \in \mathbb{R}^{m \times p}[\mathbf{r}]$, $B \in \mathbb{R}^{m \times n}$, and

$$C(\mathbf{r}) \triangleq \left[\; A(\mathbf{r}) \;\; B \;\right].$$

Also, let $V \in \mathbb{C}^{\ell \times m}$ be a basis for the left nullspace of B. Then $z \in \mathbb{C}$ is a zero of $C(\mathbf{r})$ if and only if z is a zero of $VA(\mathbf{r})$.

Proof. Let $A_1(\mathbf{r}) \triangleq A^T(\mathbf{r})$, $B_1 \triangleq B^T$, $V_1 \triangleq V^T$, and $C_1(\mathbf{r}) \triangleq C^T(\mathbf{r})$. Then from Fact A.2.4, $z \in \mathbb{C}$ is a zero of $C_1(\mathbf{r})$ if and only z is a zero of $A_1(\mathbf{r})V_1$. Furthermore, since for every $x \in \mathbb{C}$, $\text{rank}\,(C(x)) = \text{rank}\,(C_1(x))$ and $\text{rank}\,(A_1(x)V_1) = \text{rank}\,(VA(x))$, it follows that z is a zero of $C(\mathbf{r})$ if and only if z is a zero of $C_1(\mathbf{r})$, and z is a zero of $A_1(\mathbf{r})V_1$ if and only if z is a zero of $VA(\mathbf{r})$. Hence $z \in \mathbb{C}$ is a zero of $C(\mathbf{r})$ if and only if z is a zero of $VA(\mathbf{r})$. $\qquad\square$

Next, we show that the zeros of a polynomial matrix of arbitrary degree are equivalent to the zeros of an easily constructed first-degree polynomial matrix. Furthermore, since the problem of determining the zeros of a first-degree polynomial matrix can be viewed as a special case of the generalized eigenvalue problem, the problem of determining the zeros of a polynomial matrix of arbitrary degree can be viewed as a special case of the generalized eigenvalue problem.

Fact A.4.3. Let $C \in \mathbb{R}^{p \times m}[\mathbf{r}]$ be given by (A.1), and let

$$
E \triangleq
\begin{bmatrix}
C_n & 0_{p \times m} & \cdots & \cdots & 0_{p \times m} \\
0_m & I_m & 0_m & \cdots & 0_m \\
\vdots & \ddots & \ddots & \ddots & \vdots \\
\vdots & & \ddots & \ddots & 0_m \\
0_m & \cdots & \cdots & 0_m & I_m
\end{bmatrix},
$$

$$
F \triangleq
\begin{bmatrix}
-C_{n-1} & \cdots & \cdots & \cdots & -C_0 \\
I_m & 0_m & \cdots & \cdots & 0_m \\
0_m & \ddots & \ddots & & \vdots \\
\vdots & \ddots & \ddots & \ddots & 0_m \\
0_m & \cdots & 0_m & I_m & 0_m
\end{bmatrix},
$$

where 0_m denotes the $m \times m$ zero matrix, and $0_{p \times m}$ denotes the $p \times m$ zero matrix. Also, let

$$
A(\mathbf{r}) \triangleq E\mathbf{r} - F.
$$

Then $z \in \mathbb{C}$ is a zero of $C(\mathbf{r})$ if and only if z is a zero of $A(\mathbf{r})$.

Proof. Let $G \in \mathbb{R}^{p \times nm}[\mathbf{r}]$ denote the first p rows of $A(\mathbf{r})$, and let $H \in \mathbb{R}^{m(n-1) \times nm}[\mathbf{r}]$ denote the final $m(n-1)$ rows of $A(\mathbf{r})$, that is,

$$
A(\mathbf{r}) =
\begin{bmatrix}
G(\mathbf{r}) \\
H(\mathbf{r})
\end{bmatrix},
$$

where

$$G(\mathbf{r}) \triangleq \left[\begin{array}{cccc} (C_n \mathbf{r} + C_{n-1}) & C_{n-2} & \cdots & C_0 \end{array} \right],$$

$$H(\mathbf{r}) \triangleq \left[\begin{array}{cc} 0_{(n-1)m \times m} & I_{(n-1)m} \end{array} \right] \mathbf{r} - \left[\begin{array}{cc} I_{(n-1)m} & 0_{(n-1)m \times m} \end{array} \right].$$

Then for every $x \in \mathbb{C}$,

$$U(x) \triangleq \left[\begin{array}{cccc} x^{n-1} I_m & \cdots & x I_m & I_m \end{array} \right]^T,$$

is a basis for the nullspace of $H(x)$. Furthermore,

$$G(x)U(x) = C(x).$$

Hence from Lemma A.4.1, for every $x \in \mathbb{C}$, we have that

$$\text{nullity}\big(A(x)\big) = \text{nullity}\big(G(x)U(x)\big) = \text{nullity}\big(C(x)\big).$$

Therefore $z \in \mathbb{C}$ is a zero of $C(\mathbf{r})$ if and only if z is a zero of $A(\mathbf{r})$. $\square$

Remark A.4.1. Fact A.4.3 shows that the zeros of a polynomial matrix are equivalent to the zeros of an easily constructed first-degree polynomial matrix. However, even though the problem has been reduced to a first-degree matrix pencil, a generalized eigenvalue solver does not necessarily return the zeros of the original polynomial matrix, as demonstrated in Example A.2.1. The following Proposition, however, provides a method for computing the zeros of first-degree matrix pencil by first reducing the problem to a standard eigenvalue problem. $\square$

Proposition A.4.1. Let $C \in \mathbb{R}^{p \times m}[\mathbf{r}]$ be given by (A.1), and let $A(\mathbf{r}) \triangleq E_0 \mathbf{r} - F_0$ be given by Fact A.4.3. Furthermore,

i) Let $i \triangleq 0$, $\ell_0 \triangleq (p + [n-1]m)$, and $k_0 \triangleq mn$.

188

ii) Compute the singular value decomposition of E_i, that is, compute the unitary $U_i \in \mathbb{R}^{\ell_i \times \ell_i}$, unitary $V_i \in \mathbb{R}^{k_i \times k_i}$, and quasi-diagonal $S_i \in \mathbb{R}^{\ell_i \times k_i}$ such that $E_i = U_i S_i V_i$.

iii) Let $r_i \triangleq \operatorname{rank}[E_i]$.

iv) If $r_i = 0$, then go to Step vii). Otherwise, continue.

v) If $r_i = \ell_i$, then go to Step vi). Otherwise,

   a) Let $F_i' \in \mathbb{R}^{\ell_i - r_i \times k_i}$ denote the last $\ell_i - r_i$ rows of the product $U_i^T F_i$.

   b) Compute a basis $W_i \in \mathbb{R}^{k_i \times j_i}$ for the nullspace of F_i' using the singular value decomposition.

   c) Increment i, and let $\ell_i \triangleq r_{i-1}$ and $k_i \triangleq j_{i-1}$.

   d) Let E_i and F_i denote the first r_{i-1} rows of the products $U_{i-1}^T E_{i-1} W_{i-1}$ and $U_{i-1}^T F_{i-1} W_{i-1}$, respectively.

   e) Return to Step ii).

vi) If $r_i = k_i$, then go to Step vii). Otherwise,

   a) Let $F_i' \in \mathbb{R}^{\ell_i \times k_i - r_i}$ denote the last $k_i - r_i$ columns of the product $F_i V_i^T$.

   b) Compute a basis $T_i \in \mathbb{R}^{j_i \times \ell_i}$ for the left nullspace of F_i' using the singular value decomposition.

   c) Increment i, and let $\ell_i \triangleq j_{i-1}$ and $k_i \triangleq r_{i-1}$.

   d) Let E_i and F_i denote the first r_{i-1} columns of the products $T_{i-1} E_{i-1} V_{i-1}^T$ and $T_{i-1} F_{i-1} V_{i-1}^T$, respectively.

   e) Return to Step ii).

vii) If E_i is zero, then $C(\mathbf{r})$ has no zeros. Otherwise, $z \in \mathbb{C}$ is a zero of $C(\mathbf{r})$ if and only if z is an eigenvalue of $E_i^{-1} F_i$.

189

Proof. First, from Fact A.4.3, $z \in \mathbb{C}$ is a zero of $C(\mathbf{r})$ if and only if z is a zero of $A(\mathbf{r}) = E_0\mathbf{r} - F_0$.

Next, suppose that $r_0 < \ell_0$. Then

$$U_0^T (E_0\mathbf{r} - F_0) = \begin{bmatrix} E_0''\mathbf{r} - F_0'' \\ F_0' \end{bmatrix}.$$

Furthermore, since U_0 is unitary, U_0 has full rank, and it follows that $z \in \mathbb{C}$ is a zero of $E_0\mathbf{r} - F_0$ if and only if z is a zero of $U_0^T (E_0\mathbf{r} - F_0)$. Additionally, since W_0 denotes a basis for the nullspace of F_0', from Fact A.4.1, we have that $z \in \mathbb{C}$ is a zero of $U_0^T (E_0\mathbf{r} - F_0)$ if and only if z is a zero of $(E_0''\mathbf{r} - F_0'') W_0 = E_1\mathbf{r} - F_1$. Hence, $z \in \mathbb{C}$ is a zero of $C(\mathbf{r})$ if and only if z is a zero of $E_1\mathbf{r} - F_1$.

Similarly, suppose that $r_0 = \ell_0 < k_0$. Then

$$(E_0\mathbf{r} - F_0) V_0^T = \begin{bmatrix} E_0''\mathbf{r} - F_0'' & F_0' \end{bmatrix},$$

and from Fact A.4.2, we have that $z \in \mathbb{C}$ is a zero of $C(\mathbf{r})$ if and only if z is a zero of $T_0 (E_0''\mathbf{r} - F_0'') = E_1\mathbf{r} - F_1$. Hence, by induction, for every $j \in [0, i-1]$, $z \in \mathbb{C}$ is a zero of $E_j\mathbf{r} - F_j$ if and only if z is a zero of $E_{j+1}\mathbf{r} - F_{j+1}$. Therefore, it follows that $z \in \mathbb{C}$ is a zero of $C(\mathbf{r})$ if and only if z is a zero of $E_i\mathbf{r} - F_i$.

Finally, if E_i is zero, then there are no points in $\mathbb{C}$ at which the pencil $E_i\mathbf{r} - F_i = F_i$ drops rank. Hence $C(\mathbf{r})$ has no zeros. However, if E_i is not zero, then it is square and nonsingular. Hence $z \in \mathbb{C}$ is a zero of $C(\mathbf{r})$ if and only if z is an eigenvalue of $E_i^{-1}F_i$. $\qquad\square$

Remark A.4.2. Proposition A.4.1 reduces the problem of determining the zeros of an arbitrary polynomial matrix to the square, regular eigenvalue problem $E_i^{-1}F_ix = \lambda x$. $\qquad\square$

Remark A.4.3. If the final E_i in Proposition A.4.1 has full normal rank, but is

190

ill-conditioned, then more accurate estimates of the zeros of $C(\mathbf{r})$ may be obtained by computing the generalized eigenvalues of (F_i, E_i), as opposed to computing the eigenvalues of $E_i^{-1} F_i$. $\qquad\square$

A.5 Numerical Examples

Here we demonstrate the algorithm presented in Proposition A.4.1 with two examples. We begin by returning to Example A.2.1.

Example A.5.1. Let

$$
C(\mathbf{r}) \triangleq
\begin{bmatrix} 0 & 1 \\ 0 & 0 \end{bmatrix}
\mathbf{r} -
\begin{bmatrix} 0 & \alpha \\ 0 & 0 \end{bmatrix}.
$$

Then, nrank $[C(\mathbf{r})] = 1$ and the only zero of $C(\mathbf{r})$ is α. Furthermore, the QZ-algorithm yields, as generalized eigenvalues, the ratios $0/0$ and $0/0$.

Next, consider Proposition A.4.1. Then

$$
E_0 =
\begin{bmatrix} 0 & 1 \\ 0 & 0 \end{bmatrix}, \quad
F_0 =
\begin{bmatrix} 0 & \alpha \\ 0 & 0 \end{bmatrix}.
$$

Furthermore, computing the singular value decomposition of E_0, we find that

$$
U_0 =
\begin{bmatrix} 1 & 0 \\ 0 & 1 \end{bmatrix}, \quad
S_0 =
\begin{bmatrix} 1 & 0 \\ 0 & 0 \end{bmatrix}, \quad
V_0 =
\begin{bmatrix} 0 & 1 \\ -1 & 0 \end{bmatrix}.
$$

Therefore, from Step v), we have that

$$
F_0' =
\begin{bmatrix} 0 & 0 \end{bmatrix}, \quad
W_0 = I_2,
$$

191

and hence

$$E_1 = \begin{bmatrix} 0 & 1 \end{bmatrix}, \quad F_1 = \begin{bmatrix} 0 & \alpha \end{bmatrix}.$$

Finally, returning to Step ii) and computing the singular value decomposition of E_1, we find that

$$U_1 = 1, \quad S_1 = \begin{bmatrix} 1 & 0 \end{bmatrix}, \quad V_1 = \begin{bmatrix} 0 & 1 \\ -1 & 0 \end{bmatrix}.$$

Therefore, from Step vi), we have that

$$F_1' = 0, \quad T_1 = 1,$$

and hence

$$E_2 = 1, \quad F_2 = \alpha.$$

Thus α is the only eigenvalue of $E_2^{-1} F_2 = \alpha$ and the only zero of $C(\mathbf{r})$. $\quad\square$

Next, we demonstrate how Proposition A.4.1 is used to computed the zeros of a higher degree polynomial matrix. Although, Proposition A.4.1 can be applied to problems of arbitrary dimension, normal rank, and degree, we consider a problem with full normal rank and low enough dimensions so that we can compute the determinant symbolically, and compare the zeros computed using both methods. Furthermore, note that when a matrix does not have full normal rank, then one can not compute the zeros by symbolically computing the determinant.

Example A.5.2. Let

$$C(\mathbf{r}) \triangleq \begin{bmatrix} 6\mathbf{r}^3 + 4\mathbf{r}^2 + \mathbf{r} + 6 & 8\mathbf{r}^3 + 7\mathbf{r}^2 + 3\mathbf{r} + 5 \\ 3\mathbf{r}^3 + 4\mathbf{r}^2 + 4\mathbf{r} + 8 & 4\mathbf{r}^3 + 7\mathbf{r}^2 + 5\mathbf{r} + 1 \end{bmatrix}.$$

Then the degree of $C(\mathbf{r})$ is 3 and the matrix coefficients of $C(\mathbf{r})$ are given by

$$C_3 = \begin{bmatrix} 6 & 8 \\ 3 & 4 \end{bmatrix}, \quad C_2 = \begin{bmatrix} 4 & 7 \\ 4 & 7 \end{bmatrix},$$

$$C_1 = \begin{bmatrix} 1 & 3 \\ 4 & 5 \end{bmatrix}, \quad C_0 = \begin{bmatrix} 6 & 5 \\ 8 & 1 \end{bmatrix}.$$

Furthermore, symbolically computing the determinant of $C(\mathbf{r})$, we find that

$$\det [C(\mathbf{r})] = 5\mathbf{r}^5 - 7\mathbf{r}^4 - 62\mathbf{r}^3 - 37\mathbf{r}^2 - 13\mathbf{r} - 34,$$

and hence the zeros of $C(\mathbf{r})$ are

$$z\left(C(\mathbf{r})\right) = \left\{ \begin{array}{l} 4.537 \\ -2.433 \\ -1.103 \\ 0.1996 \pm \jmath 0.7202 \end{array} \right\}. \tag{A.3}$$

For this low degree example, we can now use these values as a baseline against which to check the algorithm we have proposed in Proposition A.4.1. Specifically, from

Proposition A.4.1, we have that

$$E_0 = \begin{bmatrix} C_3 & 0_{2\times2} & 0_{2\times2} \\ 0_{2\times2} & I_2 & 0_{2\times2} \\ 0_{2\times2} & 0_{2\times2} & I_2 \end{bmatrix},$$

$$F_0 = \begin{bmatrix} -C_2 & -C_1 & -C_0 \\ I_2 & 0_{2\times2} & 0_{2\times2} \\ 0_{2\times2} & I_2 & 0_{2\times2} \end{bmatrix}.$$

Furthermore, computing the singular value decomposition of E_0, we find that $r_0 = 5 < l_0 = 6$. Therefore, after performing Step v), we have that

$$E_1 = \begin{bmatrix} -4.800 & 4.144 & 4.144 & 5.92 & -1.776 \\ 0.06214 & 0.06214 & 0.06214 & 0.08877 & 0.9734 \\ -0.1450 & 0.8550 & -0.1450 & -0.2071 & 0.06214 \\ -0.1450 & -0.1450 & 0.8550 & -0.2071 & 0.06214 \\ -0.2071 & -0.2071 & -0.2071 & 0.7041 & 0.08877 \end{bmatrix},$$

$$F_1 = \begin{bmatrix} 3.103 & -3.605 & -1.369 & -0.03930 & 7.614 \\ -0.1450 & -0.1450 & 0.8550 & -0.2071 & 0.06214 \\ -0.4244 & -0.4244 & -0.4244 & -0.6063 & 0.1819 \\ 0.8550 & -0.1450 & -0.1450 & -0.2071 & 0.06214 \\ -0.1450 & 0.8550 & -0.1450 & -0.2071 & 0.06214 \end{bmatrix}.$$

Finally, since the singular values of E_1 are

$$\sigma(E_1) = \{9.79, \quad 1, \quad 1, \quad 1, \quad 0.0693\},$$

we conclude that $r_1 = 5 = l_1 = k_1$, that is, E_1 is square and nonsingular. Hence

$$E_1^{-1}F = \begin{bmatrix} 0.02797 & -6.427 & 6.204 & 6.216 & 2.481 \\ -0.3071 & -2.562 & 1.469 & 1.338 & 1.225 \\ 0.9723 & -2.282 & 1.749 & 1.737 & 1.105 \\ 0.02261 & -2.198 & 2.560 & 2.570 & 1.552 \\ -0.1953 & 0.7710 & 0.04348 & -1.040 & -0.3848 \end{bmatrix},$$

and we have that the eigenvalues of $E_1^{-1}F_1$ are

$$z\left(E_1^{-1}F_1\right) = \left\{ \begin{array}{c} 4.537 \\ -2.433 \\ -1.103 \\ 0.1996 \pm \jmath 0.7202 \end{array} \right\}. \tag{A.4}$$

Therefore comparing (A.3) and (A.4), we find that the zeros of $C(\mathbf{r})$ and the eigenvalues of $E_1^{-1}F_1$ are equal, that is, the algorithm presented in Proposition A.4.1 has indeed returned the correct zeros of $C(\mathbf{r})$. Furthermore, in this case, the QZ-algorithm applied directly to (F_0, E_0) yields the generalized eigenvalues (A.4) with an additional eigenvalue at infinity. However, in general, there is no guarantee that the generalized eigenvalues of the polynomial matrix linearization (F_0, E_0) will be a subset of the zeros of polynomial matrix as Example A.2.1 demonstrates. □

A.6 Conclusions

We have presented an algorithm for determining the zeros of polynomial matrices of arbitrary degree, normal rank, or dimension. Specifically, we used the singular value decomposition to reduce the problem to an eigenvalue problem.

BIBLIOGRAPHY

196

BIBLIOGRAPHY

[1] J. N. Juang, *Applied System Identification*. Englewood Cliffs, NJ: Prentice-Hall, 1994.

[2] R. Pintelon and J. Schoukens, *System Identification: A Frequency Domain Approach*, 1st ed. New York: Wiley-IEEE Press, 2001.

[3] G. E. P. Box, G. M. Jenkins, and G. C. Reinsel, *Time Series Analysis: Forecasting and Control*, 4th ed. Wiley, 2008.

[4] T. Söderström and P. Stoica, *System Identification*. Upper Saddle River, NJ: Prentice-Hall, 1988.

[5] P. J. Brockwell and R. A. Davis, *Time Series: Theory and Methods*, 2nd ed. New York: Springer-Verlag, 2006.

[6] L. Ljung, *System Identification: Theory for the User*, 3rd ed. Upper Saddle River, NJ: Prentice-Hall, 1999.

[7] M. Verhaegen and V. Verdult, *Filtering and System Identification: A Least Squares Approach*, 1st ed. New York: Cambridge University Press, 2007.

[8] A. Björck, *Numerical Methods for Least-Squares Problems*, 1st ed. Philadelphia: SIAM, 1996.

[9] M. Gevers, A. Bazanella, and L. Miskovic, "Informative data: How to get just sufficiently rich?" in *IEEE Conference on Decision and Control*, Cancun, Mexico, December 2008, pp. 1962–1967.

[10] H. J. Palanthandalam-Madapusi, T. H. V. Pelt, and D. S. Bernstein, "Parameter consistency and quadratically constrained errors-in-variables least-squares identification," *International Journal of Control*, vol. 83, no. 4, pp. 862–877, March 2010.

[11] M. Levin, "Estimation of a system pulse transfer function in the presence of noise," *IEEE Transactions on Automatic Control*, vol. 9, no. 3, pp. 229–235, July 1964.

[12] T. Katayama, *Subspace Methods for System Identification*, 1st ed. London: Springer-Verlag, 2005.

[13] P. J. Antsaklis and A. N. Michel, *Linear Systems.* Boston: Birkhäuser, 2006.

[14] W. J. Rugh, *Linear System Theory.* Englewood Cliffs, NJ: Prentice-Hall, 1996.

[15] A. I. G. Vardulakis, *Linear Multivariable Control: Algebraic Analysis and Synthesis Methods.* Chichester: Wiley, 1991.

[16] W. A. Wolovich, *Linear Multivariable Systems.* New York, NY: Springer-Verlag, 1974.

[17] I. Gohberg, P. Lancaster, and L. Rodman, *Matrix Polynomials.* Philadelphia: SIAM, 2009.

[18] T. L. Jordan, W. M. Langford, and J. S. Hill, "Airborne subscale transport aircraft research testbed: Aircraft model development," in *AIAA Guidance, Navigation, and Control Conference and Exhibit,* Washington, D.C., August 2005.

[19] T. L. Jordan, J. V. Foster, R. M. Bailey, and C. M. Belcastro, "Airstar: A uav platform for flight dynamics and control system testing," in *AIAA Aerodynamic Measurement Technology and Ground Testing Conference,* San Francisco, CA, June 2006.

[20] A. M. Murch, "A flight control system architecture for the nasa airstar flight test facility," in *AIAA Guidance, Navigation, and Control Conference and Exhibit,* Honolulu, HI, August 2008.

[21] M. S. Holzel and E. A. Morelli, "Real-time frequency response estimation from flight data," *AIAA Journal of Guidance, Control, and Dynamics,* accepted for publication.

[22] M. A. Santillo and D. S. Bernstein, "Adaptive control based on retrospective cost optimization," *AIAA J. Guid. Contr. Dyn.,* vol. 33, pp. 289–304, 2010.

[23] D. Xue, Y. Chen, and D. P. Atherton, *Linear Feedback Control: Analysis and Design with Matlab.* Philadelphia: SIAM, 2007.

[24] T. Kailath, *Linear Systems.* Englewood Cliffs, NJ: Prentice-Hall, 1980.

[25] W. J. Rugh, *Nonlinear System Theory: The Volterra/Wiener Approach.* Baltimore: The Johns Hopkins University Press, 1981.

[26] B. L. Ho and R. E. Kalman, "Effective construction of linear state-variable models from input/output functions," *Regelungstechnik,* vol. 14, no. 12, pp. 545–592, 1966.

[27] Z. Szabo, P. S. C. Heuberger, J. Bokora, and P. M. J. V. den Hof, "Extended hokalman algorithm for systems represented in generalized orthonormal bases," *Automatica,* vol. 36, no. 12, pp. 1809–1818, December 2000.

[28] G. C. Goodwin and K. S. Sin, *Adaptive Filtering Prediction and Control*. Mineola, New York: Dover, 2009.

[29] P. Ioannou and B. Fidan, *Adaptive Control Tutorial*. Philadelphia: SIAM, 2006.

[30] E. F. Camacho and C. Bordons, *Model Predictive Control*. London: Springer-Verlag, 2004.

[31] J. M. Maciejowski, *Predictive Control with Constraints*. Englewood Cliffs, NJ: Prentice Hall, 2002.

[32] J. E. Normay-Rico and E. F. Camacho, *Control of Dead-Time Processes*. London: Springer-Verlag, 2007.

[33] E. Reynders, R. Pintelon, and G. D. Roeck, "Consistent impulse-response estimation and system realization from noisy data," *IEEE Transactions on Signal Processing*, vol. 56, no. 7, pp. 2696–2705, July 2008.

[34] I. M. Y. Mareels, R. R. Bitmead, M. Gevers, C. R. Johnson, R. L. Kosut, and M. A. Poubelle, "How exciting can a signal really be?" *Systems & Control Letters*, vol. 8, no. 3, pp. 197–204, 1987.

[35] I. Mareels, "Sufficiency of excitation," *Systems & Control Letters*, vol. 5, no. 3, pp. 159–163, December 1984.

[36] J. C. Willems, P. Rapisarda, I. Markovsky, and B. D. Moor, "A note on persistency of excitation," *Systems & Control Letters*, vol. 54, no. 4, pp. 325–329, April 2005.

[37] M. R. Schröder, "Synthesis of low peak-factor signals and binary sequences of low autocorrelation," *IEEE Transactions on Information Theory*, vol. 16, no. 1, pp. 85–89, January 1970.

[38] D. Bayard, "Statistical plant set estimation using schroeder-phased multisinusoidal input design," in *American Control Conference*, Chicago, IL, June 1992, pp. 1707–1712.

[39] R. P. Carlyon and A. J. Datta, "Excitation produced by schroeder-phase complexes: Evidence for fast-acting compression in the auditory system," *Journal of the Acoustical Society of America*, vol. 101, no. 6, pp. 3636–3647, 1997.

[40] D. E. Riveraa, H. Lee, H. D. Mittelmann, and M. W. Braun, "Constrained multisine input signals for plant-friendly identification of chemical process systems," *Journal of Process Control*, vol. 19, no. 4, pp. 623–635, April 2009.

[41] J. C. Basilio and B. Kouvaritakis, "An algorithm for coprime matrix fraction description using sylvester matrices," *Linear Algebra and Its Applications*, vol. 266, no. 15, pp. 107–125, November 1997.

[42] A. Varga, "Computation of coprime factorizations of rational matrices," *Linear Algebra and Its Applications*, vol. 271, no. 1-3, pp. 83–115, March 1998.

[43] T. G. J. Beelen and G. W. Veltkamp, "Numerical computation of a coprime factorization of a transfer function matrix," *Systems and Control Letters*, vol. 9, no. 4, pp. 281–288, October 1987.

[44] W. X. Zheng and C. B. Feng, "Identification of a class of dynamic errors-in-variables models," *International Journal of Adaptive Control and Signal Processing*, vol. 6, no. 5, pp. 431–440, March 1992.

[45] T. Söderström, "Errors-in-variables methods in system identification," *Automatica*, vol. 43, no. 6, pp. 939–958, June 2007.

[46] T. Söderström and P. Stoica, *Instrumental Variable Methods for System Identification*. Berlin/Heidelberg: Springer-Verlag, 1983.

[47] P. C. Young, H. Garnier, and M. Gilson, "Simple refined iv methods of closed-loop system identification," in *15th IFAC Symposium on System Identification*, Saint-Malo, France, July 2009, p. 11511156.

[48] L. Ljung and B. Wahlberg, "Asymptotic properties of the least-squares method for estimating transfer functions and disturbance spectra," *Advances in Applied Probability*, vol. 24, pp. 412–440, June 1992.

[49] J. C. Akers and D. S. Bernstein, "Armarkov least-squares identification," in *American Control Conference*, Albuquerque, NM, June 1997, p. 186190.

[50] T. H. V. Pelt and D. S. Bernstein, "Least squares identification using μ-Markov parameterizations," in *Conference on Decision and Control*, Tampa, FL, December 1998, pp. 618–619.

[51] M. Kamrunnahar, B. Huang, and D. B. Fisher, "Estimation of Markov parameters and time-delay/interactor matrix," *Chemical Engineering Science*, vol. 55, no. 17, pp. 3353–3363, May 2000.

[52] M. S. Fledderjohn, M. S. Holzel, H. J. Palanthandalam-Madapusi, R. J. Fuentes, and D. S. Bernstein, "A comparison of least squares algorithms for estimating Markov parameters," in *American Control Conference*, Baltimore, MD, June 2010, pp. 3735–3740.

[53] E. W. Bai, V. Cerone, and D. Regruto, "Separable inputs for the identification of block-oriented nonlinear systems," in *American Control Conference*, New York, July 2007, pp. 1548–1553.

[54] E. W. Bai and D. Li, "Convergence of the iterative hammerstein system identification algorithm," *IEEE Transactions on Automatic Control*, vol. 49, no. 11, pp. 1929–1940, November 2004.

[55] S. A. Billings and S. Y. Fakhouri, "Identification of a class of nonlinear systems using correlation analysis," *Institution of Electrical Engineers*, vol. 125, pp. 691–697, June 1978.

[56] F. Ding and T. Chen, "Identification of hammerstein nonlinear armax systems," *Automatica*, vol. 41, pp. 1479–1489, 2005.

[57] W. Greblicki, "Continuous-time hammerstein system identification," *IEEE Transactions on Automatic Control*, vol. 45, no. 6, pp. 1232–1236, June 2000.

[58] ——, "Stochastic approximation in nonparametric identification of hammerstein systems," *IEEE Transactions on Automatic Control*, vol. 47, no. 11, pp. 1800–1810, November 2002.

[59] W. Greblicki and M. Pawlak, *Nonparametric System Identification*. Cambridge University Press, 2008.

[60] ——, "Nonparametric identification of hammerstein systems," *IEEE Transactions on Automatic Control*, vol. 35, no. 2, pp. 409–418, March 1989.

[61] B. I. Ikharia and D. T. Westwick, "Identification of time-varying hammerstein systems using a basis expansion approach," in *Canadian Conference on Electrical and Computer Engineering*, Ottawa, Canada, May 2006, pp. 1858–1861.

[62] M. J. Korenberg and I. W. Hunter, "The identification of nonlinear biological systems: Lnl cascade models," *Biological Cybernetics*, vol. 55, pp. 125–134, 1986.

[63] K. S. Narendra and P. G. Gallman, "An iterative method for the identification of nonlinear systems using a hammerstein model," *IEEE Transactions on Automatic Control*, vol. 11, no. 3, pp. 546–550, July 1966.

[64] J. C. Ralston, A. M. Zoubir, and B. Boashash, "Identification of a class of nonlinear systems under stationary non-gaussian excitation," *IEEE Transactions on Signal Processing*, vol. 45, no. 3, pp. 719–735, March 1997.

[65] J. Schoukens, T. Dobrowiecki, and R. Pintelon, "Parametric and nonparametric identification of linear systems in the presence of nonlinear distortionsa frequency domain approach," *IEEE Transactions on Automatic Control*, vol. 43, no. 2, pp. 176–190, February 1998.

[66] D. Cox, J. Little, and D. O'Shea, *Ideals, Varieties, and Algorithms*, 3rd ed. New York: Springer-Verlag, 2007.

[67] B. Buchberger, "Groebner bases: An algorithmic method in polynomial ideal theory," in *Multidimensional Systems Theory: Progress, Directions and Open Problems in Multidimensional Systems*, N. K. Bose, Ed.

[68] D. S. Bernstein, *Matrix Mathematics*, 2nd ed. Princeton, NJ: Princeton University Press, 2009.

[69] P. Lancaster and M. Tismenetsky, *The Theory of Matrices*, 2nd ed. Academic Press, 1985.

[70] J. N. Juang and R. S. Pappa, "An eigensystem realization algorithm for modal parameter identification and model reduction," *AIAA Journal of Guidance, Control, and Dynamics*, vol. 8, no. 5, pp. 620–627, 1985.

[71] R. M. Gray, *Probability, Random Processes, and Ergodic Properties*, 2nd ed. New York: Springer-Verlag, 2009.

[72] A. M. D'Amato, B. O. S. Teixeira, and D. S. Bernstein, "Semi-parametric identification of wiener systems using a single harmonic input and retrospective cost optimisation," *IET Control Theory and Applications*, vol. 5, no. 4, pp. 594–605, March 2001.

[73] A. Papoulis and S. U. Pillali, *Probability, Random Variables and Stochastic Processes*, 4th ed. McGraw-Hill, 2002.

[74] E. Weyera and M. Campi, "Non-asymptotic confidence ellipsoids for the least-squares estimate," *Automatica*, vol. 38, no. 9, pp. 1539–1547, 2002.

[75] C. T. Chen, *Linear System Theory and Design*, 3rd ed. New York: Oxford University Press, 1999.

[76] K. Ogata, *Modern Control Engineering*, 4th ed. Upper Saddle River, NJ: Prentice-Hall, 2002.

[77] M. L. Abell and J. P. Braselton, *Modern Differential Equations*, 2nd ed. Orlando: Harcourt College, 2001.

[78] J. Tokarzewski, *Finite Zeros in Discrete Time Control Systems*. Berlin/Heidelberg: Springer-Verlag, 2006.

[79] J. M. McNamee, *Numerical Methods for Roots of Polynomials: Part I*. Cambridge, MA: Elsevier Science, 2007.

[80] G. H. Golub and C. F. V. Loan, *Matrix Computations*, 3rd ed. Baltimore: The Johns Hopkins University Press, 1996.

[81] G. W. Stewart, *Matrix Algorithms Volume I: Basic Decompositions*. Philadelphia: SIAM, 1998.

[82] ——, *Matrix Algorithms Volume II: Eigensystems*. Philadelphia: SIAM, 2001.

[83] A. Amiraslani, R. M. Corless, and P. Lancaster, "Linearization of matrix polynomials expressed in polynomial bases," *IMA Journal of Numerical Analysis*, vol. 29, pp. 141–157, 2009.

[84] N. J. Higham, D. S. Mackey, N. Mackey, and F. Tisseur, "Symmetric linearizations for matrix polynomials," *SIAM Journal on Matrix Analysis and Applications*, vol. 29, pp. 143–159, 2006.

[85] F. D. Teran and F. M. Dopico, "Sharp lower bounds for the dimension of linearizations of matrix polynomials," *Electronic Journal of Linear Algebra*, vol. 17, pp. 518–531, 2008.

[86] P. Lancaster, "Linearization of regular matrix polynomials," *Electronic Journal of Linear Algebra*, vol. 17, pp. 21–27, 2008.

[87] N. J. Higham and F. Tisseur, "Bounds for eigenvalues of matrix polynomials," *Linear Algebra and its Applications*, vol. 358, no. 1-3, pp. 5–22, January 2003.

[88] D. Henrion and J. C. Zuniga, "Detecting infinite zeros in polynomial matrices," *IEEE Transactions on Circuits and Systems II: Express Briefs*, vol. 52, no. 11, pp. 744–745, 2005.

[89] D. Henrion, J. R. Leon, and M. Sebek, "Extraction of infinite zeros of polynomial matrices," in *IEEE Conference on Decision and Control*, Sydney, Australia, December 2000, pp. 4221–4226.